Praise For Ready or Not . . . There We Go!

D0197738

Also By Elizabeth Lyons

Ready or Not . . . Here We Come!
*The REAL Experts' Cannot-Live-Without Guide to the
First Year with Twins*

Acclaim for Ready or Not . . . Here We Come!

"Ready or Not . . . Here We Come! is the advice you need in the short, funny format your sleep-deprived mind can absorb. Elizabeth Lyons tells it like it is in a laugh-out-loud look at the uncertainty, craziness, and absolute joy of your first year with twins. An absolute must-have for every mother who wishes there were two of her to keep up with the two of them."
—Lisa Earle McLeod, author of *Forget Perfect*

"Elizabeth Lyons' humorous yet realistic perspective provides new parents of twins with a great starting point from which to embark on that all-important first year."
—Dr. Bob Covert, leading Chicagoland neonatologist

"Elizabeth Lyons tells it like it really is. From helping you survive back-to-back feedings, living with the stereophonic crying, and coping with a double round of diaper rash, she tells you what to do, what to buy, and what to ignore. There *is* a light at the end of the twins tunnel, and *Ready or Not . . . Here We Come!* will help you find it. Where was Elizabeth Lyons when my twins were little?"
—Kristy Lucariello, President of *Performance in Practice* (and mother of teenage twins)

"Elizabeth Lyons captures the universal discourse of sisterhood while guiding new mothers of twins through the first year."

—Kathy Voit, RNC, Labor and Delivery nurse

"Finally, a humor-filled, solution-packed tell-it-like-it-is guide to the first year with twins!"

—Betty Jean Young, BSN

Ready or Not...
There We Go!

The REAL Experts' Guide
to the Toddler Years with Twins

ELIZABETH LYONS

FINN-PHYLLIS
PRESS

Finn-Phyllis Press, Inc.

Copyright © 2006 by Elizabeth Lyons

Cover illustration and design by Samantha Wall

First edition: June 2006

This book was printed in the United States of America.

ISBN 10: 0-9746990-1-2
ISBN 13: 978-0-9746990-1-1

CONTENTS

A FEW WORDS...

A true friend is somebody who can make us do what we can.
—Ralph Waldo Emerson

It is with profound gratitude that I send this book into the world. It exists thanks to the collaboration—intentional or otherwise—of a number of people.

To Jennie Goode—thank you for your fabulous editing skills, attention to detail, knack for being professional and fun at the same time, and ability to say, "Positively nothing in this entire section works," in the nicest way. The final version is one thousand percent better for your having torn it apart.

To Mollie—thank you for allowing me to read paragraphs (or entire chapters) to you over the phone, advising me not only on the contents of this book but every aspect of my life (whether I've asked for the advice or not), and proactively calling any 800 number when necessary.

To Barb—thank you for being such a trusted, honest girlfriend. Keep in mind the words of Richard David Bach:

"Don't be dismayed at goodbyes. A farewell is necessary before you can meet again. And meeting again after a moment or lifetime is certain for those who are friends."

To Grace, Jack, Henry, and George—thank you for tolerating my need to lock myself in the office every night for almost a year. You are collectively my reason for everything. I am now locking myself *out* of the office for a while so we can spend our days hiking the desert in search of all kinds of creatures.

To David—thank you for proactively locking the office door when I forgot, and then matter-of-factly removing any child who had suction-cupped himself to it. Technically, I *could* do almost anything without you, of course, but it wouldn't be nearly as satisfying or hilarious. Thank you for always being my strongest and most constant supporter.

To all the moms who've ever written a favorable online review at Amazon or Barnes & Noble—Thank You!

To Lori and Doug at the Starbucks drive-thru in Plainfield, Illinois—thank you for consistently being the two people I could count on to speak to me nicely in the morning. Also, for speedily providing the tall, iced, nonfat latte with two Splenda that got me through the day after a long night writing. Should you ever move to Arizona, please let me know at which Starbucks you are working!

And last but most certainly not least—thank you to moms of multiples everywhere. I know you and only you will completely understand when that fateful day comes and I report that I inadvertently unloaded the one hundred items in my grocery cart onto the ten-items-or-less conveyer; subsequently lost total control over my suddenly splayed out and screaming kids; and in the midst of all the chaos, neglected to realize that I forgot to put on pants prior to leaving the house (and trade my slippers for real shoes).

GETTING HERE...

"A No. 2 pencil and a dream can take you anywhere."
—Joyce A. Myers

My journey as a mother of twins began four years ago with a dream, an ultrasound machine, and an exuberant ultrasound technician. The No. 2 pencil came later.

Not long after we got married, my husband, David, and I decided to start our family. I had little to no anxiety about the process. My seventh-grade sex education classes made the process of conception sound almost too easy. How hard could it be? I wondered. Nix the birth control, have a few "fun" evenings, pee on a stick, go celebrate. That's how it works, right?

Not always.

I took my first pregnancy test on day thirty-five of my cycle. Result: Not Pregnant. On day thirty-eight, the proverbial light bulb turned on above my head. I know, perhaps I didn't wait long enough before taking the test. Or maybe I did it wrong? With that, I was off to take test number two. And on it went until it had been eight months and my husband had set up a line item in the monthly budget for ept®. I didn't understand. It seemed as though friends and co-workers were getting pregnant left and right, even though they "weren't really even trying. Who knew it could be so easy?" I felt like Charlotte from *Sex and the City* when she found out that Miranda had gotten pregnant "by accident" while she and her husband Trey were going through what felt like orchestrated robotics every night with the hope of ultimately being deemed "with child."

Question: what do you get when you combine a Type-A personality with the obsessive intent to conceive a baby—and add to that the month-to-month reality of a barren uterus? I'll tell you: a closer relationship with a basal thermometer than with your husband and a linen closet full of pregnancy tests.

Enough was enough. My obstetrician prescribed Clomid, and approximately ten months later, our daughter Grace was born.

When we decided we were ready to try for a sibling for Grace, my obstetrician recommended that, given my history, we give Clomid a try again. Just as before, I knew there was a chance I could conceive multiples. But this time, after seeing two lines on only the fourth pregnancy test (all four taken in one afternoon to be sure the first, second, and/or third tests weren't defective), I simply had a feeling that I was carrying two babies. Of course, I'd talk myself into and out of the concept all day long, but in the end I really did believe that there were two tiny fetuses swimming around inside of me. I began having dreams both day and night about what it would be like to raise twins.

David thought I was crazy. That is, until he mulled the idea over, got mildly excited, and then started having his own fantasies about the joy of double-duty diaper changes and golf lessons. I must say, we were both a bit disappointed during my seven-week ultrasound when the technician told us that there was only one baby. We were delighted that the baby appeared healthy; we just felt a bit like someone was missing.

And then it happened. The technician grabbed my arm, in much the same way I suppose a lobster grabs its prey. "Oh!" she exclaimed. "Are you ready for this?"

I knew exactly what I should be ready for because I saw it at the same time she did. So did David. Another little heart beating right next to the first.

"There *are* two! I guess I just needed to scan from a different angle," she said. I do not understand the ultrasound machine. No matter how slowly the technicians explain it, I have never been able to figure out how to look at a cross-section of my uterus. But whether we were looking down into it or across it or through it didn't matter; there were definitely two hearts beating within it.

When the ultrasound was finished, I leapt off the table, floated into the exam room, and tried to ignore my obstetrician who—because he had two-year-old twin granddaughters at the time—immediately began regaling us with the challenges involved with raising twins from infancy through the toddler years.

I halfway listened to the spiel delivered by Dr. You-Have-No-Idea-What-You've-Gotten-Yourself-Into as he advised me on the challenges parents face while raising twin toddlers, not to mention the trials a woman who is barely over five feet tall encounters while attempting to carry them in utero. He concluded by informing me of the prospect of frequent internal exams far earlier in the pregnancy than I had them with Grace.

Feeling a bit anxious, I ordered David to drive me to the bookstore. We had less than nine months to learn all there was to know about growing, birthing, and raising twins. And a little help regarding how to do it all with an adorable fifteen-month-old in tow wouldn't hurt either.

I found a couple of great books on what to expect throughout the pregnancy. But, unfortunately, the book I wanted to guide me through the first year didn't seem to exist. I needed proven strategies. I needed funny. I needed positive and uplifting. I needed a girlfriend who'd been there, done that. I needed Vicki Iovine.

But Vicki, *Girlfriend's Guide* extraordinaire, does not have twins.

I decided right then and there that over the next couple of years, I would write the book that was missing from the bookshelves: a humorous, tell-it-like-it-is, solutions-packed guide to the first year with twins.

Six months later, David and I enrolled in a Marvelous Multiples class at our local hospital. The expectant moms in the class got along famously, as did the dads. It was as though we were meant to go through this experience together. Over time, as we each arrived at the hospital individually or within hours of one another for classes or tests or drugs to suppress pre-term labor, we became known by the medical staff as the "multiples" sorority. It was just what my little project needed: a diverse group of women to provide their opinions, strategies, and sanity-saving tips. The details of our journeys over that first year provided the material and the inspiration for my first book, *Ready or Not . . . Here We Come! The REAL Experts' Cannot-Live-Without Guide to the First Year with Twins.*

Before we knew it, the first year had come to an end. It was time to see how far we'd come in our roles as parents, how many skills we'd gained, how confident we felt in our abilities. It was time to enter The Toddler Years. And, once again seeing a need on the bookshelves, it was time to write a book.

MOVING RIGHT ALONG . . .

Motherhood is like Albania. You can't trust the descriptions in the books, you have to go there.

—Marni Jackson

This statement is as close to perfect a way to describe the toddler years with twins as I've found. I'm hard-pressed to identify just one word that accurately illustrates this time period. Truth be told, there are many ways to describe it: exhausting, humbling, frustrating, miraculous, and terrifying, for starters. I've slowly become convinced that the experts who claim that more occurs developmentally between the ages of one and four than during any other time of life are right. Ever since the moment when I officially accepted this theory, I've begun each day enjoying those last few cozy moments in bed staring at the ceiling and reminding myself that I'm responsible for nurturing and guiding said development. I won't lie to you; it's a frightening admission given that many days I believe I might be more successful completing a triple Lutz on ice or performing a quadruple bypass on a patient lying on a moving gurney than getting a child even an inch closer to understanding why spitting a mouthful of food onto a window is not acceptable. Somewhat selfishly perhaps, I set goals for *myself* during this time period in addition to those I set for my children. After all, I wanted to exit this era with as few gray hairs and premature wrinkles as possible. The solutions to the former are too messy and those to the latter are still just too expensive (and involve needles).

Many parents of twins spend at least the early portion of Year One sleepwalking through the house with "I Will Survive" by Gloria Gaynor playing in their heads—perhaps more in an effort to convince themselves that they will than because they believe it. But look at you now; you did it! You've survived the sleepless nights, the inconsolable crying (yours and the babies'), the erratic schedules, the ever-growing mountain of laundry, and the cereal dinners night after night. You've washed more bottles and changed more diapers than you ever imagined you would. You've proven yourself. You're perfectly primed to enter Phase Two: The Toddler Years.

I once read, "It takes faith to step on nothing and believe something is there." This quote hit me like the giant block that is so often hurled across the room since Jack—the older of my twins by twenty-eight minutes—has yet to accept that when he wants to play catch, he needs to inform me that the chosen object is coming *before* it lands square between my eyes. It's too bad that the boys were almost four when I first came across this most profound saying. It was quite a blessing, albeit a bit late, because it can be applied to the vast majority of life challenges: parenting, marriage, careers, illnesses, and the unknown nature of the future in general.

There will be many times during the next few years with your toddler twins when you'll wonder how on earth to proceed. People will tell you to just keep putting one foot in front of the other (duh!) but sometimes you'll argue that it's just not that simple. Might it be a wiser strategy to step in a more northwesterly direction, a more southeasterly direction, straight ahead—heel to toe—balance-beam style, or with the longest stride possible? You'll potentially question, among other things, whether or not the experts of the moment who profess precisely the perfect way to coax your children into sharing are "right," whether there's something wrong with your approach given that your neighbor recently declared with the confidence of Donald Trump that babies can be potty trained by the time they are eighteen months old, and whether or not it might just be possible that pigs (not to mention two-year-olds) really can fly.

A quick note: don't allow yourself to get overwhelmed by all the "experts" out there. They are a voluminous and endless source of suggestions no doubt, but at the end of the day, *you* are the expert on your children and on what's right for your family. If every parent did the amount of research she felt comfortable with, made the decision that seemed appropriate at that point in time, and just went with it instead of lying awake at night worrying about whether or not she should take this approach or that approach and whether, if she chose wrong, her child might end up incarcerated by the age of thirteen, the number of anxiety-related ulcers would decrease by over a third, I'm sure.

Be prepared to be forced more than once—much more than once—to close your eyes and take a leap of faith, the same way you did the day you brought those beautiful babies home. Those sorts of leaps can be quite daunting. Once in the air, you will have to believe that you'll land on solid ground. Sort of like that game you used to play at camp where you'd turn your back to your fellow campers and then fall backward with hope and a prayer that they'd catch you. (I refused to play this game because I knew what my fellow campers were actually planning to do and it did not involve catching anyone!)

The secret to surviving these leaps of faith lies in the belief that the answer that's right for you and your family will catch you. It takes an incredible amount of trust to believe—to *know*—that even though you're stepping off of a steep cliff, your feet will meet with solid ground. Work on your ability to trust that they will, and you'll change the way you approach the uncertainty that lies ahead—in parenting as well as everything else.

I once saw a commercial wherein some arbitrary question was posed to a randomly selected woman, and a choice of responses was provided. Next, miraculously, the woman was informed by angels precisely which choice was the right one for her. Sounds awfully deep, but I think it was a fast-food commercial—you know, do I choose a side salad or fries? I thought, "If we could have consistent, clear guidance like that for the toddler years with twins, for parenting period, it sure would make things a whole lot easier!"

In my first book, I suggested that there are two critical components to surviving Phase One (the first year) with twins: perspective and humor. Those traits are just as important in Phase Two. I would also like to add another: *Very Low Expectations.*

Alice Walker summed it up perfectly when she said, "Expect nothing. Live frugally on surprise." This is what you'll need to do for the majority of the toddler years with your twins. If you can manage it—most of the time—you'll survive quite nicely. Choosing to maintain very low expectations might appear a negative approach at first. If so, try thinking of it this way: this approach is not pessimistic, it's realistic. When you don't have a master plan in mind for the way things will go, you significantly reduce the potential for being disappointed when they don't go quite that way. An experience that might otherwise have been viewed as horrendous could instead be seen as "fascinating." A trip to the grocery store during which the kids were not in the most wonderful moods might be considered a success simply because you were able to keep some semblance of peace and order until everything on your list was purchased. Heed the advice of Emmet Fox:

> *Bless a thing and it will bless you.*
> *Curse it and it will curse you . . .*
> *If you bless a situation, it has no power to hurt you,*
> *and even if it is troublesome for a time,*
> *it will gradually fade out . . .*

If you bless your circumstances, no matter how dire they might appear in the moment, you'll be blessed by a new lesson learned or something to laugh about on a Friday night. If you are troubled by each and every one of the not entirely pleasant occurrences, you'll spend far too much time in the Land of the Bitter. And that's just not a pleasant place to live.

I certainly won't fib by insinuating that on every occasion I was able to turn my perspective into a positive one. That's simply not possible, and I don't believe that anyone who proclaims it is genuinely believes what is coming out of his mouth. But if you try to take the high road on challenging situations as often as possible, you'll be able to get through those really tough days and situations. You'll be able to ride the wave of insanity instead of being churned around in it.

There have been many, many moments during the last few years when I have wanted to join Buzz Lightyear and go "to infinity and beyond." I've had days when I've suddenly and urgently needed something, anything, at Linens-N-Things just so that I could stand in front of the Envirascape fountain display for a few moments while holding a Yankee lavender-scented candle under my nose because the experience made me feel as though I was sort of *close* to a spa.

That said, while my husband might disagree, I don't think I'm too much the worse for wear after these past few years. My definition of entertainment has certainly changed since I get far less time to myself than I used to. And I do seem to find myself suddenly in a confused state more often than I used to (I can't tell you the number of times I've been standing in the checkout line at the grocery store with a cart full of groceries and suddenly thought, "Ohmigod, am I in the ten-items-or-less lane? And did I remember to put on pants today?"). My body hasn't yet quite returned to the shape it was in when I was twenty-five. I'd likely have shed quite a lot of weight running after the boys all day every day, but alas, I think I ate too much ice cream in an effort to maintain my sanity.

I still keep a stash of *New York Times* crossword puzzles in my nightstand for those weeks when I'm sure I'm becoming less intelligent by the second. Thankfully, I've learned through constant observation of and interaction with other moms that I'm not alone in my concern over the loss of thousands of brain cells per hour; among the worldwide community of mothers, it's obviously a worry of epidemic proportions.

I'm still blessed to find myself consistently surrounded by and learning from amazing women, many of whom are not even mothers themselves. When Jack and Henry began preschool this year, we enrolled them in a math and science enrichment program offered one afternoon per week. At the end of each class, their teacher comes into the hallway and informs parents what concepts they studied that day. Every single mom stands there in utter amazement, wondering how on earth this adorable twenty-something teacher is able to keep their attention while teaching about inertia, density, and the rhombus. How does she do that when we can't even keep their attention long enough to discern what the heck they want for lunch? And as a side note, I'll be forever grateful to the mom who was brave enough to raise her hand and ask, "Uh, Ms. Lindsay, what exactly *is* a rhombus?"

I've been asked a few times when I would write The Toddler Book. My response has consistently been, "When I figure out how to raise twin toddlers!" The truth—the whole truth (can you handle it?): I haven't yet figured it out *completely*. But, I've successfully made it to the other side. And along the way, my girlfriends and I, not to mention the masses of twin moms I've met over the last several years, have come up with our share of suggestions, words of wisdom, and can-you-even-believe-*this* stories to share.

If you read *Ready or Not . . . Here We Come!* (the guide to the first year with twins), you already know of my "multiples" sorority sisters. You're going to get to know a few of them even better in the pages that follow. If you don't know who on earth I'm talking about, be prepared to meet a few of the women with whom I've been navigating the twin waters for just over four years now. They are awesome and nuts and hilarious and I love them to death. They have great ideas—which many times are totally different from mine—and without fail, one of our ideas has worked or we've at least found a way to crack each other up about the issue we were trying to alleviate. In one way or another, they've been the catalyst that put my left foot in front of my right most days.

Unlike many toddler books that take the reader from age one to age three, this book will cover up to age four. The overriding conclusion seems to be that with twins, it's at about age four that things start to really calm down and the light at the end of the tunnel is bright enough to make you squint. Don't get me wrong; with each passing day it will get easier and easier. But by the age of four, life will plateau and you'll start to notice a huge and consistent improvement in your overall sanity level.

It may seem as though some sections of this book are repeating themselves. I have not gone insane. It's just that the same issue seems to require a different approach depending on the kids' age. The tactic you may use to curb a biting habit when they're one will likely need to be modified if they are still biting when they are three and a half. Throwing their entire meal onto the floor when they are eighteen months old will require less patience (but more manual labor) on your part than it will when they are almost four and having nightly food fights (at which point the manual labor can become their responsibility!).

Now, if you are looking for a book that, from the first page to the last, portrays the art of raising twin toddlers as a sort of 1950s sitcom wherein everyone always smiles and never argues; Mom always knows exactly how to respond to every situation (and it's acceptable for Dad to come home from work and promptly sit in front of the TV to read the paper); and a Julia Child–worthy, five-course meal is calmly and quietly enjoyed by the entire family as they discuss the wonderful events of the day, this book is perhaps not the best choice. Frankly, if you are looking for that book, you might want to stay out of the bookstores because I don't think it exists. If it does exist, an appropriate title would be *Motherhood: Delusions of Grandeur.*

There will be challenges, and there will be solutions. There will be frustrating moments, but there will be more moments during which your heart will soar with pride and delight. There will be chaotic periods during which your husband will sit down in front of the TV to catch the scores on ESPN, seemingly oblivious to what's going on around him. I don't yet have a positive spin on that one, but I'm working on it.

So, here I sit with four kids under the age of five. Yes, I did say four kids. Keep reading for the details of that. My driver's license says I'm thirty-three; yet many days, my mind tells me something different. It is for that reason that I refuse to take Michael Roizen's "What's Your Real Age?" test. I really don't want the results of that; they may qualify me for the Guinness Book of World Records. As are all moms, I'm utterly exhausted at the end of every day, and as I lie in bed at night falling asleep to *Everybody Loves Raymond* reruns, I'm positively amazed—in a good way—at all that my life has become.

You have a wild and crazy few years ahead of you. Just think: walking, talking, climbing, duct taping your oven shut, and coming to understand the reasons why mothers pay more for the washable crayons. And lest you forget, this phase will conclude with what is often thought to be the greatest patience test of all—at least early on in parenting: potty training.

We've been through it, and we'll get you through it. So go put on a comfortable pair of pajamas, eat a big bowl of ice cream (the real stuff; none of this low-fat, low-carb garbage), and get a good night's sleep.

You're going to need it!

Secrets to Exiting the Toddler Tunnel with Sanity Intact

On the day your twins turn one year old—possibly even at the stroke of midnight—you will fall back on your bed and breathe a huge sigh of relief. After all, *no* year could be as challenging as the first, right? Right. That's the good news. Some additional news: the toddler years are going to be "interesting." I promise, you're going to make it. Here are some products and mindsets that will guarantee your success.

Your Own Phone Booth

As with many of my sanity savers, I credit my friend Mollie for this one. We were talking recently via phone and all four of our boys were screaming at us (Mollie's twins, Tommy and Kevin, are five weeks younger than Jack and Henry). Mollie proclaimed (loudly), "That's it—I'm asking Gary for my own phone booth for Christmas this year!"

The key to surviving these years of non-stop vocalization is to accept that you will have nary a moment of peace between 7:00 a.m. and 8:00 p.m. When you are playing with your children, each is vying for your attention. When you're trying to book a doctor's appointment (perhaps with a licensed therapist), at least one child will likely be hanging on to your leg and whining. When you're trying to simply take a seven-second bathroom break, one is banging on the door in fear that you've stealthily slipped out via the toilet bowl. I've tried locking myself in the pantry for eighty-four seconds to place a quick just-checking-in call to Mollie, but in the end we are usually only able to confirm that the other is alive (and in the midst of my relief that she indeed is, I end up discovering a previously hidden stash of candy and ingest far more than I should in such a short span of time).

Since you probably won't be able to have an actual phone booth installed between the refrigerator and the range, recognize that early on, the sanest way to take or make most calls is to do so while the kids are napping or after they go to bed at night.

A Warehouse-Sized Jug of Maalox

During the second year, you will likely find your twins in some precarious places—and possibly even positions attempting to get to those places. For starters, I've found my boys locked in their room (one with an appendage stuck behind the bed), on top of their bookshelf (yes, it's bolted to the wall), and hiding small toys quite deep inside their floor vent. The key to keeping your doses of Maalox infrequent: when it gets uncomfortably quiet in your home before the kids are in bed for the night, don't be thankful. Be nervous. Be very, very nervous.

Duct Tape

I never thought that an item typically reserved for home-improvement projects would come in handy for child-related challenges. I was wrong. Our sorority's first experience with duct tape came when Mollie could find no other way to keep her boys from pulling open her oven door. All of the local stores were out of the oven lock (must be a common challenge), so in the meantime she wrapped the entire front of the appliance with duct tape.

Shortly thereafter, in an effort to strategize a solution to prevent Jack from removing his diaper during naptime, Mollie suggested wrapping it with duct tape. More on that later!

The Ability to Discriminate Between an Inconvenience and an Emergency

As Richard Carlson noted in his fantastic book, *Don't Sweat the Small Stuff . . . and It's All Small Stuff,* "Although most people believe otherwise, the truth is, life *isn't* an emergency." A dirty house is an inconvenience, not an emergency (unless Oprah is on her way over). Not having time to hand-make your holiday cards one year is an inconvenience, not an emergency (unless you're my friend Barb). Don't pressure yourself to be and have it all each and every day. In most cases, the only person with unreasonably high expectations of yourself is you! There will be plenty of time once your kids are in school full-time to scrub the kitchen floor until it shines "like the top of the Chrysler Building" and craft until you can craft no more.

A Low Need for Order and Control

Newsflash: there is not going to be much of either, especially during Year Two. Toddlers are curious...period. Toddlers who have a constant partner in crime are something more significantly scary than curious. The amount of trouble these children can get into in the forty-two seconds it takes for you to switch a load of laundry to the dryer before it begins to mildew can defy even the most active imagination. Some points to keep in mind: First, while some are a bit more time-consuming than others, most messes can be cleaned up. (If necessary, review the above inconvenience-versus-emergency advice.) Second, if it's broken but not valuable, it's okay. Third, if it's broken and valuable, perhaps it shouldn't have been out in the first place!

Short-Sleeved Shirts

What is the biggest giveaway that a woman is a mother of multiples? She's wearing a short-sleeved shirt in the middle of February in Chicago. Why? Because she's constantly sweating. My poor husband suggests we build a fire most winter nights, and I have to weakly reply, "Uh . . . okay . . . I guess." I then sit in another room. And I wonder why I rush coatless to pick up my daughter from school thinking how wonderful the cool air will feel, only to develop frostbitten arms between the parking lot and the front door.

Patience

While it may sound ridiculous at times, the effect of slowly counting to ten is highly underestimated. You could even learn to do it in various languages to create a calming experience for yourself and a learning experience should your children actually be listening. There will probably be many occasions when your first instinct will be to yell when something inconvenient occurs. This is perfectly understandable. After all, finding the entire contents of a tube of bubble-gum-flavored, blue toothpaste all over the bathroom floor can be frustrating. Do your best to determine which incidents are indeed accidents—and, quite possibly, the result of your child simply learning and becoming more independent—and which are behaviors that your child knows aren't acceptable. When the latter occurs, have a plan for a natural or logical consequence. Most important, be calm and consistent with your response. Sometimes, the entire point of the wrongdoing was to work you into an uproar. Try not to allow yourself to lose this battle to a toddler.

A Lot of Paper Towels

Yet another good reason to join a warehouse club. Do not buy the cheapest paper towels—the ones that break in half when you attempt to fold them. At the same time, don't assume that the most expensive brand is your best bet. What you want is the most absorbent paper towel your dollar can buy. I'm personally a huge fan of Bounty—you know, the "quicker picker-upper." Maybe my preference is due in large part to the jingle associated with this product because I do find myself singing it on occasion as I'm cleaning up the latest flood. By all means, please don't rinse and reuse paper towels in an effort to conserve money or anything else. I have a penchant for bargain shopping, but even I draw the line on this one. Our family goes through approximately one roll of paper towels every two days or so, and that's just fine with me. I don't have the time to do multiple loads of laundry each day to wash the again dirty (yet pretty) dishtowels.

A Reliable Sitter (or Two)

By the time your multiples reach the age of one, you're going to be ultracomfortable leaving them for an evening, believe me. It's extremely important to ensure that you have a reliable sitter with whom you are comfortable leaving your children for a few hours so that you and your husband can get out together. Once you get comfortable with actually leaving your children, you may get uncomfortable with how much it will cost to leave them. It's easy to think that going out isn't worth the expense, but look at it as an investment in your marriage, and allocate part of your monthly budget to babysitting services. This way, none of it is an unexpected expense.

Yoga (or at least the ability to breathe deeply)

The ability to transform yourself immediately into a relaxed state will come in handy when you hear someone yell, "That wary bad! Crayon only go on paper!"

Ketchup, Lots of Ketchup

This is the surefire can't-beat-it sanity saver for mealtimes. My kids put ketchup on their ketchup. I bet many kids would eat even brussels sprouts if they were covered in ketchup.

20/ Ready or Not...There We Go!

THE SECOND YEAR
(TWELVE- TO TWENTY-FOUR-MONTH-OLDS)

Serenity Now!
—Frank Costanza, *Seinfeld*

Early in Jack's and Henry's second year, I went to watch fellow "multiples" sorority members Sonya and Barb, plus our friend Stacey, compete as a relay team in a local triathlon. I was simply in awe. I couldn't even run to the stop sign at the end of the street, and here they were swimming half a mile, biking fifteen miles, and then running 3.2 miles. As usual, I was happy on the sidelines with my chocolate ice cream cone.

The fact that I had no desire to do so notwithstanding, it truly was amazing to me that I couldn't successfully participate in any of these endeavors. My children moved so much at that point (and, as promised by more than a handful of clairvoyant strangers, never in the same direction) that I was often convinced that the sum total of my daily running segments surely equaled a marathon—at least. Due to their constant motion—rivaled only by the level of their curiosity— I quickly developed enormous interest in sheep herding and childproofing.

Big changes occur in the six months following the first birthday. It's hard to decide which is more chaotic: working with newborns to get them onto a schedule or chasing after them once they realize that putting one foot in front of the other can be fun. Sooner than you think, your toddlers will begin walking (and almost immediately thereafter, running), talking (though you may rarely understand them at first), and standing firm in their conviction that they are in charge.

Have you ever had a conversation with someone who talks so quickly and/or loudly that you find yourself suddenly whispering (slowly) in an effort to coax her into a quieter state? During this second year, one of my most common thoughts was "God bless Mr. Rogers." Albeit through a television screen, he became that person in my life whose voice relaxed my mind almost instantly. Apparently, my mother used to look forward to the Mr. Rogers time slot with great anticipation for the same reason. He was on at four in the afternoon when I was younger, and nowadays, at least in my time zone, he's on at 10:30 a.m. It's a good thing; I need him long before four o'clock.

Beyond Mr. Rogers, there are a number of items all moms of twin toddlers need.

Absolute Necessities for Moms of Twin Toddlers

A Proper Key Chain

By "proper," I mean easy to locate immediately. There's nothing like standing in the middle of a parking lot (possibly in the rain) with two kids who are none-too-pleased to be out and about in the first place, an impatient civilian waiting for your parking spot, and the inability to find your car keys inside the bottomless pit you call a purse. I have a key chain that's more like a bracelet. I literally wear it through stores, and when I need it, I know exactly where it is. The only problem with it is that it allows me to put so many keys on it that I believe it's seriously damaging my car's ignition.

A fabulous product that recently hit the market is called Finders Key Purse™. It's brilliant. It's a little J hook like thing that slips onto the outside of your purse. Your keys suspend from the clip that hangs inside your purse, and the portion that's outside your purse is a cute charm or design of one form or another. Do a search for the product on the Internet and you'll find a whole slew of retailers that carry them. I discovered them at our local Bob Evans restaurant of all places.

Laid-back Friends

It is important to ensure that you have friends who truly do not care what condition you or your house is in when they come over.

A Proper Broom

One of the cleaning activities you'll do most frequently over the next few years is sweep crumbs off of the floor. Keep a broom and dustpan combo near the kitchen. It is tiring to get down on your hands and knees to clean up the remnants of each meal. With this combination product, you can sweep up the crumbs and dump them right into the sink or the trash can.

A Sanitizer for Oft-Touched Surfaces

Store a can of Lysol sanitizing spray on each floor of the house. Your twins are toddlers—need I say more? Spray door handles, light switches, and faucet handles on occasion—especially during cold and flu season. Store this product up high; don't trust any of the childproof cabinet locks except the Tot-Lok where cleaning products, medicines, or any other toxic product is kept. My kids learned to work most childproof products remarkably quickly.

Floral Wire Cutters

Don't panic. I would never suggest that making your own wreathes or floral arrangements is an integral part of raising twin toddlers. You will need wire cutters not for adult craft projects, but for cutting the wires that hold toys hostage in the manufacturer's boxes. Most toys are wired into these boxes so well that it makes me wonder whether or not the toy companies actually want us to get them out!

An additional note: Before any holiday or special event, free the toys from their boxes and either rewrap them or put them into gift bags. When a toddler gets his hands on the toy of the century and then has to wait fifteen minutes while you cut or twist the toy loose, it's not pretty.

Antibacterial Hand Sanitizer

As Lysol's partner in keeping germs at bay, antibacterial hand sanitizing gel should be kept in abundant supply. Store it everywhere. Use it often.

A Memory Box

As many times as I was asked, "How do you do it?" when the boys were babies, during the toddler years a new phrase came precariously close to booting that one out of its first-place status. Friends and strangers alike demanded, "Write that down!" every time something even remotely funny happened around here (which was often). I knew I should, but really, when? My solution was to quickly jot down the basics—a comment one of the kids made or a hilarious question one of them asked—on a Post-it note and stick it in a little box inside my kitchen cupboard. One day I'll get around to sorting through them and writing them out more formally, but this way, at least they don't get lost in that big black hole that is my brain.

THEY'RE ON THE MOVE!

You spend so much time asking, "When will they walk? When will they talk?" And then they do and you spend even more time asking, "Will you please sit down and be quiet?"
—Steve, father of three

It's hard to keep up with twin toddlers on the move. Remember all those people who drove you crazy asking what form of fertility drugs you took, or informing you with great insight that you had your hands full? When your babies get close to being vertically mobile, these same people will proclaim, "Just wait because when they start walking, they'll always go in different directions!" As much as it pains me to admit it, they are by and large right on this one. Twins think alike and differently at rather inconvenient times. They think alike when they are trying to navigate to the top of the fridge and differently when they are deciding which direction to flee when they are frightened or curious (or simply defying authority!).

If they have not already, sometime during this year your children are going to get mobile. Vertically mobile, that is. They may do it at the same time and they may not. Honestly, there are pros and cons to either alternative. If they begin to walk at the same point in time, you don't have to worry about one wanting to be carried simply because the other needs to be. However, you'll be dealing with two little beings who are concurrently ecstatic to realize that there are ways to get somewhere other than on one's hands and knees or by scooting across the room on one's bum.

This newfound skill alters the daily dynamic quite a bit. On a positive note, the kids have a completely new activity for which you didn't have to spend a dime. They derive immense satisfaction from seeing the world at a whole new level. At the same time, they quickly realize that the higher level at which they can now function also affords them the luxury of access to a whole new world of fun provided by cabinets, drawers, tabletop knickknacks, window blind cords, and oven knobs. Therefore, the most immediate challenge on your end will be to ensure that your home is as safe as it can possibly be.

CHILDPROOFING FOR TODDLERS

Only adults have difficulty with childproof caps.

—Unknown

Truthfully, without effective childproofing you'll often feel like a robot whose batteries are on overdrive. You'll not only understand the word "pivot" much better than Chandler did on the *Friends* episode when Ross used it repeatedly, yet ineffectively, to direct the process of moving his new sofa up an oddly shaped stairway, you'll also find yourself doing it every 1.2 seconds—either to find a temporarily lost child or to determine what toy or lamp caused the most recent crash.

Think about it. There's a whole new level of stuff (literally) that your kids can get into once they are vertical. Many childproofing experts recommend that parents get down on their hands and knees and crawl around their home so that they can be fully aware of all of the fascinating items that small crawlers and walkers can get their hands on (or into). I've done this in my home, and I've done it in hotel rooms. Actually, performing this exercise in hotel rooms was particularly enlightening. It taught me not only that there are tons of hidden dangers there, but also that the carpets are usually so disgusting that letting the kids down on them any more than necessary was potentially more hazardous than allowing them to experiment with ways to climb into each of the six dresser drawers in search of the requisite hotel Bible.

I realize it may not seem possible, but the childproofing necessity may actually be greater with twelve- to eighteen-month-old twins than it was when they were crawling around gaining interest in every outlet plug or minute piece of mulch that migrated from the patio to the carpet and frankly, was so small that even the vacuum cleaner missed it. Once standing, your kids have access to intriguing items such as tabletop décor, door knobs, fireplace hearths and tools, and dishwasher and oven controls.

Rule Number 1: Get rid of anything that you do not want your children playing with. Put away all crystal, all expensive picture frames, and all knife blocks. If you own a Grammy or an Oscar or an Emmy, move it to higher ground as well. This stinks, I know. You'll have to decide which is harder: putting these things away for a while or saying "No" to your kids all day long. Of course, there are going to be a few items that you choose to leave out—or leave out thinking that there's no way the kids will be interested in them. When your kids get into them, you'll have to let them know in no uncertain terms that those aren't to be played with or around. However, unless you want your kids to be yelling "No" at you at every turn (and believe me, you do not), do what you can to ensure that you aren't yelling it at *them* at every turn.

In the "multiples" sorority's experience, the most important elements to childproof are the fireplace, television, any heavy furniture that could tip over, lamps, unlocked cabinets, chairs that can be moved across the kitchen to gain access to counter tops and thereafter the top of the refrigerator, the dishwasher, crystal chandeliers . . . You see where I'm going with this. There's not a lot that's respected as "off limits" by a curious set of twins who are in the process of discovering that their legs, when put one in front of the other, can get them places. Add to that the realization that their minds, when put together, would make Einstein proud and you've got the recipe for a science experiment gone awry. Even though they may be barely talking, trust me, they are communicating with one another. And their world is about getting into everything "off limits." I think it's sort of the same logic they use after opening a gift and deciding that the best part of it is the box in which it came. As a parent, you don't really understand what's so fascinating about the goo under the seat of the chair or the torn box in which the Weeble Wobbles were packaged, but to young children, they are potentially the most fascinating discoveries on earth (at least for the moment), and we have to respect—albeit question—that natural curiosity while keeping them safe.

One thing you're also likely to discover early on is that many of the childproofing products on the market weren't designed with twins in mind.

And so I say, Thank God for Duct Tape.

I remember the day I went over to Mollie's for one reason or another and nearly fell over when I got into her kitchen. The oven door was duct taped shut, the knobs had been completely removed, and the dishwasher was also duct taped shut (this part, she assured me, was only temporary). Her boys had been opening the oven door and playing with the buttons, and since she never cooks (her husband, Gary, has been known to hide her birthday and holiday gifts in there since he knows she's not likely to open it), duct tape seemed perfectly logical.

Jack learned to work the cabinet door locks incredibly quickly. I've become convinced that the only cabinet door locks that make sense when you absolutely, unconditionally do not want kids in a particular cabinet are the magnetic Tot-Loks. Though more expensive than other varieties, they prevent a drawer or cabinet from being opened even a little bit. This not only solves the problem of kids learning how to work the locks, but also the dilemma of those same kids slamming their fingers in the doors and drawers over and over again.

The one potential problem with this type of magnetic lock (and the reason I did not purchase them initially) is that if you lose the magnet that unlocks them, you're hosed. Since I can rarely find my car keys (in the house—when I'm not wearing them on my wrist), I knew this was a disaster waiting to happen. Also, it's not always easy to get the magnet in just the right position to unlock the lock, and it can be frustrating to stand there running the magnetic key over the cabinet façade for what feels like hours on end just waiting for the magic *click*. My husband has never been able to open a single cabinet locked with this type of lock. This may speak to his abilities (or lack thereof) in the home improvement arena, or it may suggest that the batch we purchased is functioning on the extreme end of the way in which they were intended, I'm not entirely sure.

I left one cabinet unlocked and designated it the boys' Funland. I filled it with Tupperware and thought it would be enough to curb their curiosity. I was sort of right. They opened that cabinet and fought over who got to go in first (at thirteen months old, and I have the video to prove it). Then, when one got in to retrieve something in the back, the other would shut the door on him and lock him in the dark. The screaming would commence, I'd save the kid who was confined to darkness, and they'd start all over again. This went on for a while, until they got bored, and then they started trying to figure out how to get into the other cabinets. So, lock them however you want. But again, don't leave anything in them that would be horribly dangerous for them to get to, certainly not cleaning products, medicines, or knives.

For those of you who are reading this and thinking, "No way, I am not going to live in a house that is completely stripped of everything that makes it a home and not a barn," I understand. Barb's house always amazed me because she was somehow able to keep picture frames on top of end tables, vases on top of coffee tables, and the dining room table set as though a feast for twelve would be served any minute. In addition, her house was always immaculate. She claims this is not true and that she had taken *tons* of stuff down, but believe me, if you compared my house to hers at that point in time, it was like comparing the cheapest room at the Four Seasons to a room reserved for someone requiring solitary confinement at an insane asylum. Do your best to keep those things available that make you feel "at home." If you can pull it off without saying "No" all day long, replacing fourteen objects per week, or sweating over what might break in the next ten minutes, then as I tell Barb almost constantly, You Rock.

And finally, please ensure that you are up-to-date on your CPR certification. The American Red Cross recommends that you take a refresher course every two years. Of course, we all hope we never have to use these skills, but in the event that we do, it would be unfortunate not to have the knowledge. I've heard that some Red Cross chapters are now offering at-home CPR courses. For as few as six and as many as twelve participants, a Red Cross volunteer will come to your home and provide the instruction. You can enjoy a social opportunity and receive a life-saving lesson in one afternoon. If this sounds fun, check with your local Red Cross chapter to see if such an opportunity is available in your area.

Childproofing for Twin Toddlers: The Specifics

There's a lot to keep in mind when ensuring that your home is safe for your toddlers. In an effort to alert you to hazards you may not have thought of, I've included as many potential dangers as I could.

- Post the number for Poison Control by each phone in your home. Program it into your cell phone as well. The national number is (800) 222-1222. Many cities have a local number as well. Check with your local hospital to see if they have one.

- Ensure that all outlets are covered with outlet plugs.

- Remove all knives and scissors from accessible cabinets and drawers and from the countertops.

- Lock all cabinets and drawers that you do not want the kids to get into—whether you believe that they can get into them or not.

- Do not assume that the kids are listening or understand when you explain that pens, pencils, and permanent markers are Mommy's. Just put them out of reach.

- Keep all bathroom doors shut.

- Once the kids are able to reach the doorknobs, whether or not they've demonstrated the ability to actually turn them, attach doorknob covers. Thankfully, these deterrents are even made for French-door handles nowadays.

- Protect fireplace hearths. The foam cushions that attach to the edges of the hearth with Velcro probably won't work. Kids quickly figure out that if they pull hard enough, the cushions come right off. In the end, most of us had to put a large gate in front of the hearth or move our furniture around so that a few chairs or a couch blocked the kids' access to it.

- Bolt all furniture that's heavy, especially in their rooms, to the wall (you should do this even for a singleton, but trust me, twins will find a way to crawl into drawers or jointly pull on something with just the right leverage to bring it down). The holes in the wall are inconvenient, but you'd far prefer to spackle and repaint in a few years than worry, or worse, hear a loud crash and find a potentially hurt child.

- Clean when your kids aren't around. Most poisoning accidents occur when parents are using products such as window or bathroom cleaners. All too quickly, one kid goes running for the steps, and as you lurch to grab him, the other grabs the Scrubbing Bubbles. The stress just isn't worth it.

- Ensure that you keep your exterior doors, especially screen doors, locked to ensure that a child can't sneak out when you aren't looking.

- Prevent the kids from breaking and falling through screen doors by keeping the main door closed or purchasing a screen-door child protector.

- If you have a deadbolt that does not use a key but instead only has to be turned to the left or right to unlock it, consider installing a second lock at the top of front/back doors. You could install a second deadbolt or a slide-bolt lock. The goal is to provide a lock that the kids can't reach and unlock (or lock after you've run out to get the mail). As the kids get taller, it will be too easy for them to reach up and unlock doors to open them—to either solicitors or deliverymen who've rung the bell, or simply to get out. Don't assume that you'll always hear them when they're engaging in activities like this. Remember, the times during the day when you should be the most concerned are those when it's the quietest.

- Put a lock on any accordion-style doors in common areas. Opening and closing these doors is more fun for children than you might believe . . . that is, until someone's fingers get pinched.

- Make sure all window blind cords are childproofed. Most newer models come childproofed from the factory. On older models, you should cut the looped cords. Also, wind the cords around S-hooks. Even if a cord is childproofed so that your child doesn't get tangled up in it, he might have a bit too much fun using it as a pulley or pretending he's a monkey and the cord is his vine. It's better to keep it out of his reach completely.

- Install gates at the top and bottom of your steps. If you

have a banister at the top and/or bottom (even I would not drill into my banister to install a gate), there's a wide gate called the Extra-Wide Soft Gate by Evenflo that you can slip in between the spindles. For a more aesthetically pleasing look, take cues from Sonya. She took a piece of plywood, cut it to the proper size, and covered it with batting and a fabric that matched her décor. She then slipped that between the spindles. If you have a wall on one side of your staircase and a banister on the other, look for a gate with a no-holes post mount for the banister side.

- Many newer cars have a button on the driver's side that allows the driver to prevent passengers from raising or lowering their windows. If your car has this feature, use it. And if you have the ability to lock all doors from your pole-position, do that as well. If not, utilize the child lock feature on the kids' doors. Opening the doors will be difficult for them while they are in a car seat with a five-point harness, but I've personally known children who figured out how to use their foot to open the window (and throw things out of it before their mother was able to recover from her momentary state of hysteria and figure out which button to push to raise it back up).

- Be aware of hazards posed by lamps. A lamp often provides the finishing touch to a room, but when a toddler has access to and pulls on its cord and the lamp comes crashing down (and the light bulb breaks on the kid's head; it happened here, folks), it ruins the ambience. Don't even get me started on floor lamps. Mollie insisted on keeping her floor lamps, so she screwed an eyehook into the wall and used a cable tie to secure the lamp post to the eyehook.

- Beware of tablecloths. They're pretty, yes. What is not pretty is the aftermath of a child (or children) pulling them and their contents onto the floor (or their heads).

- Keep your purse out of reach. Kids love to go through bags, and in all likelihood, there are a few things in your purse to which toddlers should not have access. A hook on which to consistently hang your purse is a great idea anyhow; it will ensure that you always know where it is when you need it. (An equally great idea: keep your keys on the same hook.)

- Don't neglect visitors' purses. Many times, visitors are used to setting their purses just inside the front door or on the kitchen table in their own home. Without thinking about it they may drop it in the same place while visiting your house. While you and your guest are chatting, your kids may be having a scavenger hunt. Additionally, grandparents' purses pose a hazard as they may contain medicines that don't have childproof caps.

- Rid your home of all toxic houseplants. A quick Internet search will provide you with a list of the dangerous varieties.

- If your oven knobs are accessible, either remove them (and reattach them when you cook) or purchase a product that will prevent your children from being able to turn them.

- If you have a gas cook top, install a carbon monoxide (CO) detector in your home. Our cook top is built into our kitchen island, and the knobs are, therefore, also on top of the island. One day, Henry used a stool to get something off of the island, and in the process, became curious about the fun-looking knobs. He turned one, and while the burner didn't light, the gas line was open and gas was spilling into the kitchen. Thankfully, I was nearby and heard the clicking sound the cook top makes when the gas has been activated. But if I hadn't, it would have been critical to be alerted to the unsafe level of carbon monoxide in the home.

- Keep a fire extinguisher in the pantry. (Don't worry, I don't know anyone who's ever had to use one, but just in case, it's a good thing to have. Frankly, it's a good thing to have whether you have children or not.)

- Ensure that all trash cans are inaccessible.

- If you have a wood burning fireplace with a gas starter, store the key to the starter out of reach. If you have a gas fireplace with a glass front that gets hot when the fire is on, set up a gate to prevent children from touching the glass. In many cases, the glass can get hot enough to cause third-degree burns if touched.

- If you have an in-ground pool, ensure that you have a four-foot-high fence with a self-closing and self-latching gate around it.

- Be sure to empty wading pools after each use.

- Don't leave even small amounts of water in buckets or other containers. Toddlers are top-heavy and can fall into, and drown in, even small amounts of water.

- If you have any guns in the house, ensure that they are stored in a spot that is completely inaccessible to kids. It's best to store weapons in a locked gun safe. A combination lock is safest because there's no chance of kids obtaining the key and unlocking it.

As an additional note, at some point I read that parents should mark sliding doors or other large pieces of glass with stickers. I assume that this is meant to prevent the kids from accidentally walking into the door, much as it's meant to protect birds from flying into windows that are so clean that they appear invisible. These are toddlers, not birds. How many homes with mobile toddlers have sliding doors that are so clean that the kids might mistake them for an open door? If any exist, I want the name of the owners' cleaning product or person immediately.

Home-Proofing for Twin Toddlers

While we're at it, although it's most important to protect one's children from dangers in the home, the "multiples" sorority feels that it is also necessary to protect one's home from the dangers posed by children. To that end, there are a few requisite cleaning supplies all parents of toddlers should keep on hand.

- Mr. Clean Magic Eraser (It even gets permanent marker off a computer screen; see the three- to four-year section for further details.)

- A plunger—with strong suction

- A powerful carpet cleaner

- A quality window and wall cleaner. Wipes pre-saturated with window cleaner—or any other kind of cleaner—are great because they limit any cleaning job to one step.

- Lots of paper towels

- Spackle and sandpaper (to repair holes from toys ridden—or rammed—into the wall). Spackle now comes in varieties that go on pink or blue and then dry white so that you know when it's safe to sand it. This can prove most helpful. I understand all too well that when a wall has been damaged, you want it fixed as soon as possible. But trust me, sanding spackle before it's dried is *not* a fun experience.

- Tide-to-Go Pen (to prevent you from refusing to buy that incredibly cute shirt because you are convinced that the first time you wear it someone will "accidentally" pour a glass of purple grape juice right down your front).

GOTTA GET OUTTA THIS PLACE!

Vacation is what you take when you can't take what you've been taking any longer!
— The Cowardly Lion, *The Wizard of Oz*

Next to childproofing, the most important focus over the next few years is undeniably taking care of yourself. The phrase "get outta this place" is meant both literally and figuratively. There is no doubt that you'll need to get out of your home now and then to get some space, some time to regenerate and reflect, and the opportunity to finish a gossip magazine so you're crystal clear on whether or not Brad and Angelina really are engaged. You'll also need to get out of the place in your head that is preventing you from putting a positive spin on less-than-positive experiences.

When the boys were nearly four years old, we joined a fitness club. David wanted to join to get into better shape in case he ever came face to face with Faith Hill. He talked me into the membership by touting the benefits of the complimentary childcare available at the facility (it didn't take long for me to acquiesce). I do not enjoy formal exercise. However, on many levels, it had become clear that I needed to start some kind of a routine. The little diet-that-allows-no-fruit regimen I'd started early in the boys' toddler years hadn't lasted more than seventeen days, and what better reason to start a fitness routine than the grand opening of a facility where the kids could spend an hour loving life on basketball courts sized just for them while I did what I could to lose the ten pounds that *still* had not dropped off of me?

After the requisite sixty minutes of suffering through an exercise class while praying that the woman next to me was a trained EMT (in case I passed out from sweating too much or breathing too heavily), or thirty minutes of tolerating the treadmill right beneath a TV showing *The View* with closed-captioning and my iPod in one ear and my cell phone in the other—so as to render myself as unaware as possible of the sweat and heavy breathing—I had to laugh at what I often found in the locker room. Undoubtedly, on any given day I could count on discovering three or four women—complete strangers to one another—sitting in the lounge area watching the television. One day, they were sitting there watching the advertisement for that Space Saver apparatus. I kid you not. I thought, "I'm glad I'm not the only one. Clearly other women need a break at least as badly as I do and are willing to watch very bad infomercials to get it!"

When raising young children, it's easy to feel completely overwhelmed. As with anything else, if you perceive the length of your to-do lists, the challenges in your relationship with your spouse, or your concerns over just how to keep your kids within ten feet of you at the mall to be mountains instead of mole hills, you'll always be behind the eight ball instead of in front of it.

Truthfully, I had a hard time with the concept of getting away in the beginning. Part of the issue with leaving the house was that I have always had a need to control things. I arrived into this world three weeks overdue for heaven's sake (thank goodness they don't allow women to stay pregnant this long anymore). I suppose I've done things on my own terms since the get-go.

While David is more than competent as a father and caregiver, I was nervous about leaving the kids for an extended period of time. After all, I was the one who had cared for them each and every day since the moment they had first been placed in my arms. As much as I needed a break, in some ironically masochistic way it was hard to bring myself to walk out the front door.

As Brenna, a mom of boy/girl twins and an older son, noted, "I learned that leaving my kids for the weekend meant giving up control. Sure, I could write down their schedule and tape it to the fridge. I could make a list of acceptable menus, but was anyone really going to follow it?" Ultimately, she concluded that it wasn't going to hurt anyone if the kids ended up eating an occasional McDonald's Happy Meal or going to bed a half-hour later than usual. She took her trip, and ended up relaxed, rejuvenated, and ready to face life again with a lot less stress and a little more patience to offer her children and husband. She also learned that it was important for her husband to know that he could take care of all three kids. It helped to build his confidence as a father, and he had a great time with them to boot. Dads who are full-time working parents don't get that one-on-one quality time with all of their kids on a consistent basis. These kinds of opportunities are really positive for them on the enlightenment as well as the confidence fronts, and the kids look forward to them with great anticipation.

With regard to getting out of my mind and changing my way of thinking (I already was out of my mind many days, which was ninety-six percent of the problem), I believe that it's challenging to diametrically change your way of thinking at any point in your life. When your days are chock full of myriad parenting and household or career duties, it multiplies the difficulty level by quite a bit. Commented Brenna, "I am a mother, but before I was a mother I was a person with interests and thoughts of my own, and I owe it not just to myself, but also to my children, to reconnect every once in a while with this woman I used to be, so that I can remember who I am and have more to offer my family."

Important advice regarding getting away (and so much more): ensure that your perspective motivates you, not debilitates you. We have the ability to choose how we will perceive any situation. I have learned this to an enormous degree over the last few years. I've watched friends and acquaintances have a challenge dropped on their doorstep— one that I believe would have blown me away had it landed on mine. But in the end, what did blow me away was the way they chose to look at and address the situation.

We have, in essence, the ability to create and even modify our reality on a minute-to-minute basis without doing anything more than changing our way of thinking. As an example, let me take you back to the days and nights when your babies were eating constantly. You were so tired you were using toothpicks to prop your eyelids open at 3:00 a.m. The debilitating perspective would be: I can't do this. This is impossible. These babies are never going to get onto a schedule and I'm going to lose my mind. The motivating perspective would be: there are parents out there right now doing this same thing with quadruplets or quintuplets. I can do this too. Suddenly, with a quick change in perspective, your reality can appear a little bit more manageable and a little less dire, can't it?

In the case of going away for a night or a weekend (or longer), your perspective can be that the kids simply won't make it without you, or it can be that this is as good for the kids as it is for you. You can believe that you don't need some time away (and then proceed to yell at someone two seconds later for reasons that are unclear even to you), or you can believe that a small break will refresh you to a point where someone throwing a ball into a hanging plant which then delivers a tidal wave of dirt to your carpet frustrates you, but you know it can be vacuumed up rather quickly. I say all of this from experience because I did not get away by myself until *way* too late; my perspective for far too long was of the debilitating variety.

Over the course of the boys' toddler years, my need to get out and create some variety in my life on a consistent basis made itself clear in various ways, subtle and otherwise. One of the less subtle messages came directly from my husband's mouth the night he looked at the television, sighed loudly, and said, "Um, at what point in your reality-TV obsession do you become concerned that it's gone too far? Because I think that the fact that you're watching *Meet the Barkers* at eleven thirty on a Sunday night may just be a cry for help."

Another initial challenge was the fact that it truly took about forty-eight hours for me just to wind down. I loved getting out for a trip to the mall by myself, but sometimes I was so preoccupied with what would be going on when I got home that it was hard to truly be in the moment.

Mollie had the same problem. One afternoon after she'd gotten a facial, she called to check in. I asked her how the treatment was and she reported that it was nice, but she felt that the aesthetician "could have been more efficient." For only the third or fourth time in my life I was stunned into silence.

"What?" I asked.

"Well, it's just that she spent a *lot* of time cleansing and a *lot* of time massaging my temples and I just spent most of that time thinking, 'You know, if you multitasked this way or that way, you could cut down this facial from fifty minutes to thirty-five.'"

"Mollie," I quietly advised, "a facial is supposed to take a while. You're not supposed to *want* it to be over. It's not about multitasking. It's about the silence."

So please, to right the universal balance that surely is still out of whack after this need-for-efficiency-gone-haywire episode, would everyone please go get a facial sometime this month and think of nothing but the silence? And pray that the aesthetician massages those temples forever!

My first big break—meaning more than four hours—came when the boys were about eighteen months old. I went to a nice resort about three hours away. Far enough away to feel like I had left town, and yet close enough that I could get home in an emergency without having to rebook a flight. I checked in to the hotel, carried my too-cute-ever-to-be-checked-on-an-airline bag to my room, plopped down on the bed, and became instantly confused. No one was yelling. There were no diapers to change. There was no food to prepare. It was just me and a bed and a room service menu. Oh, and a spa. And frankly, I had no idea what the hell to do!

So I did what I always do in those types of situations: I called Mollie.

"Hello?" she answered.

"Hi!" I animatedly began, as though I hadn't talked to her in weeks. "What are you doing?"

(Pause)

"Um, where are you? You're supposed to be out of town."

"Well, I am. I am out of town."

"Are you okay? Ohmigod, is everything all right at home?"

"To the best of my knowledge."

"Well, what's the problem? Oh lord, is your room a pit? Did they put you in a pit?"

"No, no," I reassured her. "The room is very nice. I have a robe and slippers and everything."

Another moment of silence.

"And you're calling me *why*?"

"Well, um, because . . . and I feel really weird about saying this . . . but, I have no idea what to do!"

At this point some statements came out of Mollie's mouth that bordered on inappropriate, and I wouldn't want to embarrass her by continuing to transcribe the dialogue. Though to be fair, I may have misunderstood a few of those words because there were two smaller beings screaming loudly right next to her.

When the boys were two, my mom and I splurged on four days at a spa. It was truly a splurge, but I really, really needed it (refer to the "Fecal Fascination" section for more information on exactly why). So we modified our lifestyle for a few months to allow it to occur. When I say modified, I mean that I really thought that I had eaten my last package of Ramen noodles in my dorm room a good number of years earlier. But it was worth it and I've never looked back and regretted it even for a second. And that's how it usually goes; you hesitate and hesitate and finally acquiesce and then wonder why the heck you waited so long!

A couple of years later, I had the opportunity to attend a business function with David. You know, the kind of husband's "business function" that lasts three days but only two hours of that time is set aside for an actual meeting while the remaining time is allocated to a round of golf, an afternoon at the spa, and a whole lot of food consumption? It was one of those functions. And I told him that under those circumstances, if I didn't go, neither did he.

I chose to get crazy and try a new water treatment at the spa. I lay down on a table as the therapist rubbed a sugar scrub exfoliant all over me. I tried not to wince as my legs felt as though they were being stung by thousands of bees simultaneously because I was dumb enough to shave ten minutes prior to the appointment out of fear that my unshaven legs would horrify the staff. After being hosed off (literally), I was invited to hop into a Kohler shower with a body spray on the back wall and a waterfall above it. My wonderful masseuse, Pam, explained how to use it. Seemed easy.

I sat down on the seat, plunged my feet into the twelve-inch-deep warm water, and turned around to hit Body Spray. Out of four holes came four jets of water. I adjusted the pressure to be a bit more intense. I then thought, "Wonder how the waterfall feels?" I turned around, selected Waterfall, and just about melted as it cascaded down with the perfect pressure over my aching shoulders and neck. Oh, the relief.

After a few minutes more, I decided to return to the jets. I turned around to reactivate them, but when I pushed the applicable button, it appeared that they had reset to the highest pressure possible. The water surged out of the holes like rockets being propelled into orbit. Reminded me of that frozen dinner commercial where the large burly man is blown into a wall by his hair dryer because he claims he ate sprouts and cucumbers for dinner instead of the manly frozen dinner being advertised. Without warning, I was pushed right off the seat into the basin below. There was water shooting everywhere and truth be told, it hurt! I could not turn around to fix the problem for fear I'd lose an eye (and if water at that pressure went up my nose, it would surely make it to my brain and I couldn't afford to lose any more of that). So, I lay there for a minute somewhat paralyzed, and then, instead of worrying about the very real possibility that I might lose my vision through a strange version of water torture, I thought, "Please don't let Pam walk in right now and see me like this." There's not much that's less relaxing than having your masseuse perform CPR on you before applying a lime-mint lotion.

I fought back the broken dam of water and got my rear on the seat, used my feet to hold me in place, and waved my arm frantically behind me until I found a button—any button would do at that point—and activated the waterfall again, which thankfully came down quite peacefully. About thirty seconds later, Pam walked in and draped a dry towel over the top of the shower, letting me know it was time to get out. I could barely contain myself. Truly, it was like a cartoon. So, in addition to a little R&R, a day or a weekend away may provide you with some humor and something to write about in the journal you should be keeping, since you likely will remember little of this time period fifty (or even four) years from now.

Sometimes, when you're in the thick of it, it's hard to justify the money or the time away—or both. Keep in mind that relaxation and rejuvenation do not have to come in the form of a weeklong stay at one of the top spas in the world.

Mollie is a firm advocate of "mini outings" several times a year as opposed to a big vacation once a year. As she puts it, "You need to get a haircut by yourself. You need to browse the mall by yourself." As she frequently reminds me, Mother Teresa was the one who said that you can't take care of others until you take care of yourself. Mollie's physician actually wrote her a prescription for three hours per week of

"Mollie time." She instructed Mollie to give it to Gary so that he would help ensure that she stay on her "medication." Frankly, I love this doctor even though I've never met her. Not for lack of effort however. She has been closed to new patients for three years. Gee, I wonder why.

Deciding when they are ready to leave their children for some time away is often a challenge for moms. If going away by themselves, moms sometimes have trouble turning it all over to dad or another family member or friend. If going away with their spouse, moms occasionally have concerns about how things will go while they're gone. One mom confided in me (after she made me swear to protect her anonymity) that the hardest part about going away with her husband for the first time was the knowledge that she would return home to a laundry list of things that her mother-in-law wanted her to start doing so that the kids would have a prayer at being raised properly! Sometimes, being able to let go of that need for control—and being able to trust that although things may be done a bit differently while you're gone, the children will be loved and well taken care of—is the hardest part.

A few moms I've spoken with (and, frankly, I'm included in this group) have been somewhat frustrated by one fact. Inevitably, after a nice day, weekend, week (whatever) away, the minute they walk back in the door expecting some glowing made-for-TV moment when all the kids rush to them in slow motion, freshly bathed and proclaiming their glory in their Sunday best, they are instead pounced on at the door by the whining, crying, and yelling that they left in the first place. That said, I have yet to meet a woman who claims she won't leave again just because she knows what she has to look forward to upon returning home. I usually spend the last hour of my time away (driving home from the airport or wherever I've been) listening to a classical music station and doing some serious deep breathing. I do not expect the kids to be in pinafores or for Grace's hair to be perfectly braided à la American Girl (which I can barely do myself). I expect the chaos. That way, if it's chaos, it's exactly what I expected. If it's anything better than that, I'm thrilled.

GOTTA GET OUTTA THIS PLACE!
(WITH MY SPOUSE)

Do not wait for ideal circumstances, nor the best opportunities; they will never come.

—Janet Erskine Stuart

I know all too well that it may not be possible to have frequent out-of-town getaways with your spouse while the kids are young. It can be hard to find someone to care for two (or more) small children for an extended period of time, especially if most of your family lives out of town. At a minimum, be sure to schedule frequent dates with your spouse so that you can get out and spend time together without any interruptions.

One of Barb's friends came up with a great plan. She put her sitter on retainer to come every Wednesday evening. She and her husband budgeted for it every month so there was no stress over where the money would come from. They went out to dinner, took in a movie, or just ran errands. Regardless of the activity, they were spending time together and it broke up the week. They had something to look forward to midweek instead of waking up Monday morning and thinking, "That was the fastest forty-eight hours in history and I'll talk to you in five days."

It's possible that over the next year or so (and certainly over the next few years), a dinner out here and there with your spouse, while fabulous, might not be enough to give the two of you sufficient time alone, away from the yelling, and even the mundane tasks of bed making, laundry folding, and menu planning. It's fun to get away by yourself or with girlfriends, but it's important to get away with your spouse, if for no other reason than to have a great time and remember why you got together in the first place!

Over the past six years, David and I have gone away together overnight only four times. For various reasons, it's been hard to find someone to stay with the kids. The closeness in age of our kids makes our house more like a daycare center than a home and is a lot for *us*, let alone for folks who aren't used to providing this sort of care twenty-four/seven.

Our most recent trip was to Las Vegas. David had a business conference there (tag along on these whenever possible; it's very cost effective), and I now strongly urge that Las Vegas is the place to go if you are looking to get as far away from the feeling of being a parent as possible. That said, do not walk the strip after 10:00 p.m. because you'll want to call child protective services on the tens of parents who are literally dragging their two- and three-year-olds down it that late at night.

Restaurants are open all night long, casinos as well, and there are so many fabulous shows to see it's unbelievable. Las Vegas most certainly is not all about gambling anymore. Obviously, if you want to gamble, you aren't going to have a problem doing so, but if you are strongly against it for some reason, there is a whole slew of other stuff you can do to keep yourself completely entertained for a few days (and nights). One thing that has always been tricky for me about traveling to a place that is more kid-friendly than not is that I'm always thinking, "Oh, Grace would love this!" or "Jack has *got* to see this!" When I'm thinking about the kids constantly and therefore missing them even more, I don't get as much of a true reprieve as I might otherwise.

The first time Mollie and Gary took a trip without their boys (the boys were twenty-one months old), they went to an out-of-town wedding. Gary's parents came and stayed at their house with Tommy and Kevin. On this trip, Mollie felt that the hardest part was calling and not being able to talk to the boys because they did not yet talk. But although she vowed upon returning that she'd never leave them again (she did), she acknowledges that she felt completely refreshed. Most important, getting away either alone or with Gary has reinforced for Mollie how important Gary, Tommy, and Kevin are to her. It also reminds her that there is more to life than the crumbs constantly on the floor, and that she has a name other than "MAAAAAHHHHHMMMM!"

Most moms I've talked to were so anxious initially about leaving their children—even for a night—to spend some quality time with their spouses that in hindsight, they believe they waited far too long. Once they did it, they thought, "Why didn't we do that sooner?" Stephanie reported, "The first time away just breaks you in regarding what a wonderful thing it is to do. You will be looking for excuses to get away once you realize how wonderful it is and that your kids will be okay while you're gone. It doesn't matter if it's for a day, an overnight, or a week. You have to make time for yourself. And you have to make time for your marriage. If you don't, you'll look in the mirror one day and wonder, 'Who am I?' You'll then look at your spouse and wonder, 'Who are *you*?'"

Another important thing to remember (in honor of perspective and all) is that the kids won't be kids forever. They will get older and there will come a point when they will be easier for a family member or friend to manage if you are simply not comfortable leaving them when they are really young. We're not talking high school here (frankly, I'll be more nervous about leaving town when my kids are in high school than when they are much younger). But once they are potty trained and can dress themselves and fluently communicate their needs, it may be more feasible for others to care for them for a few days.

NEW CAR SEATS

Change is inevitable. Change is constant.

—Benjamin Disraeli

Part of Getting Outta This Place, at least on a day-to-day basis, will likely involve the car. You won't need new car seats per se, but it's time to turn them to a new position. Once your babies turn one year old *and* weigh twenty pounds (it's important that they meet both criteria), it is time to turn their car seats around so that they are forward facing.

This change provides several benefits. You can see your children without having to strain to get the perfect angle; you can (provided you aren't driving down the road) hand them their sippy cups or pacifiers with greater ease; and, because facing forward provides a new and improved panorama, the kids may actually enjoy road trips for a while.

One of the most frequent questions moms of twins have once they graduate their babies to the convertible car seats whether facing forward or backward—is, "How do I get them both out of the car once I can no longer put their infant car seats in the stroller and before they are able to get out of their convertible seats themselves?" Answer: most likely the same way you did with the infant car seats, you just don't realize it!

Getting the Babies from Car Seat to Stroller or Cart

Step 1

If you are using a stroller, get it out of the trunk before you do anything else. If you are using a cart, park near a cart stall that has an available cart in it and bring a cart over to your car. (Do not leave your car running while you do this. Turn the car off, lock the doors, and take the keys with you. I'm not trying to be Debbie Downer from *Saturday Night Live*, but it's a frightening world.)

Step 2

If you have a car that allows you to get into the back seat with ease (such as a minivan or SUV), and one of your children is walking even a little bit, you can climb in, unbuckle the child farthest from you, set him on the floor, and then unbuckle the child closest to you. Put the child closest to you in the stroller or cart, have the other child walk over to you, and then put him in the stroller. If neither of your children is able to walk even while holding on to something, or if you have a car, such as a sedan, that does not allow you to climb into the back seat easily, take your stroller to one side of the car, get a child out and put him in the stroller, then take the stroller to the other side and repeat. If it is pouring, either use an umbrella or wait to see if it lets up. (I became a frequent viewer of the online weather channel when my boys were this age. The day's forecast meant little to nothing; I wanted actual radar proof of any and all storms' locations.)

If you are using a cart and are unable to park near a cart stall or the employees of the store are being extra vigilant that day and there are simply no carts outside of the store, you can either carry both kids in and then put them in the cart, or do what Mollie did: put them in their stroller, and push the stroller while pulling a cart behind you.

CAPTURING THE KIDS

You can learn many things from children. How much patience you have, for instance.
                                                                —Franklin P. Adams

We're talking about capturing the kids on film, folks, not a game of supermarket catch and confine. I laughed when I was asked how on earth to go about attempting a professional portrait session with twin toddlers. Come look around my house and you'll see that we have very few professional photos of the kids. It was seriously way too stressful, not to mention exhausting, to attempt a public picture-taking session with them at any stage of toddlerhood. Sometimes I feel badly when I go to other people's houses and they have on display all of their professionally taken annual pictures (or monthly in some cases for babies under the age of one). But, as I look back through albums, there is not one time period that was not captured on one of my own cameras. The shots often aren't posed, and the kids aren't always smiling, but there is proof that the kids were, at some point, fourteen months old.

Right before Christmas one year, Mollie and I took all of our kids to a photo studio at the mall. Mollie was not there to have photos of her own boys taken; she was there to help me. The boys were all two and Grace was four. It was about thirty below zero out, and of course, both Mollie and I were in short-sleeved shirts. It should be noted that we ran into another woman attempting to get photos of her six-month-old twins who didn't even move yet—but still weren't real happy to be involved in this activity—and she was also in a short-sleeved shirt.

After sweating away six pounds in seven minutes, we had one nice shot. Was it worth it? I suppose—it's a great shot. But it wasn't great enough that I've done it since.

Barb didn't go anywhere for formal pictures during her girls' toddler years (or their first year) because she, too, feared the chaos. For Father's Day the year after Olivia and Kambria turned one, Barb hired a professional photographer to do a photo shoot of the girls in a wooded park near her home. The photo was mounted on a sixteen-by-twenty canvas and it's absolutely incredible. She took all the money she would have spent on monthly or seasonal photos at the mall and put it into this project. Again, there's no time period for which Barb doesn't have fantastic pictures of the girls. She whips out her digital camera and takes candid shots all the time, and I would challenge many professional photographers to get the quality shots she's gotten because the girls are in a relaxed environment and there's no pressure—on anyone!

To be fair to those who can't figure out how to open the lens of their camera and therefore choose to leave this chore to the professionals (I'm referring to Mollie here, but don't tell), if you can find a way to head to the photo studio without the stress taking years off of your life, go for it. Ask friends which photo outlets in your area they've had luck with. Find out which studios have employees who are good with kids and make the process fun. Those folks can usually get a good shot in less than three minutes.

Mollie seriously is camera-phobic. She admits to taking pictures here and there for the scrapbooks or to prove that an event (such as a birthday celebration) indeed took place. However, in most cases, she claims that there ends up being some lewd object in the background or some other embarrassment rendering most of these shots unusable.

Our friend Holly, who has triplets, took her girls every single month to have their photo taken. She took a helper most times, but honestly, she took three or four changes of clothing. It was like a Calvin Klein shoot. I've seen most of the pictures, and they all came out incredibly well.

I love taking pictures, and I'm a fan of candid shots, which are far easier to get if the kids aren't expected to think that the duck the photographer is balancing on his head is hysterical. Sadly, a few of my shots inadvertently captured one kid biting the other, so I have those lovely escapades captured forever, but I've gotten some great ones as well.

VENTURING OUT

The kids really just don't listen yet, so telling them to sit down when they're in a wagon or trying to get out of a stroller or cart is like talking to a wall.

—Amy, mom of boy/girl twins

Can you guess where I went the first time I ventured out with Jack and Henry for a "serious" outing after they turned one? Yep, that place I vowed I'd spend little to no time: the mall. I positively had to get something (I have no idea what it was), so after we dropped off Grace at preschool, we headed over. The boys were fourteen months old and rode well in the stroller so I figured I could almost certainly get a couple of hours out of them. Given that it was late October and therefore—in the retail world at least—Christmas was practically yesterday's news, I hoped that they'd be so entranced with the pervasive holiday displays that they wouldn't even notice that we were making our third lap around the women's department of Marshall Field's in search of the perfect whatever-it-was that I so desperately had to have that day.

My wish was granted, and they did quite well in the stroller. They didn't hit each other; whoever was in back didn't pull the hair of whoever was in front; they didn't scream, cry, or otherwise complain. At least not for the first hour and a half.

You see, with thirty minutes to go, I found the have-to-have-it-today clothing item I was seeking. I approached the register. I was behind three or four people, all with seemingly serious return/exchange issues. So I sought out another register. I did this three or four times until I finally realized I was going to have to just pick a line and stand in it.

I picked the wrong line.

There was only one person in front of me, so I thought surely it was my best bet. The woman was purchasing no fewer than thirty-seven clothing items, but most of them had already been rung up. The saleswoman was folding them with perfect precision—the customer was at no risk of getting them home and finding a wrinkle anywhere.

After we'd waited for about six minutes, the saleswoman began to put the items into bags. She filled five bags and was moving on to the sixth. By this point, Jack and Henry were getting a bit impatient. After all, we were no longer moving, and there were no snowmen or reindeer in this part of the store. They started to squirm, and I started to sweat.

The customer behind whom we were waiting was well-aware that we were there. She didn't seem to care. She waited until the saleswoman was putting the very last item into the very last bag before she said, and I am not kidding, "You know what? I think I would like to have these items left on the hangers."

"Just these?" the saleswoman asked, holding up the three or so items she was gingerly putting into the last bag.

"No, all of them."

I thought I would scream, and I thought the saleswoman's face had actually frozen with her mouth hanging wide open. I couldn't bring myself to go to another line at that point. I had one chance to walk out of the store with a bag in hand, and I was quite confident that this was the only register that could grant me that privilege. So, I just stood there, right foot tapping, lips pursed, praying for the boys to have such a meltdown that this woman would realize that she had made a horrible and calculated mistake.

My prayers were answered.

Within three minutes, the hitting, hair pulling, screaming, crying, kicking, and tossing of sippy cups began. The most pathetic component of this tirade was that the woman truly could not have cared less. She wanted her items on hangers, and she was going to get them on hangers even if she had to stand there for fifteen minutes listening to fourteen-month-old twins tell her off in lieu of their mother doing it.

Finally, I got my item purchased, and I realized on my way to the car that due to the anxiety involved in finding it in the first place, I'd never even looked at the price tag. I found what I needed and that was all that mattered in that instance. Once inside the car, I checked the receipt and, thankfully, the shirt or sweater or whatever-it-was was on sale. Frankly, it was a steal. And then I thought, "You know, even if it had been outrageously expensive, I think I would have just told David that I'm too tired to notice the prices on things anymore. I'm sure he'd understand."

In this circumstance, the tantrum truly was not the boys' fault. However, shortly after twins turn one, many parents realize that the days of plopping their infant car seats into the stroller and getting in a quick hour or so of shopping while the babies take a little catnap are over. Babies at this age aren't always altogether happy at the mall, or the dry cleaners, or Blockbuster, or the grocery store, or anywhere else where they are confined and bored. And they convey this in no uncertain terms.

While they may not be able to actually unfasten their stroller belts, they might do everything else in their power to get out. Whether toddlers choose kicking and screaming, violently jostling themselves left to right in an attempt to perhaps break the belts, bothering the sibling to such a degree that the sibling starts to pitch a gigantic fit, trying to climb out of the stroller, or grabbing and throwing anything within reach into orbit (or, heaven forbid, at other customers), parents often begin to wonder whether or not it's even worth it to attempt to go out with the kids at this age.

Nancy Bowers, a nurse and the mother of now fifteen-year-old boy/girl twins and a nineteen-year-old son, remembers all too well the challenges that came with outings when her kids were toddlers. Because she found that they were always fussier and grumpier during the trip if they were hungry, she always made sure that they were fed just prior to leaving the house. She also made sure she had snacks with her at all times.

The real challenge with public tantrums (whether had by one child or both) is the fact that at this young age, the kids don't yet reason very well. Bribery and threats have zero effect, so the promise of an extra-huge sundae or, conversely, the loss of dessert, means nothing to them. If it makes you feel any better, when Jack and Henry were four, there were still occasions (though far fewer, don't worry) when they pitched a fit in a store. Most often, a fit would ensue when I had to remove a privilege in, say, the feminine hygiene aisle because one of them was refusing to stand still for six seconds and instead insisting that his brother go long to catch a box of super absorbent winged Kotex Hail-Mary style (which their sister was trying to intercept).

An example of such a tirade: just recently, I had to inform

Henry no fewer than fifteen times that if he asked me again when we were going to leave Target (yes, we spend a lot of time there), he would not be able to get the bag of goldfish crackers I had promised him for good behavior. After the fifteenth warning, he asked probably another twenty-two times. So as to put off his public display of displeasure for as long as possible, I waited until we were almost through checkout to inform him that he was not getting the crackers. When he grabbed them in line, and I had to say "No," he broke loose. He was completely hysterical—crying and yelling and swatting at invisible objects in the air.

I realized in that instant that I had become the mother I'd previously sworn I'd never be—the mother who not only *appears* to have no control over her child, but in fact *has* no control. I thought, "At least when they did this and were under two, I *could* pick them up and carry them out." At this point, Henry weighed forty pounds, and given that I was pushing a completely full cart with his fourteen-month-old brother in the front seat (more on that later), there was no way I could carry him out. Also, as I learned, other adults—typically those without children—may look at you somewhat condescendingly when your child (or children) is having a public tantrum at any age. But believe me, far more of them take pity on you when the kids are under two than when they're four. So, at least take comfort in *that* when an episode presents itself during this second year.

For many of the sorority sisters, there was a period of time during the second year when it made more sense to run certain errands in the evening or on weekends when we could do it alone. Yes, this made our days longer on occasion. I would meet David in the driveway when he arrived home from work, not so much because I needed to get out for a while, but because I needed to leave *right then* in order to get home before it was the next day already. It was frustrating at the time, but in hindsight, it wasn't long before the kids could be entertained in some way when we were out, and I was able to do my grocery shopping or make a quick trip to the mall with no problem whatsoever. Exactly when did this happen for us? I don't remember exactly. But it was before they were two, I can promise you that.

As for keeping the kids organized when they are not confined to a stroller or cart, I have one big piece of advice: you can't. I strongly suggest keeping them confined to a stroller or cart—at least while shopping. We have a grocery store nearby that has carts with tandem child seats, and we were able to use those with success for a while—until the kid in back learned that he could annoy the bejeepers out of the kid in front. Our Costco has side-by-side child seats, which worked well for a while—again until the boys realized they could go to war in the frozen foods section. We tried the carts with the kid benches attached that allowed the boys to either sit side by side facing forward or sit diagonally across from one another. These last two were the worst options in our case because until the sport of intra-cart fighting lost its appeal (which it did), they truly did just hit each or steal each other's toy-of-the-moment the entire time. This type of cart is also quite large, and in my opinion, should require a license to drive. I noted as much one day to another mom who was struggling to get her tractor-trailer-sized cart by another normal-sized cart. Her response: "Yeah, and a turn signal would be helpful as well!"

Some moms have great success with these sorts of arrangements, so I'd encourage you to give them a try. Even if they only work once, that makes for one successful trip. Just know that if they do not work, or if at any time they cease working, you are not alone.

Barb's rule was plain and simple: her girls were not allowed out of their stroller while shopping until they were much older. This way, they never realized that freedom was an option. At times, Barb's mother-in-law or another adult accompanied her and offered to take one of the girls out of the stroller or take both out and be responsible for one. Barb always said "No" because she knew that if the girls did it once, they would want to do it every time thereafter. Unless her mother-in-law was volunteering to join her on every single outing, Barb knew it was a disaster waiting to happen. Once she knew that the girls would walk next to the stroller and actually stay with her, she allowed them to do so. But again, it wasn't until they were much older—probably closer to three.

The only foolproof method I'm aware of to keep kids organized when in public (and not in a stroller or cart) is to leash them. You know, I'm all for each parent choosing what works best for him or her. At the same time, as anyone who knows me will attest, I have *no* problem sharing my opinions on virtually any subject. I am an information gatherer to the core, so I'll listen until the cows come home to anyone who claims to know something about anything, and then I'll decide whether or not any of it makes sense to me and might be worth exploring further. That's how we figure out who we are as parents and as people; we take in a lot of information, weed out the stuff that doesn't work for us, incorporate the stuff that does, and go to bed feeling A-OK about the job we're doing.

Unfortunately, no one has ever tried to tout the benefits of the human leash to me. Therefore, I must convey my position on it based purely on my own opinion, which is that it is, in the vast majority of applications, nothing short of inhumane. Now, there are two settings in which I can get to a place of understanding regarding its value: busy airports and Walt Disney World. Venues that contain hordes of people as well as the potential for you to become distracted for a split second (either to stop someone from pilfering your luggage or to consult your map of the Magic Kingdom to ensure you are indeed headed toward the infamous and ever-popular Dumbo ride) certainly might provide a viable reason to utilize this sort of a contraption to keep your children safe. I've braved busy airports with four kids and I've braved Walt Disney World with them and, frankly, there have been moments during both excursions when it might have been a good idea for my husband to have *me* on a leash. If having a

way to ensure that your children stay with you
make the difference between traveling a
purchase an aesthetically pleasing toddler teth

What gets me particularly crazy is when
use in malls, grocery stores, and parks. Yes, I've seen the
use at parks. Once, I even saw one in use at a mothers' group
meeting. Honestly, the kid moved and the mother tugged. I
half expected her to pull out a dog bowl instead of a sippy
cup. The only thing more ridiculous in my mind than a kid on
a leash is a parent being dragged by a kid on a leash, which I
have witnessed at the mall on more than one occasion. I ask
you, if your children aren't responding to your verbal request
to stay by your side, do you really think they are going to act
differently once you put this apparatus on them? When
you've reached the point where you have to tug on a kid (or
kids) every six seconds as though he were a canine, ask
yourself, does it possibly make sense to find a way to run this
particular errand in the evening or on the weekend? I say yes,
it does.

Apparently parents and manufacturers alike felt as though
the marketing angle on this device needed tweaking, so now
many tethers are being made to look like stuffed animal
backpacks, and part of the advertising includes the benefit
that your child can use the animal's head as a pillow. When—
while he's attempting to run away from you? Because if your
child is calm enough to lay his head back on this "pillow"
while walking next to you, I'm thinking you don't need a
leash. But if you're trying to get through a crowded airport
without losing anybody, and to passersby your child appears
to be resting his weary head on the top of his monkey
backpack (until one notices you or your husband holding on
to the monkey's tail), it's a far preferable look than a plain,
sterile-looking harness, which is how they were initially
manufactured.

Another common question I hear: "What do I do when
they are *simultaneously* throwing tantrums in public?" Answer:
at this age, if they are in a stroller or cart, just keep going.

Seriously, they'll get over themselves. Give them a few minutes and they'll find something interesting to point at (and then possibly demand, provoking another tantrum when you say "No," but at least the issue has changed), or they'll get tired of their own voice. Okay, the latter isn't likely, but optimism is the best medicine sometimes.

While these tantrums are ensuing, the people staring at you will either completely understand because they have been there, or they'll give you "the look" either because they have no children or because they are in denial regarding the way their own children behaved thirty years ago. If you avoid eye contact and train your vision on the location of the next item on your list (you're on a mission at this point), you won't know of their reaction either way.

Should your children be walking with you in a place like the grocery store—meaning that they are probably closer to two years of age or on the other side of their second birthday—and throw a simultaneous tantrum, just stand there. This has happened to me on only a few occasions (none of them pretty). My approach has always been to stand there, announce that when they could get themselves together we'd continue shopping, and wait (and giggle as I thought about how I would regale their future potential spouses with this story the first time I met them). Should they be disturbing other shoppers in some way, consider utilizing the approach I resorted to once: Operation Lift and Leave (described shortly). But if you're on your own in the dairy section, give it a minute and see if you can find a way to finish your shopping.

Should they throw simultaneous tantrums while walking in a place such as the mall, vow never to let them out of the stroller again until they are older! In the short term, do what you have to do to get them back into the stroller and get yourself to the car. I can pretty much guarantee that the only chance you have of getting them to regroup so that you can finish your search for a bra that actually fits is finding the nearest food venue and getting them something on the no-no list (french fries work every time).

A critical time to intervene is when your kids are outside of their stroller or cart and blocking traffic. This did occur once in my case. The boys were weeks from turning two and after they asked to get out of their side-by-side cart bench for the thirty-seventh time, I thought, "Well, maybe it'll be okay." After all, they were almost two and I had only five or so more items to get.

We were in the cookie aisle. Do you really need an explanation of what happened next? Honestly, I should have just handed each kid the bag of cookies he requested, but for some reason (apparently I remembered to put on pants that day but left my brain at home on a hanger) I said, "No." Not wise. They were lying head to head, each with his feet touching opposite sides of the aisle. So, when the fifty-nine-year-old woman—who apparently had never had children or, as I said, was in denial over the fact that her children had ever done anything like this—suddenly started heading our way, I had to do something.

I picked them both up—one under each arm—told Grace to follow (thank God she followed most directions by that point without asking a lot of questions—or perhaps just recognized a real crisis when one presented itself), and I left. I felt horrible, and I wanted to go back later and help someone put back all my non-perishable items. It was my number one Lesson of the Week. They just were not ready to join me on foot during shopping expeditions. There was no recovering from the tantrum they were having, and I knew it. I know I'm not the only one who's been in such a boat because I've seen a few other fully loaded and clearly abandoned carts before and since. But I still felt horrible. They probably had to throw away the deli meat. There are times, however, when you've got to admit that you're past the point of no return, whether your kids are lying head to head in the grocery aisle or leaning out of the cart on opposite sides wailing and grabbing everything within reach (or smacking their heads on clothing displays and therefore screaming even louder). At that point, it's best to just leave. With any luck, this won't happen more than once because you won't be willing to test fate again until you are *darn* sure you'll make it out *with* the contents of your cart!

During this time period, I could take one of the boys shopping with me and let him walk, and I did on occasion as it provided a way for me to get some extremely rare one-on-one time with each of them. But I was more likely to do that when I needed fewer than ten items; otherwise we would still be there today. Of course, whomever I took with me spent the entire time asking, "Where's Henny?" or "Where's Jack?" They didn't even know how to ride to the gas station without the other being present. I think they truly felt like I do when I have the distinct feeling I've left the house without a key item but am not entirely sure what it is.

Accept that there will be bad days, and remember that there will be good days. Just because you can't take them to the Gap on Monday doesn't mean that a trip to the same store the next Monday won't go swimmingly.

CREATING VARIETY IN DAY-TO-DAY LIFE

The mother—poor invaded soul—finds even the bathroom door no bar to hammering little hands.
—Charlotte Perkins Gilman

Many moms who left their jobs to raise their children full-time start to feel at some point during the toddler years as though they'd like just a bit of variety in their week, i.e., to be able to work maybe two days per week doing something they enjoy. At some point, many moms who continued to work full-time after their babies were born begin to consider the possibility of switching careers or exploring options for working fewer days, perhaps through job sharing.

One of the underlying reasons women feel the need to do something outside the home during this time is that they need an activity for which they feel validated. I know that David works really hard at his job; he's very good at it, and he enjoys it, which is a real bonus. At times, I've unintentionally minimized the work he does all day because I've been overly focused on the fact that he's permitted a snack and the use of a bathroom when necessary. One day, the reason why I was subconsciously jealous and even a bit resentful of his life from 8:00 a.m. until 5:00 p.m. dawned on me.

His job is compartmentalized. His goals are defined, and it is clear at the end of the day (or week, or whatever) whether or not he's met his goals. If he has, he's rewarded in some way—monetarily or otherwise. At a minimum, the guy for whom he works gives him the proverbial pat on the back and says "Good job."

However, parenting metrics and measures (not to mention their associated rewards) aren't always as cut and dry. Kids don't typically thank their parents at the end of the day for making all the meals, cleaning carrots out of the carpet, doing the laundry, researching preschools, getting all the other items on the to-do list accomplished, and even completing four tasks that *weren't* on the to-do list. It's understandable, therefore, that moms often feel slightly underappreciated.

I won't speak for every other mom on the planet, but I know that I've spent my fair share of days wondering if I was coming even close to meeting my goal of raising happy, healthy, well-behaved children with strong values. Or whether—if in another environment—the boss would be on her way to my office with my walking papers. It becomes necessary for a stay-at-home mom to find some fairly consistent source of validation, which in turn will allow her to continue to pour such an immense amount of love and energy into her children each and every day.

Mollie, who was a teacher prior to having her boys, started privately tutoring high school students when her boys were eighteen months old. She was fortunate to have a babysitter with whom she felt completely comfortable leaving the boys while she worked with her students. She needed that time away, loved what she was doing, and loved that she made money doing it. As the boys reached their third birthday, she became aware of the fact that they would go to preschool the following year. Additionally, her boys have severe asthma and one has a life-threatening peanut allergy. It became harder for her to turn their care over to someone other than Gary. She consciously made the decision to stop tutoring in order to focus on the boys during this year. She ensured that she always had a trustworthy sitter or two on speed dial so that she and Gary could go on dates with some regularity, and she continued to follow her doctor's order for three hours per week to herself. For her, that level of variety was just right.

When Barb's girls were just two months old, she resumed work as a dental hygienist one night per week. She did this solely to get out of the house. Later, when her girls were fourteen months old, Barb—who is also a teacher—began tutoring as well. She waited until that point only because she needed time to find a good sitter, and she wanted to get the girls on a solid schedule so that her time away would be as positive for everyone involved as possible. She tutored to earn extra money for this or that, but the evenings working at the dental office were for sanity. She was escaping the physical exhaustion early on, but when the girls were around two and a half and were talking non-stop, she felt almost mentally deranged and needed a way to escape that exhaustion.

She made a great point the other day that I hadn't thought about in a while. In the beginning, you need a break now and then because of the physical exhaustion. You may just check yourself into a hotel for an evening or inform your husband that you are going to bed at 6:00 p.m. because you just *have* to rest. But when the kids start talking—really talking—you'll find yourself needing a mental health break now and then. Barb has confirmed with many of her friends that the earlier your kids start talking, the earlier you'll need to find a way to get consistent breaks from the soundtrack of toddlerhood.

It's beautiful music. Really, it is. But you can't listen to any genre of music all day every day without needing to change the station now and then. Even if you switch from beautiful opera music that soothes you to hard core punk rock, the change for the sake of change is likely to be refreshing—even if only for twelve minutes.

Bari, who continued to work full-time after her boy/girl twins were born, ultimately succumbed to her desire to work for herself. While pregnant with her twins, she was frustrated not to be able to find a retail outlet that catered to expectant and new parents of multiples by providing some level of personalized service and knowledge about which products are really necessary and which aren't (not to mention which products actually work as advertised!). She saw a perfect opportunity. So, in her "spare time," she and a friend founded Multiple Matters, an online boutique that provides exactly what she felt was missing. She hopes that one day not too far in the future, she will be able to open a brick-and-mortar store as well. She takes it one day at a time and loves the variety—albeit extra work—it provides.

ADDING VARIETY WITH THE KIDS

Without adventure, civilization is in full decay.
—Alfred North Whitehead

When kids turn one year of age or so, parents may begin to explore opportunities to get involved in an extracurricular activity or two with the kids (if they have not already). Many times when the kids are this young, these sorts of activities are, in all honesty, more for the parent than for the child. They provide a way to get out and socialize a bit, especially during the winter months. Parents of twins are often concerned about which activities might work for them and which might end up being so much work that by the end of the class, they conclude that it would have been a better idea to facilitate a block-stacking contest in their own living room.

One of the biggest issues that plagues registering twin toddlers for formal programs is that, due to the age group being addressed, many programs require a one-to-one ratio of parents to children. I took a parent/tot tumbling class with Grace when she was about eighteen months old, and I was exhausted afterward just from chasing one child around. I could not imagine trying to chase two who would likely be traveling in different directions. The park district apparently could not imagine it either because they do require a one-to-one parent-to-child ratio for that particular class.

Obviously, if you have family nearby or another adult you can take with you to such events, you'll be fine. Barb signed Olivia and Kambria up for a parent/tot swim class when they were between one and two years of age, and she and Tim both went, so each took responsibility for one child. On the occasions when Tim could not attend, Barb took her mother or her mother-in-law.

But what about parents who simply don't have another adult who can accompany them to such events? Are they basically stuck inside until their kids are old enough to attend classes that don't require that one-to-one ratio?

Thankfully, no. But you'll have to be resourceful, which fortunately is one of your greatest strengths. Almost every public library has some sort of story time. These sessions are usually quite short, no more than thirty minutes, and many times as few as fifteen minutes long. The other benefit of these programs: they are free! I know moms who've been successful keeping their twins in the stroller for these sessions because the kids were so engaged by the storyteller (who usually had puppets or some other prop) that they almost forgot they were restrained. My boys screamed so loudly at not being allowed to get out of their stroller that this did not work for us. I had to find another option.

My church offered Musikgarten classes at a discounted rate, which was further prorated for twins. The teacher was perfectly comfortable with my bringing both Jack and Henry on my own. The boys loved it. They were closer to two at the time, and they didn't always participate, but they threw no fits and, if not interested in participating, were always content to watch and listen.

Be sure to inquire about a discount for registering more than one child for a program. Oftentimes, the registration fee (if there is one) will be discounted or removed altogether for the second child, and in most cases, the second child will receive at least ten percent off. Even so, I could never bring myself to sign up for some of the more popular tumbling classes because the one-time initiation fee plus the per-session fee to sign up both boys was sky high. Unsure whether they'd even like it (not to mention whether or not I could manage them during it without going into cardiac arrest), I was too uncomfortable to try when they were younger than two. However, Gymboree, as an example, does offer trial classes (or they did at one time). If you are interested, check your local listings and see if they offer such a trial. If so, you could get a good feel for what such an experience would be like, and whether or not it would make sense for you and your kids at any particular point in time.

Until the boys were two, we spent our social time on playdates. Accept in advance that there's no such thing this early on as a playdate where the kids play and you and your girlfriends sit and chat over coffee and bon bons. But just getting together with people you enjoy while giving your kids the experience of interacting with other children their age is a great reason to arrange a playdate now and then. If you and your friends are able to complete a conversation in the midst, it's an added bonus! (By the way, playdates don't necessarily get any less noisy or chaotic as the toddler years progress, but you will be able to spend more time directing your children to "work it out" and "use your words" from your most-comfortable spot on the couch.)

BEWARE OF INCORPORATING
TOO MUCH VARIETY

Everyone is always trying to cram so much into their schedules. I say fight back, take a stand, take a nap.

—Margot Black

In what was apparently a subconscious effort to prove just how capable I was (or crazy, the jury's still out), we acquired two Weimaraner puppies when the boys were about eighteen months old. David has been in love with this breed forever, and one night he took me out to dinner, plied me with sangria, and mentioned he had found an available puppy. As he laid out his plan in a style similar to Franck Eggelhoffer, the eccentric wedding coordinator played by Martin Short in the 1991 remake of *Father of the Bride*, it became apparent that he had clearly considered all of the details involved in raising a puppy along with three young children. He seemed to have it all worked out (or maybe it was the wine talking). After several hours, I hesitantly acquiesced. It was at that time that he chose to casually suggest that we continue the "twin tradition" and get two—so they'd each have a friend.

By this point, I guess I was drunk, so I agreed to that as well. Two days later, he drove eight hundred miles round trip to pick them up. He was elated. I'll admit, they were cute. But within two days, it became painfully clear that twin puppies are very much like twin toddlers, except that you can't even begin to make the argument that they should understand the words "Sit," "Move," or "Not on the rug!" They grew and grew (and grew), and before I knew it they were six months old, weighed seventy-five pounds each, followed *no* commands, peed everywhere, and ate their own feces—a fact humorous only in hindsight due to the fact that Jack and Henry were simultaneously fascinated with spreading their own feces all over their sheets, carpet, and walls during nearly every naptime.

What took the situation from bad to worse was David's

conviction that they were well behaved. I had to reiterate nightly that when a man has to resort to yelling "Get off of her!" more than once a night, the dogs are not trained.

So, when trying to figure out just the right amount of variety to add to your life, go slowly. And whether you add one new thing or twenty-one, beware of adding anything that is difficult to get rid of.

FINDING A CAREGIVER
WHO CAN HANDLE TWINS

All things are possible until they are proven impossible—and even the impossible may only be so as of now.
—Pearl S. Buck

A reliable, trustworthy sitter is going to come in quite handy over the next few years. This is the person upon whom you'll rely when you need to get out during the day for, say, a gynecology appointment that you'd prefer to attend alone, or when you and your spouse need a night out together.

Whenever you begin leaving your children in the care of another, it can be challenging in the anxiety department. Along with the usual list of emergency contact numbers and directions on dinner and bedtime routines, one mom I know even leaves her and her husband's will out on the counter! But still, the period of time between driving out of the driveway and pulling back into the garage can be a bit stressful the first few times.

Even though you believe wholeheartedly that no one will do as good a job as you would comforting your children should they awaken prematurely, it's critical to find someone who you believe will do as good a job as possible, and will tend to all of your children's needs while you are away.

Many parents spend more time searching for someone to watch twins, or getting comfortable with someone watching twins, than they would (or did) a singleton. It's far easier to put a one-year-old in the care of a fifteen-year-old than to put twins in the care of the same person. After all, this person potentially has to be chasing kids who are getting into two different kinds of mischief.

One idea: try having the sitter come the first time when you will be home, maybe even just for an hour or two. Use the time to clean or relax, but let it be an opportunity to get a feel for how comfortable the sitter is and how she handles the job. It will give her a chance to ask any questions she might have. Most important, it will give the kids an opportunity to meet and become familiar with her before you've gotten dressed up for the first time in months and are prepared to walk out that door, kids screaming or not.

Another idea: have the sitter come after the kids are in bed. This way, at worst, she'll have to go in to replace a pacifier or comfort a baby, but won't be tasked with feeding them or putting them both down for the night. Some parents worry that if they put their children to bed and then a child awakens to Suzy Sitter at ten o'clock without warning, the child might flip. And she might. Or she might not. If you're concerned, don't take this approach the first time you use a particular sitter. At a minimum, ensure that your children have met and spent time with any sitter who will begin her duties after the kids' bedtime. That way, while not your face, it's at least a familiar face your child will be met with if she needs something.

We've had great luck with two sources for sitters: preschool and church. One day, when I was picking up Grace from preschool (the boys were just over a year old), her preschool teacher said, "If you ever need a sitter . . . " That was as far as she got. I lunged forward with pen and paper to get her number. She was twenty-six, I knew her well, the kids knew and liked her—it was a no-brainer. Worked great . . . until she had a baby of her own a few years later. Just after the boys turned three, David asked the girl who helped run the toddler nursery at church if she ever babysat. She was seventeen, great with all the kids, and they knew and loved her. This girl was seriously amazing. She would come over for six hours in the middle of the day, and I'd pray the entire time that things weren't going so poorly that she'd refuse to come back. Each time, I'd return home to the litany of games they played, stories she read, meals she prepared (without my even asking), etc. Worked great . . . but she goes off to college in the fall. When the boys were newborns, our good friend Stephanie occasionally watched one of them while I took the other to his physical therapy appointment. Again, great trust, kids loved her. Worked great . . . until *she* had a baby a couple of years later. (At least caring for my kids didn't convince anyone that babysitting was as far as they wanted to venture into the childrearing tunnel.)

We're now on the search for another candidate. In the end, you'll know you've found the right person when you feel at peace leaving your children with her. Remember, the sitter is not you, so don't set your standards *too* high. Of course, if you have family living nearby, you may have an advantage that we don't. Not that you have to use them every time, and not that they'll be available or willing every time, but perhaps even once a month they'll be available to lend a hand.

I know friends who've used a sitter service at the recommendation of other friends whom they trust. Mollie found out about one in the area from a friend who frequently leaves all four of her children in the care of one of their sitters. They charge $14 per hour plus a $15 booking fee each time, which I'm not sure I could swallow, but Mollie believes it's worth every penny. And remember, Mollie checks and double-checks everything *and* has to leave an Epi-pen in the hands of whoever watches the boys. Many of the sitters from this service have experience with Epi-pens, which, in Mollie's mind, is probably more than can be said for the fourteen-year-old down the street.

Another source for sitters: friends. Beware, however, that this can turn into a friendly (or not) bidding war at times. I remember New Year's Eve 2000 when sitters in our neighborhood (fourteen-year-olds, mind you) were going for $100 an hour. Can you believe that? I almost took up babysitting for a night. Absurd. But they are guided by the same supply/demand theory as anyone else, I suppose. More of an issue than money, some sitters just end up getting bombarded by phone calls on Wednesday night, some from their usual sittees and others from newcomers begging for their services. So, once you find a sitter you really like, be careful when you give out her name/number. Or establish some kind of silly rule with your friends, such as: if your friend wants the sitter for a particular night, she must call you first to ensure you don't need her as well! When we found Sarah, the sitter from the nursery at our church, Mollie was like, "Who is this girl? You really seem to like her." My response: "Sarah. Her name is Sarah. No last name. Like Cher or Madonna." To this day, Mollie does not know her last name, and Sarah isn't even accepting new clients.

Once you've left for the evening, especially the first few times, you're bound to have some anxiety. The first time our friend Stephanie and her husband, Kevin, left their daughter to go on a dinner date (the baby was about ten months old), she was in the care of Stephanie's sister and brother-in-law who were visiting from out of town. Ava was already in bed asleep when they left, and Stephanie still had a hard time focusing. She kept the cell phone sitting on the table in front of her dinner plate anxiously awaiting its ring with the news that Ava was crying uncontrollably. She and Kevin devoured their food much too fast in an effort to get home as soon as possible. It was as though they were racing to beat the call that they knew would inevitably come. It was the first time Stephanie felt as though she had deserted her responsibility of being "in charge" as the mom. They didn't relax as they had promised each other they would, and upon returning home, she really wished they had. For although Ava did wake up, Stephanie's sister rocked her back to sleep and not another peep was heard. Even though Stephanie and Kevin had just one baby to leave, this scenario is all-too-common whether

you're leaving one, two, three, or sixty (
time.

Leaving your children in the care of
adult will get easier and easier each t
slowly if you need to (or dive right in-
time David and I got a night out togeth
since we'd done it that I practically threw the contact-num
sheet and pajamas at Stephanie as she was walking in the door
and I was walking out).

MARRIAGE

*When my husband wants to get his hair cut, he makes an appointment
and goes. When I want to get my hair cut, I've got to get six people
involved and plan three weeks in advance.*

— Annie, mother of three

I am beginning to believe that ninety-five percent of all
marital issues post-children boil down to what this statement
represents. Women often feel as though their spouses are
simply never going to *get* how many balls they constantly have
in the air, not to mention the fact that half of them are on fire
and a quarter of them are covered in oil.

There's a little story that often circulates via e-mail. Any
mother, whether at home full-time or not, reads this and gets
about as excited as a lone monkey in a banana factory. She
then hits "forward" and includes the entire female contingent
of her address book as she proclaims a whole lot of Amens
and Hallelujahs. In case you haven't seen it, and even if you
have, here it is:

A man came home from work and found his three
children outside, still in their pajamas, playing in the
mud with empty food boxes and wrappers strewn all
around the front yard. The door of his wife's car was

pen, as was the front door to the house and there was no sign of the dog. Proceeding into the entry, he found an even bigger mess. A lamp had been knocked over, and the throw rug was wadded against one wall. In the front room the TV was loudly blaring a cartoon channel, and the family room was strewn with toys and various items of clothing. In the kitchen, dishes filled the sink, breakfast food was spilled on the counter, the fridge door was open wide, dog food was spilled on the floor, a broken glass lay under the table, and a small pile of sand was spread by the back door. He quickly headed up the stairs, stepping over toys and more piles of clothes, looking for his wife. He was worried she might be ill, or that something serious had happened. He was met with a small trickle of water as it made its way out the bathroom door. As he peered inside he found wet towels, scummy soap and more toys strewn over the floor. Miles of toilet paper lay in a heap and toothpaste had been smeared over the mirror and walls. As he rushed to the bedroom, he found his wife still curled up in the bed in her pajamas, reading a novel. She looked up at him, smiled, and asked how his day went. He looked at her bewildered and asked, "What happened here today?" She again smiled and answered, "You know every day when you come home from work and you ask me what in the world I did that day?"

"Yes," was his incredulous reply.

She answered, "Well, today, I didn't do it."

Moms often report feeling as though their husbands just do not understand. Anything. Because a large part of successfully getting through the process of raising children involves successfully keeping your marriage intact, let's take some time to address this topic.

Stop rolling your eyes. I know, I know. If you're a stay-at-home mom (let's be honest, stay-at-home moms work completely unreasonable hours that frankly border on abuse; where are the labor laws for this profession?), you're all too aware that your spouse gets to leave the house each morning. He has time to leisurely sip a cappuccino with an extra shot of espresso instead of downing the entire contents of the sixteen-ounce cup in the same amount of time in which college students down shots of Jägermeister. He may be allowed the luxury of a business trip on occasion. Believe me, I've had more than one hair-pulling moment when David has called me from his out-of-town locale to discuss the rigors of his business trip—reminding me that "It's business; I'm not on vacation"—when I hear a waiter in the background, ask where he is, and find out he's sitting in a "meeting" in Morton's Steakhouse awaiting the $500 lobster appetizer.

Many women I've spoken with who work full-time outside the home report that at the end of the day, they still maintain most of the responsibility for the kids' schedule and developmental needs, not to mention the strategy for getting them to eat something other than chocolate pudding. They no doubt feel somewhat like Lynette Scavo from the ever-popular (and really, is it any secret why?) *Desperate Housewives*, who switched roles with her husband to work full-time outside the home while he cared for their four children (including twin boys). She spent her days in the office trying to fit her son's first day of school and holiday party into her schedule between conference calls and status meetings. Her husband, perhaps somewhat defensively, probably had to admit at some point that when he was the one working full-time, he wasn't trying to juggle quite as many work/family needs.

I was blown away by the introductory monologue delivered by Mary Alice on one recent *Desperate Housewives* episode. The storyline was still exploring poor Lynette's efforts to juggle her personal and professional lives, and Mary Alice poetically noted: "There was one thing all the fathers on Wisteria Lane had in common: they could return home from a hard day's work to the family they left behind and not feel at all guilty about the precious moments they had missed. Sadly, the same could not be said for the working mothers."

For those of you as addicted to the Housewives as I am, you likely also remember that Lynette came home to a house in complete disarray almost every night. Her husband claimed he had a "system." But by the end of the week, it became clear that his "system" wasn't working very well. The house looked much like the one described in the oft-forwarded adage I shared earlier.

To be clear, I'm not insinuating that men can't competently hold down the role of primary caregiver. One of my closest friends is a stay-at-home dad. His house is *far* cleaner than mine is, and he is *far* less uptight than I am. He's utterly amazing. What I'm getting at is simply that there is a reason why the Scavo storyline on *Desperate Housewives* works: more than a handful of women identify with it.

At the top of the list for many women is getting to a place where we feel validated by our spouses for all that we do in our role, and staying connected to the person we used to know like the back of our hand (but who recently declared that unbeknownst to me, he stopped wearing Armani cologne two years ago).

To be fair, the opposing issue is that our spouses often feel as though we don't understand them either (or so I'm told). The pressure to single-handedly provide for the day-to-day needs of an entire family (not to mention fund college educations, a possible wedding or two, and retirement) is a lot. Men need and want to be validated for the work that they do as well.

I know many a mom who's gotten into an argument with her husband wherein he professes, "You have no idea how many offers I've turned down, professional or otherwise, to spend time at home with you and the kids." I know one mom whose husband claims he turns down "over eighty percent" of all offers that come his way. This woman communicates with her friends via e-mail or phone only, orders her clothes over the Internet at 3:30 a.m., and has been cutting her own hair for over a year. She's honestly having some trouble figuring out how she's supposed to feel bad about the fact that her husband goes to one happy hour per week instead of four, but . . .

The rumor is that men think differently. John Gray came quite close to proving so many years ago. *Men Are From Mars, Women Are From Venus* was a bestseller for a reason. Men and women have been trying to understand each other for centuries . . . probably longer. Women supposedly fail to understand the male perspective, and men are often reported to not only fail to understand but fail to even pay attention to the female perspective. My friend Annie summed up the post-baby resentment she's experienced brilliantly when she said, "He has no idea what it feels like to never be able to do anything without asking someone for help." For the majority of us who are Type A personalities to begin with, admitting that we need help, not to mention continually asking for it, can be difficult. The logistical problems involved in merely getting our hair cut, getting a blood test to discern whether or not the daily oatmeal breakfast is helping decrease our cholesterol level, or picking up kids from two different schools that let out at the same time are underestimated because they've become so routine.

I was recently listening to an XM radio segment of *Satellite Sisters* in my car. I love the Satellite Sisters; one of my kids could proclaim from the back seat, "Mom, I think I finally understand why I can't stop whining!" and I'd counter with "*Shhhhh!* I can't hear the sisters!" On this particular segment, attorney and communications expert Laurie Puhn was being interviewed. The author of *Instant Persuasion: How to Change Your Words to Change Your Life*, Laurie argues quite convincingly that this notion of men and women being wired differently is absurd, and it provides nothing more than an excuse for our frustrations. As she puts it, men aren't from Mars and women aren't from Venus. We're all from Earth.

She made more than a little bit of sense, I must tell you. One point she made that really got me thinking was that, stereotypically, most men don't express emotion, but, stereotypically, most women don't take on home improvement projects.

On any given Saturday in our home, you can count on finding David in the kitchen over a pot of roux à la Emeril while I'm in the garage cutting something with a miter saw. I don't trust him any more with a hammer than he trusts me with an egg poacher. We go against the stereotypes in this particular area, so aren't we doing damage by assuming that we fit them in communication style or the ways we need to be validated and loved?

Another point Laurie made brilliantly was that women need to let go not only of stereotypes, but also of trying to get their spouses to read between the lines to figure out what to do and how to do it. Comments Puhn, "The reality is that most husbands want their wives to be happy, but they don't know how to accomplish this. Unfortunately, many women don't communicate their needs because of the self-fulfilling belief that 'men are men' and they won't change anyway. If, instead, a woman rejects the stereotypes, expresses her needs, and offers constructive suggestions by telling him what she *does* want, not what she *doesn't* want, she will get results."

As convinced as I am that I can match or top any challenge placed in front of me regarding toddler behavior, I also believe I can match anyone in terms of a relationship gone awry in the midst of raising young children. It's been said that if something doesn't kill you, it makes you stronger. There have been many days when I was convinced that trying to get my husband to "get it" while trying to determine how to help him understand my needs when I wasn't sure even I understood them hadn't yet killed me, and yet I did not feel as though I was making any great strides in the strength department either.

I'll let you in on a little secret: Barb and I are each other's unofficial marriage therapist. With few exceptions, if you can imagine it, Barb or I have experienced it and complained to the other about it. We're constantly recommending books to each other, only to then spend an hour complaining about the fact that our spouses never read them.

In an effort to make herself feel better about the challenges involved in keeping marriage alive while raising a family, Barb recently developed the Relationship Barometer, by which she is confident that with eighty-three percent accuracy, she can assess the exact status of a marriage in 9.4 seconds or less. She spends a lot of time watching other couples to determine where on the barometer they fall, and she's assured me that at least eighty-seven percent of them are exactly where we are (or have been), while the other thirteen percent are obliviously floating down the River of Delusion completely unaware that there's a massive waterfall just around the corner.

Some birds mate for life.
There's no divorce in the aviary world, apparently.
I think that's why they fly into windows; it's the only way out.
—Robin Fairbanks

Maybe it would be easier if we were birds. The journey of marriage and the bumps in the road that come with it may force you to greet your sense of humor at the front door more often than any other challenge. But, as I said, on those days when you believe you can do nothing else about it, call a girlfriend and have a good laugh. I can almost guarantee you that on any given day you can find a friend who's dealing with the same issues. Because really, there are only so many core issues all women deal with where men are involved, and we're *all* dealing with them to one degree or another. So, know that you are not alone, and be comforted (albeit disgusted) by that fact.

While it's important to be clear about exactly what you need to feel validated, and it's important for your spouse to do the same, that alone doesn't necessarily hold the key to a fabulous marriage. Issues such as a lack of compliments and thank yous and a lack of willingness to put a diaper in the trash or a pair of pants on a hanger are not the real problems. They're annoying, but they aren't what send us running for the hills. Wives spend a lot of time believing that "if only he'd help out more with this or with that, we'd be so happy." I'd be willing to bet that these little annoyances are merely symptoms of a greater problem: you and your spouse have become less connected. You don't understand how to make your spouse feel important anymore and vice versa.

Here is the Number One surefire solution to ensuring a long and happy (most of the time) marriage: *do whatever you must do to stay connected.* I cannot emphasize strongly enough the degree of importance I place on these words. Maintaining a connection with your spouse when there are young children and housework and bills and an overgrown lawn and mountains of laundry and a milk jug in the refrigerator with half a centimeter of milk in it and diapers everywhere is difficult, no doubt. Rebuilding your connection once it's completely dissolved is as close to insurmountable a challenge as any I've experienced as a parent or a person. I'm not kidding.

Let me be completely candid (do you expect anything less of me at this point?). When our fourth baby was almost one, that fateful day arrived: David and I looked at each other and said "Who Are You?" After nearly six years of raising kids, washing dishes, changing diapers, researching dog-training strategies, and otherwise passing in the night, David and I coexisted just fine, but we were no longer connected in that way that gets you through the days when no one is listening and you find permanent marker artistically and irrevocably scribbled on the dining room furniture. And it was the scariest experience I've ever encountered.

When, I wondered, would we find the time we needed to reconnect for more than a night? We needed basically to start from scratch, and our circumstances simply were not going to allow that. Our favorite sitter had just given birth herself; our families lived on opposite sides of the country; we had barely the ability to go out to dinner, let alone get some real quality time together on a consistent basis to discuss anything other than the next week's schedule.

While this didn't occur until well after the time period during which Jack and Henry were one- to two-years-old, it didn't happen overnight. It would be a disservice to wait to mention it until the three- to four-year-old section when the issue was at its peak because the strategy for ensuring that you don't end up in the same boat needs to be employed *now*, not later.

I went to see my internist one day for an issue over which she decided to order a CT scan. She said she wanted to make sure I wasn't pregnant before she did it. I assured her that there was no way I could be pregnant. She said, "Oh, you'd be surprised, honey." I told her that truly, there was no way that I was pregnant.

"What are you using for birth control?" she asked skeptically.

"Abstinence."

She said, "Okay, of course you're not having sex because you're a parent. Parenting is hard work and it leaves you little time for much else. Do you still love your husband? Do you want to stay with him?" Yes on both counts. Not in the heat of many battles, but at the core, yes.

She pulled up a chair. She pulled out her prescription pad. She said, "Well then, I am writing you a prescription. You and your husband are to get away together every two months, even if it's just for one night. I don't care what you have to do to ensure that this happens. I don't care if you *think* you have no one to leave the kids with. You put it on the calendar and you make it happen. In the end, if you do not do this, your kids will be the ones who suffer."

Of course, I argued that we just didn't have anyone to watch the kids that often. She did not care. She gave me the prescription and told me to go home and start making calls. So, in the end, I guess I did get a prescription like Mollie had gotten, I just wasn't sure how to fill it because I wasn't going to put an ad in the paper in order to find a caretaker for my kids!

After a few days, I realized that whether or not we actually left town, the message was that we had to work to make time to spend together. Consistently. I realized that it had to be a joint effort; I couldn't always be the one to find and call a sitter and make reservations at a restaurant, and yet I couldn't expect that he'd do it every time either. I realized that when we had that innate, deep connection, I didn't care as much when the two items on his at-home to-do list didn't get done right away. It didn't bother me as much when he asked, "What's for dinner tonight?" as though if I personally didn't create the menu, we'd all starve.

We had to step back, cut each other some slack, and make a decision: start over and stick with it, or call it quits. I knew that I wanted the former, as did David. We took it a day at a time. I let go of a lot of my unrealistic and unfair expectations, and he accepted that good intentions only go so far. We swallowed our pride and our frustration and made pacts with ourselves and each other that we would tell each other how to give exactly what we needed. It wasn't sweep-me-off-my-feet romantic, but my hope was that it would lead to that once we rebuilt the connection and maintained it with a new set of guidelines.

> *Love is a fire. But whether it is going to warm your heart*
> *or burn down your house, you can never tell.*
> —Joan Crawford

The bottom line is that if you can find a way to maintain the connection that made you want to have a family together in the first place, you will find humor in many of the challenges that come with raising that family.

I firmly believe, having lived through all of this, that every couple should identify a marriage therapist early on for larger emergencies. This really is very posh, I'm sure. I mean, everyone who's anyone in L.A. has a therapist of some sort, right? Every couple should have a marriage therapist on standby once they decide to have children. I know very few couples, in fact perhaps none, who would testify that they have never been in a place where they could have used a little extra "expert" assistance. Whether or not they got that assistance is another matter entirely, but they believe they could have benefited from it. What keeps many couples from seeking it out is the reality that in order to get to the here's-what-you-can-do-to-make-it-better segment of therapy, they'd have to endure what would likely be several sessions communicating the history that got them to this place to begin with! And getting a sitter for all of that is usually what puts the wife over the edge.

This is why I am a firm believer in getting established with someone early on. See her once a month, every three months, or every six months if things are going well. Develop a rapport with her. (I am using the pronoun "her" simply because our therapist happens to be a woman, but I'm sure there are very qualified and helpful men out there in this capacity.) This way, when you really do have a problem, you have someone with whom you feel comfortable. You can make the appointment, talk it through, and move forward. It's far more seamless both mentally and realistically than having to find someone, make an appointment, make sure she's covered by your health insurance plan, identify an appointment time that works for everyone involved, secure a sitter, and then stand at the base of the mountain of history you'll have to climb over before you can even address the issue that's currently got you sleeping in the guest room.

Another thing that will make not only your marriage easier, but your life in general, is to try your best to "chill out," as our daughter, Grace, says. As mothers, and especially as mothers of multiples, we tend to be a bit rigid in the schedule and organization departments. We have rules and a plan for almost everything, and we become convinced that without them, the world might spin completely out of control.

In the midst of working through our challenges, my

husband sent me an e-mail that was totally unlike him. Like many men, David is completely logical and rational, which works in many situations but not always in personal relationships because relationships aren't always logical or rational. But because it was so unlike him, the e-mail caught me completely off guard. It was almost poetry. And it will probably stick with me for the rest of my life. Because I believe that the contents of it can truly benefit so many who have unknowingly traded their previously fun and spontaneous selves for a life of perfectly honed, not-to-be-deviated-from bath schedules and bedtime routines, I'll share it with his permission.

"Why can't we always make sure that we eat dinner as a family?

"And why can't we make sure that we always do something with the kids after dinner every night as a family?

"And why can't we say thank you to each other for everything instead of nothing? For dinners and breakfasts and cleaning and going to the office and writing and running baths and bathing kids and driving to school and making appointments, regardless of whether or not we were thanked for doing the exact same thing yesterday and accepting that if we weren't thanked yesterday it probably wasn't personal because we assume the other person must have been having a bad day?

"Why do we have to cry when we are sad? Why can't we cry when we are happy?

"And why can't we have more good days?

"What is the definition of a good day?

"And why can't we go to the park with the kids every weekend? Every weekend.

"And why can't we make sure that after the kids go to bed at night we talk about our day? Why do we need to wait to be asked?

"Why can't we ask for what we want, knowing that we will get it if at all possible and that if we don't it is okay?

"Why can't we be truthful about our feelings the first time? With ourselves and each other?

"Why do we care if the house is a mess occasionally?

"Why do we have to be in bed at 10:00 p.m. on weekdays? Why can't we be tired tomorrow?

"Why isn't it okay if I say I will be home at 6:00 p.m. and it turns into 6:30?

"Why isn't it okay if you have to paint the bedroom at 12:18 p.m. on Saturday the fourth?

"Why do we have to argue every time we are angry? Why do we have to walk away mad? Why not walk away laughing? And why does one person always talk and the other one always listen?

"Why do we always want something in return? And why don't we get something in return?

"Why can't Henry ask the same question fifty times and not be answered fifty times?

"Why can't Jack interrupt when we are on the phone for an hour?

"Why can't Grace do more projects?

"Why can't George scream and throw his entire dinner on the floor?

"Why can't Jack and Henry laugh in their room until 9:30 p.m. occasionally?

"Why can't I play hooky from work on Friday?

"Why can't I read a book you ask me to read? Why do I have to finish the book by Friday?

"Why don't I go to the mall at lunch and buy you something? Why don't you go to the mall and only look for things for you?

"Why don't I buy presents before the last minute? Why does it matter?

"Why don't we eat sushi every night of the week?

"Why can't I tell you when I am upset? Why can't you tell me when you are happy?

"All of the answers are the same."

Of course, being dense as I can be at times—due to the

loss of most of my brain cells and all—I had to call him and ask him what the answer was. But it really wasn't all that shocking that I couldn't figure it out because the answer to all of these questions is about as obvious as the underlying issue that often causes the rift. It's so clear that it's overlooked.

Choice. It's all about what we choose to believe, how we choose to view things, how we choose to react, how structured we choose to be, how much of our pride we're willing to stuff behind the couch with half the kids' toys, how hard we're willing to work to meet our partner's needs without proclaiming "I'll take care of you once you start taking care of me." As much as I talk about the importance of teaching children how much they can be empowered by choice, the fact is that we *all* are empowered by choice. And our reality is defined by the choices we make and the perceptions we choose to adopt and maintain. I was so focused on maintaining order and control and schedules and perspective regarding parenting that I lost it all regarding marriage and the bigger picture that is our journey together as a family. David was so focused on his belief that he was trying to understand my perspective and change his approach accordingly that he neglected to realize that good intentions are worthless unless they are backed up by actions that reinforce those intentions. I know David wrote these questions as pure stream of consciousness, but I believe the prose is incredibly powerful. I read it often, and it reminds me of how many choices we have each and every day to create our own experience—for better or for worse.

Here's a little story to reinforce the importance—and with any luck ultimate result—of being specific about one's needs. I have spent years telling David that I needed to feel more validated, more appreciated, more respected, more everything basically. I know he was trying, but he just couldn't seem to nail it. I was as direct as I knew how to be at the time. I'd say, "Do anything. Draw me a bath. Buy me a magazine. Bring me coffee one night when you know it's been a never-ending day. And then try to make these thoughtful gestures part of your repertoire, not just one-time deeds intended to coerce me into zipping my mouth for a few more weeks."

One night, I returned home from a brief trip to the salon to have my eyebrows waxed (one of the few moments of luxury I insist upon since I so enjoy looking into the mirror when it's done). It had been a crazy week of carpools and gymnastics and swimming lessons gone awry, and I really needed a little respite. A respite didn't seem to be in the cards, as I got very nervous when approaching the front hallway because I smelled smoke.

"David," I said nervously, "I smell smoke. Do you smell that?"

"No. Why don't you go upstairs and rest."

"But David," I said, somewhat irritated that he appeared not to smell the smoke or more importantly, not to care—"something appears to be on fire."

"Yeah, I doubt it," he replied cavalierly.

Annoyed, I started looking behind doors and in closets, trying to follow the scent, which ultimately took me upstairs.

"Holy crap," I thought, "one of the kids' rooms is on fire!" I got up there, followed my nose, and ended up in my own bedroom.

"David, seriously, would you *help* me?"

"For crying out loud Liz, I lit candles in the bathroom. Would you just go in there already?"

"Oh," I quietly replied.

The bathroom was filled not only with candles, but with bottles and bottles of my favorite beer, which he had brilliantly and correctly suspected I would need for the "vacation" I was taking with the kids and my mother-in-law the following week. During the same week, he would be on his own vacation fishing with friends on a lake in Canada. (A lake that provided no electricity, cell phone tower, or bathroom. And he regards those sorts of accommodations in combination with the word "vacation" as an exciting experience to which one looks forward for 364 days? Enough said regarding different perspectives.)

He had also purchased several magazines he thought I'd enjoy reading on the "vacation," and some bottled Starbucks Frappaccinos to ensure I could function after having slept poorly next to my adorable but very restless sleeper of a daughter.

It was all going so well. And then I saw it. The package of all packages reared its ugly head. Somewhat buried to ensure I saw it last (and perhaps was so elated by the preceding ones that I didn't care) was the Victoria's Secret gift box.

"For God's sake, David. How many times do I need to reiterate that anything from this store is a gift for *you*, not *me*?"

But, truth be told, it was a fabulous little number—in the right size even, which is an area in which many husbands get it horribly wrong in one direction or the other after their wives have had babies—and it was a style I could actually wear out of the house without having to yank on it every six steps to get it back in its proper place. The only person who's seen me in it is me, as I sought out any excuse to hide in the bedroom for four minutes while chasing the Belgian beer with a Frappaccino three nights into the "vacation," but that should be okay because after all, it was a gift for me, not for him. Right? But he had heard what I'd been saying for years about needing to be taken care of. He had thought through a whole slew of my needs. I provided him with the specifics of how to fill those needs. And as somewhat of a team, we had come through.

For those of you who saw the remake of *The Stepford Wives* with Nicole Kidman and Matthew Broderick, might I divulge that I personally believe that the solution to all of this is to have Stepford Husbands who are robotically programmed to say and do precisely the right thing at precisely the right time. David believes that the solution is for all women—no matter how neurotic or emotional—to look like Faith Hill. Because I am aware (though heavily dismayed) that both wishes are no more than pipe dreams, I've listed some other important lessons Barb and I have learned over the past few years regarding marriage.

Secrets to Not Killing Your Spouse

Be Realistic

Accept that many of the traits that drew you to your spouse initially will drive you completely crazy once you have children. For example, David is very laid-back, which was initially very appealing. However, when three out of four children are screaming and the fourth is climbing into the dishwasher, it's not a helpful approach.

Additionally, regarding your desire for your husband to "get it," know this: he won't. Not because he doesn't want to, but because he can't. He doesn't do what you do all day. Even if he did, just as Tom Scavo demonstrated, he'd do it differently. Do everything you can to let go of your need for your spouse to "get it." Instead, focus your energy on helping him to understand what you need to feel validated and appreciated for the work that you do. Once you get to a point where you feel valued at the end of each day because you're connected to your spouse and know he appreciates your efforts (and vice versa), the need for either of you to "get it" will miraculously disappear.

Respect What You Didn't Know BK (Before Kids)

Realize that when you marry someone, in most cases you can't possibly imagine how they will respond to the job of parenting. Even if your spouse has children from a previous marriage, unless you've seen him or her actively parenting a newborn or toddler, you may not fully know what to expect. Realize that you are going to have to work through needs and expectations on both sides, and that doing so will be more challenging than it was back in the day when you were able to go out to dinner every night of the week to discuss whether you'd serve chicken or filet at your wedding. After all, whether chicken or filet was served, several hours later the wedding was over. Working to merge different approaches regarding roles you'll be in for the rest of your lives is a much larger and more significant proposition.

Accept Responsibility

Be prepared to acknowledge the ways you are adding to the tension. This is difficult because, let's face it, you're right 99.9 percent of the time! However, if you're willing to really look at the way you're dealing with a particular situation, you can almost always find a way your approach is not working for your spouse.

Accept Those Things You'll Likely Never Understand

Men claim they'll simply never understand some of their wives' approaches or responses to life circumstances. Women feel the same way about their husbands. Don't waste too much time trying to understand those things that aren't likely ever to make sense. Accept that you'll never understand why your husband couldn't care less that the family room is an utter disaster area but is losing sleep over the state of the garage. Accept that you'll never understand why it's necessary to mow the lawn in mid-November in the Midwest. I ran into Mollie and her boys in the store the Saturday after Thanksgiving. I asked her what Gary was doing, and she replied, "Um, he's mowing the lawn. It's so ridiculous I could scream. I swear, next year I'm replacing all of the grass with gravel."

Avoid Power Struggles

Do not sit around vowing you'll give your husband what he needs as soon as he gives you what you need. The reality is that your husband is unable to give you what you need because he's so devoid of what he needs and vice versa. Stay away from this dynamic. I can tell you with absolute certainty that a war over which will come first—the chicken or the egg—is a war that ends in a stalemate every time. Just focus on doing your part. Do the right thing because it's the right thing to do, not to provide you with justification to then sit around stewing and counting how many seconds it takes for him to reciprocate (and after he does, do not communicate that he waited 12.6 seconds too long). Cut each other some slack. If you each vow to work on loving the other in the way that he or she needs, and worry more about your own part than your partner's, you'll make your way down the aisle toward wedded bliss far faster than you otherwise would.

Know Your Needs

It is important to be crystal clear about what you need. You need to be clear not just with your spouse, but with yourself. How many times have you been in a rut and a friend has asked, "What do you want to happen?" or "What could he do or say that would make this better?" and your answer is "I don't know!" You *can't* not know—if you don't know, how the heck is *he* supposed to know? Take some time to identify what you need, and then communicate it to your spouse.

When you do communicate your needs, beware of saying simply, "I want to feel validated." You need to be more specific by telling him what you need him to say or do to validate you. Many times, as Laurie Puhn mentioned, men want to make women happy, but they have no idea what the hell to do! Of course, this theory was blown to bits the year I sent my husband an e-mail with a link to a lovely Jeanine Payer necklace and said, "This necklace with this saying on it would make me feel quite validated this Mother's Day" and then received a gift that, although lovely, was not the necklace. Apparently, getting me something I specifically request isn't special—or something to that effect. No matter how many times he's attempted to explain it, I still don't get it, but I'm quite sure that necklace will make its way to my neck sometime in the next fourteen months (or so).

Choose Your Confidants Wisely

David took one critical point from our premarital session

with a priest: when you are choosing a confidant with whom to discuss your marriage difficulties, choose someone who supports not just you but also your marriage. You know which friends these are. You have friends who, as they would have in high school, might say "You deserve better" or "Divorce isn't that bad" or some such thing. These are not the friends to go to for help during difficult times. You need to count on the friends who know you and know the strengths of your marriage and your spouse. You need to go to the friends who, in the end, want you and your husband to work out your issues because they are supportive of your journey together as a couple.

Keep Your Cool

In the heat of an argument, when you're about to blow, do everything you can to walk away and come back to the discussion when you've had some time to calm down. Some of the most hurtful things are said in moments of frustration. Most of those things you might mean in the moment, but you don't mean them overall—they are merely a reflection of your level of frustration. Many adults need time and practice to learn to "fight fair." But it's a very valuable lesson because it teaches your children a healthy way to resolve conflict. They are listening far more often than you might realize.

Focus on Your Own Personalities, Not Stereotypes

Don't worry about what the stereotypes say about the ways men respond to challenges or crises or mountains of laundry. Almost every person on earth defies the stereotype of his or her gender in some area. I install crown molding. David makes a mean chili. Barb's husband, Tim, irons like nobody's business. Mollie has no desire to be a fantastic chef—even when the in-laws are over. And Sonya's husband, Bob, is so good at vacuuming that the White House would be lucky to have him on staff. By assuming that general this-is-the-way-they're-wired stereotypes apply to your spouse, you're merely providing yourself with an excuse to be more frustrated than you perhaps need to be. The best way to find out exactly how your husband operates and what he needs to feel valued is to ask him—and ask him for specifics. It's easy to assume that others receive love and validation the same way you do. You may show your love for your spouse in precisely the way you need to receive it, but unfortunately, it may not hit the same emotional chord with your partner. After you ascertain what your spouse needs, be sure to provide him with the same information about what you need.

Be Resourceful

In addition to girlfriends who can understand and a standby therapist, there are a few good books to keep handy. Let me save you some frustration: your husband is likely not going to read them. However, try not to feel as though this means you are making an effort and he isn't (which is very easy to do). This is your way, just as it was when you were pregnant or a new mom and reading as though the printed word would cease to exist at any moment. Anything you might be able to glean from any resource, printed or otherwise, that could give you a better understanding of his position, or help you to identify an approach that may work, is valuable.

Two books we've found of value are *Couple Talk: How to Talk Your Way to a Great Relationship* by Chick Moorman (this guy is great and you'll hear about him again shortly) and *The Five Love Languages: How to Express Heartfelt Commitment to Your Mate* by Gary Chapman. This book truly helped me to understand that everyone needs to receive messages of love differently, and what works for your closest friend may not work for you. Likewise what works for you may not work for your spouse. You have to learn how to speak his love language, and vice versa. David did actually read this book at one point, and found it quite interesting and valuable. The author also wrote a book called *The Five Love Languages for Children*, which can help you identify how each of your children gives and receives messages of love.

Respect the Journey

It has been said many times that life is a journey. Marriage and parenting are segments of that journey. At times their paths cross, and at other times they must be walked separately. What's important is that you and your husband take the trip together.

Think of the overall journey in terms of the letter H. You and your spouse each travel your individual paths, but you must ensure that those paths are always connected. In this way, you make certain that you continue to grow—as individuals, as parents, and as a couple—but your journeys don't become completely detached from each other's at any point in the process. In reference to the breakup of Harrison Ford's first marriage, Walter Beakel said, "It wasn't because he became a star. In all relationships, there are changes and the point is both partners have to change together." Amen to that.

COMMUNICATING WITH YOUR CHILDREN

My friend has a baby. I'm recording all the noises he makes so later I can ask him what he meant.

—Stephen Wright

In the early toddler years, parents must weather the time period when their children are learning to coherently pronounce words and form sentences. They must also patiently wait as their children master the ability to communicate their thoughts and needs as quickly as they become aware of them (which frankly may take longer than a year or two).

Babies begin babbling at around two months of age. To the parent who isn't too exhausted to identify the difference, infants have distinguishable cries for hunger, pain, and pleasure. By six months or so, babies are usually quite pleased with the sounds they can make (not to mention the amount of saliva they can produce while making them). They can repeat single syllables and begin listening more intently to those around them.

By one year of age, most babies can follow simple instructions, and should recognize their name when called. They typically have a five- to six-word vocabulary, and in some sick twist of fate, one of those words (and likely their favorite) is quite possibly "No." As I've mentioned, one way for parents to keep this word out of their children's vocabulary for as long as possible is to use it as infrequently as possible themselves! Remember, if your babies were premature, they may not follow these guidelines exactly. Work with your pediatrician to determine whether or not your children are on track given their gestational age at birth.

According to Katherine Cook, an Illinois-based speech-language pathologist, "Many children have quite a limited vocabulary by their first birthday, and this does not necessarily mean that they are delayed. Speech milestones are approximations, and there is a wide range of 'normal' in the first nine to fifteen months."

By the time they celebrate the end of their first year with what is possibly their first taste of cake, most babies begin making more obvious attempts to communicate specific needs. The frustration that can result when parents don't respond exactly as the child wishes can be hard on everyone involved. When two children are trying to communicate simultaneously, a parent can begin to wonder if her own head might soon start to spin around exorcist-style as she tries to figure out what each of them wants amidst the garbled yelling.

One approach to communicating with children who are this young—an approach that has gained increasing popularity in recent years—is sign language. Notes Tracy Kunce, a speech-language pathologist in the Western Chicago suburbs (and heavily responsible for the fact that Henry, while not knowing his own name until he was sixteen months old, will now not stop talking), "Sign language is a wonderful way to enrich the language environment and ease communication with little ones who aren't speaking much yet."

Parents can begin teaching a baby signs for common words such as "more," "eat," "sleep," and "all done," between four and six months of age. With consistent reinforcement many children will begin using these signs between seven and eleven months of age to communicate their needs and desires. Until they were at least three years old, Jack and Henry remembered the signs for "more," and "please." Even at three and a half years of age, Henry was so fascinated by sign language that he continued to pick up new signs even though he could communicate orally on par with any other child his age. There is a whole slew of books available on teaching your child sign language as well as several video tapes and DVDs, should you need the instruction to be more visual.

According to Cook, "If, by one year of age, a child doesn't appear to know his name, isn't babbling at all, or if parents believe their child's overall speech and language skills are leap years behind those of his peers, a consult with their doctor and/or a speech-pathologist or audiologist should ease their concern or confirm the need for intervention."

The toddler years are notoriously trying when it comes to communication. The greatest frustration parents experience is perhaps the feeling that their child can understand what they are asking or requesting of him, but can't effectively communicate his needs in response.

A one- to two-year-old should be able to identify body parts and speak in two- to three-word combinations. Remember, a lot of growth occurs between the ages of one and two. Most newly turned one-year-olds are not speaking in two-word sentences. Many don't yet produce any recognizable words. But a lot can happen in 364 days, so don't fear that when your child is almost two, he still won't be speaking in two- to three-word sentences. Even if he is, he may not be able to voice his needs fluently. However, he will usually figure out a way to get what he wants.

Continuing to use sign language during this time is not only appropriate, it might even prove quite beneficial. A toddler is capable of far more signs than a baby, and while his pronunciation is developing, signs will assist in making hard-to-pronounce words easier to understand. Some parents worry that at this age, using sign language might hinder a child's speech development. Not true. Kunce reassures that "baby signs are not a replacement for speech; they actually help facilitate language development" and recommends that parents always use words and signs together.

Additionally, beware of supporting the apparent invention of a word by your child. It's easy to fall into a pattern where you refer to a shoe as a "doo" because your child refers to it that way. But the only way your child will learn to ultimately pronounce the word properly is by hearing it spoken properly by others.

Case in point: Grace always referred to a blanket as a muckley. That's how she reproduced the sounds she heard early on. David and I therefore began to refer to blankets as "muckleys." Today, all six of us refer to blankets as "muckleys," and while the older three kids (and obviously David and I as well) do indeed know that a blanket and a "muckley" are the same thing, we tend to forget that the rest of the world does not. It's fun when we have guests over and a kid says, "I need a muckley." David or I throw a blanket to him while our guests look on as though they must have been asleep the day that the definition of "muckley" was taught in English class.

As with everything else in parenting, it is so important to trust your instincts when it comes to your child's speech and language development. If you are concerned that something is just not right in terms of your child's development in this area, make an appointment with his doctor to discuss it. If your primary physician isn't concerned, but you aren't reassured in a short timeframe, contact a qualified speech professional on your own.

When Phase Two started, Jack and Henry didn't yet talk.

They screamed, and I tried anything, including sign language, to help them communicate what on earth they were screaming about. But we really were not yet communicating by any official definition of the word. By the time they were almost three, I heard Henry say, "Jack, you no hit me again. I'm tired of this." Later that morning in the car, as Henry attempted to steal a few of Jack's pretzels, Jack yelled, "Henry, don't even think about it!" Obviously, they learned the language, and unfortunately, my own words came back to haunt me more often than not.

One week past their third birthday, Jack said, "Mommy, Henny's my best friend." And those are the moments to live for as a mother of twin toddlers. The moments when they can clearly communicate how important they are to each other, and we can feel absolutely fabulous for getting them to a place where they can not only coexist (at least part of the time) but love each other as well.

These days, Jack and Henry fight all the way to preschool, and then cannot walk through the front doors without holding hands. After a particularly loud morning at home, their teacher informed me that during center time, Henry got frustrated and took a small swing at Jack. Jack "used his words" and asked Henry to please not hit him. Henry threw himself at Jack, bear-hug style, and said, "I'm sorry, Jack. I love you." I was stunned. I said, "*What? Are you sure? I've never heard Henry say anything like that!*" Those are the moments when all of the hitting, the climbing, the signing, the screaming, and the running in opposite directions are worth every second. I could cry just thinking about it.

I promise, over the next few years, the kids *will* learn to communicate, and much of what they say is going to make you keel over with laughter. I am stopped dead in my tracks several times a week—and have been ever since we got over that whole I-refuse-to-communicate-by-any-method-other-than-wailing period—over comments I can hardly believe are exiting the mouth of one of my kids. An example: the day Jack left his room, tripping over clothes, books, and toys on the way out (it often resembles the aftermath of an F5 tornado in there) and went straight to my office. He saw Post-it notes everywhere (it's my own unique—and very effective, I swear—form of organization), and yelled, "Who put all this paper all over my mom's office? This place is a *mess!*"

One day sooner than you can imagine, you'll surely be able to have lengthy discussions with your child about the theories of Freud or the views of Socrates. And when that happens, it might just be you who's in the position of trying to keep up!

GUIDING TWIN TODDLERS

Believe it is possible to solve your problem. Tremendous things happen to the believer. So believe the answer will come. It will.
                                                            —Normal Vincent Peale

I use the word "guiding" instead of "disciplining" because, frankly, it sounds better. It's what you're going to be doing for the next several years (at least), so might as well make it sound pleasant. The word "disciplining" sounds so negative. As parents, we shouldn't necessarily focus on punishing our children for behaving inappropriately—though sometimes that is indeed what occurs—but instead on guiding them toward proper reactions and approaches to life's challenges (I wish it were as easy as it sounds!).

The one time you might read more about raising your children than you did when you were pregnant is when you're trying to teach children who barely talk—and certainly don't understand the proper way to negotiate or reason—how to behave in a manner that will prevent you from opting to wear a baseball hat and sunglasses everywhere you go as though you were Jessica Simpson. Just as with any subject, the number of experts available to help you with this task is immeasurable. And of course, each has a different view of what makes for a successful approach. If they all thought the same way, it would certainly make our lives easier, but they would never get their unique viewpoint displayed on the shelf next to their competitor whose approach has quickly become yesterday's news. It's consumerism gone haywire to some degree.

It is going to be very important early on for you to accept a few things about guiding your children, whether you are doing it with a singleton, twins, or more. First, it is critical that you find an approach that works for *you*. Realize this may not be the approach that works for your neighbor, your pediatrician, or your friends; it more than likely will not be the one that worked for your parents or your in-laws; it may even need to be modified to accommodate the varying needs of each of your children. Everyone has an opinion. Don't allow yourself to get caught up in someone else's approach unless you believe it might work for you. Don't worry about your mother, who swears by her approach even though you believe it caused irreparable damage. Pray that your in-laws leave their opinions at the door (unless you believe that their ideas are brilliant).

Second, accept that not only may different approaches be necessary for different children, but that different approaches may be necessary (strike that, *will* be necessary) based on the age of your children at any point in time.

Finally, every expert believes wholeheartedly that his or her entire approach is the "right" one. And the opinions run the gamut: Use time-outs, don't use time-outs; count to three, don't count to three; don't use the word "bad," but don't use the word "good" either because every word has an opposite and the opposite of "bad" is "good," which is a word you aren't supposed to use. Don't praise your kids too much. Be sure to say at least four kind things to your child each day. But not more than six. Fewer than four creates a self-conscious child. More than six creates an egomaniac. It can send you into a tailspin wondering *what* to do. Trust yourself. Take bits and pieces that make sense at any point in time from a variety of experts. Know that an approach that sounds absurd today might just sound like an option in two years. And if all else fails, take comfort in the fact that next week a new "expert" will likely be sitting in a chair directly opposite Katie Couric at 9:37 a.m. on NBC, and she may just have the answers you've been seeking.

The challenge when teaching twins proper behavior is that you have two children at the same age who are, in all likelihood, completely different from one another and therefore require different approaches. The other big challenge: you will often contend with the fact that you don't know who started the current battle—or what the issue actually is!

> *Children are unpredictable. You never know what*
> *inconsistency they are going to catch you in next.*
> —Henry Ward Beecher

While the issues you'll be addressing and the approach you'll choose to address them will change over the three or so toddler years, one aspect of your approach will remain critical: consistency. Whatever solution you employ, be sure that you employ it consistently. It's just not fair to let a child bite one day because you're too tired to address it, but give her a time-out for it the next day. Consistency is what will (hopefully) ultimately teach the lesson.

In this chapter, I'll address guiding twins from the age of one to two. I'll isolate some of the more common challenges parents face while raising children in this age group and provide potential solutions. I'll do the same in the chapter on two- to three-year-olds and again in the one on three- to four-year-olds.

GUIDING YOUR ONE- TO TWO-YEAR-OLD TWINS

The pessimist sees the difficulty in every opportunity; the optimist the opportunity in every difficulty.

—L.P. Jacks

Remember this: by and large, kids younger than eighteen to twenty-four months old aren't "misbehaving" on purpose. They aren't consciously breaking the rules for any other reason than to test their boundaries. They aren't trying to make you angry at them or defy the system just because they want to do it a different way. In fact, toddlers' biggest joy comes from your approval. This may seem crazy now, but wait until they are between three and a half and four years of age. Only then will you be able to look back and acknowledge that there truly is a difference between the ways a one-year-old "misbehaves" and the ways a four-year-old does.

Additionally, unless your children understand why you are doing what you are doing when you provide a consequence for their actions, the consequence serves no purpose. It makes you feel as though you are doing something, and it gets the child out of your way for a few minutes, but until he begins to link an action with its natural or logical consequence (if you fall off the couch you're jumping on, it will hurt; if you throw the sippy cup, it goes in the sink), he's going to continue to repeat the behavior, if for no other reason, because one thing he *has* learned is that it pushes your buttons!

With one- to two-year-olds, the crux of the challenge is distinguishing the babies' comprehension abilities from their communication abilities. You may spend quite a bit of time wondering, "Does he really *get* that he's not allowed to color the floor? And if not, is the consequence fair?" (By the way, I've read tales of moms walking into their dining rooms to find a newly created mural by their eighteen-month-old on the wall. While I agree that the child was probably trying to create a beautiful work of art for his mother and had no idea that such a thing was unacceptable, I've never been sure I could muster the attitude to say, "Oh, honey, this is just beautiful" without shedding a tear or two while burying the expletives.)

For starters, ensure that you minimize the number of issues you'll be faced with by making sure that the toddlers' environment is free of those items that will excite them into doing something they should not be doing. For example, if you don't want them climbing on the fireplace, block that area off. If you don't want them coloring without you around, store all crayons up high. Gate off rooms with valuables you prefer they not be near, such as fine china. Store Play-Doh out of sight *and* out of reach. During this timeframe, babies are incredibly curious. If they know they are not supposed to have something or be somewhere, they want it all the more. The theory that forbidden fruit always tastes sweeter is especially true when toddlers are involved. Don't tempt them into doing something that will frustrate you but truly is not their fault.

I recently heard an interview with a prominent L.A.-based interior decorator on XM radio (I don't know what I did before XM radio). At one point, the woman conducting the interview mentioned that a friend of hers believes that while raising young children, parents should not alter any part of their lives in the decorating department. This friend claims that parents should do whatever they would do if they didn't have kids, and then take it upon themselves to teach their young children that certain things in the house are "art" and to be looked at only with their eyes, not their hands. This way, they develop a respect for those things they aren't to mess with, and their parents are able to maintain a home that actually resembles a home. The decorator was asked for her opinion on this.

I loved her answer. She agreed that this approach works, but only to a point. It is indeed important to teach children to respect things that are not for them to play with, but it's also important to respect that their curiosity at this age is stronger than their ability to remember each and every time that they aren't supposed to play Frisbee with the thousand-dollar artifact from Chile. It's important to ensure that those things that would truly hurt them are up and away for a short time. This protects both them and you. They are less tempted and therefore get into less, and you spend less time saying "No" and replacing broken artifacts.

There is a reason why many babies' first word is "no." It's easy to say, and more telling, many of them hear it non-stop (and I realize that's about the third time I've mentioned that fact myself, but repetition of important points can be helpful). Of course there are times when you'll use the N-word. There are times when you'll *scream* that word (like the second you see the glimmer of your one-year-old's plan to throw a sippy cup into a roaring fireplace or hurl a remote control at a stained-glass window). However, if you limit the number of times you have to use it by ensuring that there aren't too many enticements lurking on table tops or in easily accessible drawers, it'll keep everyone happier.

My home during the one- to two-year-old timeframe looked more like one giant toy box than an actual home. There were gates *everywhere*. All cabinets were locked. All drawers to entertainment centers and other furniture were locked. All books or video games (David's video games; I'll never forgive Microsoft for the Xbox concept) that might have tempted the boys to climb onto anything at all to get to them were put out of sight. Any art work I might have acquired anywhere nicer than a drugstore was put in storage. Was it a pain? Yes. Was it worth it? Absolutely.

As I mentioned earlier, the real problem I experienced during this time was the difference between the boys' ability to understand me and their ability to communicate their needs to me. They'd scream and I'd ask questions and they'd keep screaming. Many times, I had no idea what they wanted. Sign language was one strategy I used quite successfully. Of course, it takes time and patience to teach them the signs they'll use most often, and unfortunately they never learned to sign "I needed a sugar fix so I ate a whole bag of marshmallows" or "I thought the glass tasted good so I licked all six lower panes of the front door." But many times, it helped a great deal.

You're likely to come up against certain other issues during this timeframe that, unfortunately, you can't eliminate by locking a cabinet or inquiring via sign language. These might include biting, throwing food at mealtimes, or standing up in the bathtub, to name a few.

Mollie's boys used to throw their food off of their trays constantly. Mollie had the big highchairs—two of them—as opposed to the reclining feeding chairs you can attach to your own chairs. So, this game was potentially more exciting for her boys because the food had farther to fall. Food wasn't the only thing they'd throw; sippy cups often made it into the game as well. The key with this challenge is not to draw attention to it. It's annoying, but it's temporary. It may not go away fast enough, but it should only last a few months at worst.

Since my boys were sitting in their feeding chairs on the floor, I went to the fabric store and got about three yards of picnic table covering. It cost next to nothing and I even got to pick my pattern. I just put it underneath the boys' chairs and when they were finished eating, I picked it up, opened the sliding door, and fed the birds. If they dropped food such as applesauce or yogurt on it, I ran it under the kitchen faucet.

This is the time period when you'll learn that babies think that any word that communicates your displeasure is hilarious. Even a look that communicates that a particular behavior isn't going to fly can be enough to send toddlers into hysterics. So, even if you don't want them throwing food, saying "No" or giving them "the look" is not likely to curb their interest in doing it. Mollie would tell the boys "No" or say "Stop" one time when they threw their sippy cups. If they did it again, she took the sippy cups and put them on the counter. That was the rule: you throw it, you lose it. While the words "no" and "stop" are hilarious, losing one's meal isn't. While you will spend a lot of time wondering what they understand and what they don't, they seem to get this particular lesson of cause and effect rather quickly and choose to cease and desist.

It's hard to find a parent who hasn't experienced frustration at their child's realization that tremendous fun can be derived from watching food drop to the floor or fly toward the wall—over and over (and over) again. When two children encourage each other in this game of Lob and Laugh, it can be even more trying. "Toddlers have a way of putting O's in their ears and spaghetti sauce on their heads, all in the millisecond your back is turned to refill their sippy cups," notes Jennifer Margulis, editor of *Toddler: Real-Life Stories of Those Fickle, Irrational, Urgent, Tiny People We Love.*

The simplest, time-tested solution to this game is to inform your children that dropping (or throwing) food isn't allowed. If it continues, the meal ends. Kids quickly learn to stop behaviors that have an unpleasant consequence. The removal of their meal is often incentive enough for toddlers to stop this activity—at least for that particular meal.

Honestly, the best parenting book I've read yet (or should I say the one from which I've utilized the most strategies) is *Parent Talk: How to Talk to Your Children in Language That Builds Self-Esteem and Encourages Responsibility* by Chick Moorman. The strategies in this book likely won't work on a one-year-old, but if you buy it now and begin to make some of these phrases part of your life, they'll be solidly in place by the time your kids can understand them. I bought it when Jack and Henry were almost three. Grace was almost five. I saw immediate improvement with Grace in several areas. Not all, but more than enough. The book is basically made up of phrases you can use—as well as those you should not use—to get the desired result while encouraging responsibility in your child and keeping her self-esteem intact. For several months, I kept this book on the kitchen island and every time there was a meltdown, I went running for it. The kids stared at me like I was crazy as I said, "Hang on. Just stop yelling for two seconds while I find an appropriate phrase to use." So get this particular book sooner rather than later if you believe Moorman's approach might work for you.

Another book that I highly recommend is *How to Talk So Kids Will Listen & Listen So Kids Will Talk* by Adele Faber and Elaine Mazlish. While initially published in the early '80s, its authors share Moorman's philosophy. Because it's organized a bit differently from *Parent Talk*, it gives the reader additional perspectives on the strategies she can use to elicit cooperation from her children.

Specific Approaches to Behavior Modification

Time-Outs

Many of the sorority sisters learned that time-outs don't work terribly well during this phase. First, you will have to carry the child to the designated time-out spot, which creates more manual labor for you. Because your child isn't likely to fully understand why she is there, she's probably going to escape unless she's confined somewhere such as her crib or a Pack 'n Play. Some people do utilize Pack 'n Plays or cribs for time-outs, but I've heard more than once (and tend to agree) that using a child's crib for a time-out is not the best idea. You do not want your child to develop any negative associations with his crib—at least beyond the fact that it's time for lights out even though he would prefer to crawl in and out of the Tupperware cabinet for another hour.

That said, time-outs worked quite well for Chrissy's twenty-month-old twin girls. As many of us were when it first debuted, Chrissy was a loyal watcher of CBS's *Super Nanny*. (Did anyone else ponder the minor detail that the majority of Super Nanny's clients seemed to be parents of multiples?) Whenever Chrissy so much as made mention of the Naughty Chair, her daughters would immediately cease and desist the problematic behavior. Thus, for a period, she became known as Super Chrissy.

1 . . . 2 . . . 3

When Jack and Henry were two years old, there was a large craze over the concept of counting to three. The premise was that when you began counting, your child would realize that he could choose to stop what he was doing, or, when you got to three, there would be a consequence (of which he was informed ahead of time). The problem with this strategy in the experience of many of my fellow moms is that kids learn fairly quickly that before anything unfortunate happens, mom has to get to "Three." They continue the behavior until Mom's said "Two," and then they stop.

The main problem with this approach, especially early on in the second year, is that young children don't have a clue what you are doing when you start counting. Most of the time, they'll just continue what they're doing. As they reach the latter half of this year, they'll look at you with a wow-I've-sure-got-you-frustrated grin on their face the minute you say "One."

I knew a mother once who not only counted incessantly, but each "strike" required three sub-strikes. So, the mom would begin counting, and inevitably just after she said "Two," the kid would stop doing what he was doing. If he didn't, and she actually uttered the word "Three," he'd get Strike One. Once she got to Strike Three, the child received one "official" strike. He required three "official" strikes before he was punished. So, the mom had to successfully get to "Three" *nine times* before the child suffered a consequence. It was insane. This kid acted up all day long. He knew the way the game was played, and the mom was so terrified of her son being angry with her because she punished him (regardless of the fact that the punishment resulted from his misbehaving nine times) that she ensured that she never had to make good on the consequences, but was being a responsible mother by doing something to enforce good behavior. When I witnessed these counting episodes day-in and day-out, the child was three or four years old. But clearly, this sort of laissez-faire approach had been utilized all his life because trust me, he had no interest in behaving for any longer than it took his mother to stop counting—for twenty seconds.

Barb, who has been the exception to the rule in a few areas, was just that when it came to counting. When her girls were between eighteen and twenty months old, Olivia was having such frequent and mind-blowing tantrums that counting to three was the only thing that worked—for Barb. I remember this stage of beautiful Olivia's life as though it were yesterday, and I remember Barb uttering numbers more times during a five-minute phone call with me than any other type of word. She recently informed me that the counting wasn't entirely or even predominantly for Olivia's benefit. It was for Barb's. She was so frustrated by Olivia's behavior that counting to three kept her as calm as possible while she attempted to deal with the latest outburst. If Olivia actually responded to the tactic by stopping her tantrum, all the better.

Ignoring

Flat-out ignoring your child's less-than-acceptable behavior doesn't work terribly well at this age for anything other than full-blown tantrums. At this age, a child's ability to understand cause and effect is still maturing. It's easier for her to understand that if she throws her food on the floor, her plate goes in the sink than it is for her to understand why you're not helping her when her outburst is the only way she knows to communicate a particular need. She'll understand that if she's throwing a major tantrum to get your attention and you walk away, she's not getting the desired effect. However, if she's whining or having a disagreement with her brother over who gets the yellow block, she won't understand why you've left the room. She's not trying to get your attention at this point; she's trying to get through a frustrating situation as best she can. She needs your help (and will for some time) to learn how to handle it properly.

Distraction
Distraction works better at this age than at any other because while they appear to be getting more persistent (and they are), one-year-olds really don't have the attention span to be attached to anything for very long, including the conviction that the red toy on the other side of the room that her brother is playing with is different from the exact same red toy right in front of her. Many times, diverting a child's attention with another toy, a butterfly sitting on a flower outside, a plane flying overhead, or the appearance of the floating teddy bear in a commercial for fabric softener will be enough to help your child to forget the frustration she was previously focused on.

Praise/Positive Reinforcement
Positive reinforcement is a wonderful tool to use at any age. It doesn't matter how old you are; it always feels good to know that someone else approves of something you have done. When your children share nicely, tell them what a good job they did sharing. When they follow directions, tell them what good listeners they are.

If you have extraordinarily sensitive kids, as Mollie did at this age, you may be able to just give "the look" and get the exact result you are seeking. There were days when, if Mollie even looked at Tommy or Kevin funny, he'd cry. They were very receptive to her approval and almost anxious about the alternative. So, Mollie didn't often have to go too far to squelch the problem of the moment. But don't worry, this extreme level of sensitivity didn't last long so don't get mad at her.

ADDRESSING THE MORE
FRUSTRATING BEHAVIORS

As the light changed from red to green to yellow and back to red again, I sat there thinking about life. Was it nothing more than a bunch of honking and yelling? Sometimes it seemed that way.
—Jack Handey [Deep Thoughts]

Tantrums

Temper tantrums are nothing more than an immature expression of anger and/or frustration. This doesn't explain why a full-grown man went into a rage and nearly threw himself over the customer service counter at the grocery store a few weeks ago simply because the deli meat that was supposed to be on sale was not, but thankfully I didn't have to take that man home with me. Temper tantrums are in no way an indication of poor parenting skills on your part. What's most important in terms of guiding your child toward a more appropriate way to handle moments of anger or frustration is the way you choose to handle him while he's melting down (and don't discount the way you handle your own moments of frustration and anger in front of your child!).

When your child is throwing himself on the floor and thrashing in a manner that has you wondering exactly what you spawned, there are a variety of approaches you can use to help get him through the challenge. Following are some strategies for taming tantrums:

- Stay near your child (in case he actually starts levitating or something), but remove yourself emotionally from the situation. Sometimes kids just need to get their frustration out, and at a young age they don't yet know how to do it in an appropriate or rational manner.

- Let your child know that when he's calmed down, you are

there to hug him and discuss his frustration. Prior to age two or even three, kids will typically get their frustration out and then either wish for a hug or some other form of comfort or simply crawl or walk away because they spotted a toy that's seemingly been hiding for two days.

- Try to identify the cause of your child's frustration. Many times when children are frustrated, it's because they can't complete a task (such as getting a toy to work properly) or can't effectively communicate their needs. The latter occurs with frequency in the one- to two-year-old group. For strategies on making communication easier for everyone, refer to the "Communicating with Your Children" section. Let your child know that you understand that she's frustrated. Speak slowly and in short sentences. Encourage her and let her know you care and want to help. Ask her to show or tell you what you can do to help.

On occasion, Jack or Henry would come to me and clearly want something, but the word they used to describe that something was "Uh." The back-and-forth dialogue that consisted only of "What?" and "Uh" got challenging for both of us. At one point, I started saying, "Show me," and putting out my hand for him to take me to wherever it was that the desired object lived. Inevitably, it was almost always the pantry, as all those two wanted to do was eat, but if the sixth cereal bar of the day was enough to end the What?-Uh discussion, that was fine by me.

- Be on the lookout for a pattern. Try to identify common instigators of your child's temper tantrums. Did she miss her nap or take an unusually short nap? Could she be hungry? Did you just return from a vacation during which her schedule was modified? Do your best during these occasions to steer your child to bed, to the kitchen table, or to the bathtub or another calming activity. Once she's gotten the rest, food, or relaxation she needed, her temperament will likely improve. Another way to look at it: when you are exhausted, you might think, I'd love to take a hot bath right now, or settle down with a good book, or go to bed early. Or you might just snap at someone for something that ordinarily wouldn't elicit that sort of response from you. Your toddler doesn't have any knowledge of why she's out of whack or a clue what to do about it. It will be up to you for the next few years to help identify the culprit (when possible) and steer her to a solution so that she'll learn to do so on her own over time.

- Don't play into her hands. When your child is throwing a tantrum merely to get his way, a different approach is warranted. These are the times when no matter how bad it gets, you simply cannot give in. It's like the time period when you were sleep training. Each time you acquiesced and got a screaming baby out of his bed, he learned that if he screamed for twenty or thirty or forty-eight minutes, you'd rescue him. Do not give your child an audience for these types of tantrums. Stay close, but move to a different room or otherwise make it clear that you are not paying attention. Let him know that you are aware that he's quite frustrated and that when he can calm down you'll be happy to talk with him and try to work things out together. Yes, I do remember that I'm advising you on speaking to a one-year-old, not a twenty-year-old. Sometimes, it's not what you say, it's how you say it, and it's hard to utter the above phrase with anything less than a compassionate tone. Even if he doesn't understand every word, he'll hear your tone and perceive your intent. Once you've worked things through, do your best to keep an upbeat attitude. It's very hard on children to have their parents' obvious annoyance and frustration with them continue well past a tantrum or otherwise negative situation.

- When possible, use the words that your child cannot. When she's somewhat calmed down (don't attempt this as she's flipping around like a fish on the hardwood), acknowledge that you can see that she's upset because she wants to play some more or watch another movie or use her brother as a stepping stone to get on top of the dining room table in order to swing from the chandelier. Explain that it's time to go to bed or have dinner or play with a truck instead of a light fixture. This is a time when distraction may work wonders. Get as excited as you can about the truck to which you are now calmly escorting—or downright dragging—her and she may find something equally exciting (yet hopefully far more appropriate) to do. That is, until her brother takes the thing from her.

If a child's tantrum is utterly disruptive because he's damaging property, physically hurting another person, or "pulling a Henry" as we said at our house when it appeared as though no matter what we said or did, he could in all likelihood scream at the top of his lungs for the next twenty-four hours, consider removing him by putting him somewhere that is safe for him and for others. Again, I am not a strong supporter of using cribs for time-outs, but on the rare occasion when he's really out of control, it might be the best (and possibly only) option. Squeeze him tightly as you carry him there, as his complete lack of control may actually scare him. This will help him to relax. He may throw everything out of his crib, and he may continue to scream for a time. But eventually, he'll calm down. And in our experience, he'll then likely fall asleep for about two hours, making it clear that he was not only frustrated about something, but unbelievably exhausted to boot.

Different approaches work for different families and different situations. One approach, however, that I strongly advise you to avoid is spanking. You may have had it up to your eyeballs, and you are well within your rights to need a break, a bath, or a beer (or all three), but spanking your child, especially in moments of frustration, only shows him that you are out of control as well, and communicates that a solution to being out of control is hitting. You are responsible for teaching your children how to handle their frustration and their anger. And if you, as an adult, resort to spanking, it's only fitting that they'll be a bit confused the next time you impose a consequence for hitting.

Many parents wonder when the tantrums their child is throwing are of concern. If your child has hurt himself (by smacking his head against the floor, for example) or others during a tantrum, is having severe tantrums more than five times per day, has a parent with a tendency toward tantrums that he (or she) has not been able to divest himself of, is continuing to have violent or long-lasting tantrums after two weeks of your using the above techniques, or if you simply feel uncomfortable with what you're seeing and/or your ability to handle it, please call your child's health care provider. They see and hear about these behaviors day-in and day-out, and they will be able to reassure you. They can also provide you with additional strategies and input regarding possible causes for the tantrums that you may not have considered.

Biting

More often than not in this age group, biting, hitting, or jumping on top of a sibling is not so much a deliberate act of aggression as it is a result of a toddler's inability to express his needs and frustrations. If you did not have words to tell someone that he was bothering you or that you wanted the toy she had, at the absolute peak of your frustration wouldn't you think to bite or hit? Truthfully, as an adult who *does* have the words, there have been occasions—such as when I'm waiting for a parking space with fourteen cars behind me, and the occupant of the car with her reverse lights on is taking far too long to reapply her lipstick before backing out of the space, seemingly expecting to be seen by Orlando Bloom as she's driving down the street—when my desire to use kind, tactful words has gone out the window too.

Nonetheless, age-appropriate coping mechanism or not, parents often want to put an end to this activity in short order. I was one of those parents. In fact, Jack has a permanent scar on his back that, if you look closely, is quite clearly in the shape of Henry's one-year-old bite.

Try to patiently instruct your children on the proper way to handle frustrations that cause them to react in an inappropriate manner. When they bite, intervene and firmly advise, "We do not bite. Biting hurts." If your child persists in physical punishment of her twin or another child, remove her from the situation temporarily or try to distract her with another toy. (Do that subtly because the instant the other toddler realizes that a "new" toy is in play, you'll once again have two kids fighting over the same toy.)

Sometimes, biting is done not aggressively, but in response to your child's need to chew on something as he is teething. If you suspect this is the case, try saying, "Please don't bite me. That hurts," and replace your shoulder with a teething toy of some sort. On the occasions when one of my kids persisted in chewing on me to alleviate teething discomfort, I resorted to putting him down after advising, "It hurts when you bite me. If you keep biting me, I'll have to put you down." I had no idea if they fully understood that, but while it occasionally appeared otherwise, neither my shoulder nor my kneecap is a raw piece of meat. Usually, once I removed myself from the situation, he either used the teething toy or found another, more appropriate object to gnaw on (or, to convey his extreme displeasure at my walking away, wrapped his arms around one of my thighs, forcing me to hobble around with a living, breathing, twenty-five pound weight glued to me. But hey, I had to get my exercise somehow, right?) The reality is that even if your child no longer needs to chew, or throw, or scream, or whatever, the knowledge that it's ticking you off is all she needs to continue doing it indefinitely if you don't squelch the game.

Throwing

Once they can do it, kids love to throw things. The bad news: it doesn't necessarily go away as they get older. The good news: perhaps if you work with them, they can be future NFL quarterbacks or major league pitchers.

The biggest issue we had with throwing in our house was that Jack's favorite target was Henry's head. On most occasions, we'd just take away whatever he was throwing and try to distract him with something else. There were a few occasions when we'd tell him that if he kept throwing, he'd have to go to time-out. Once he ended up there (we were using a Pack 'n Play in the dining room), he'd sit in there happy as a clam and Henry would crawl in and entertain Jack from outside his confined quarters. As I mentioned, we learned rather quickly that time-outs simply did not work.

Mollie took away the toy that was thrown and comforted the victim. The attention went to the child who was hurt and his brother could not stand it.

When I called Barb and asked her to remind me how she handled throwing in her house, she said, "What, you mean like sippy cups?"

"Well, yes, but we just took those away once they'd been thrown too many times. What about toys and books and holiday decorations and such?"

She started laughing.

"Why are you laughing?" I asked.

"Oh," she answered, sounding somewhat embarrassed. "You're serious? Your guys threw books and holiday decorations?"

"Honey, Jack once hurled David's laptop at me for absolutely no apparent reason whatsoever."

Once again I was left feeling annoyed with the dynamic in Barb's house. And once again I reminded myself of the impending demise of her sanity in nine years when her girls turn thirteen.

Fighting over Toys

Kids fight over toys. Period. This pastime is in no way exclusively limited to twins. However, having two children of precisely the same age in the house can pose a challenge that might not be present with a six-year-old and a one-year-old running around.

When the boys were young and we hadn't yet ascertained what kinds of toys each of them liked, we'd often find something we thought they'd both enjoy and buy them each one, perhaps in different colors. Or we'd buy one a puzzle with fish and the other one with farm animals. We rarely bought the exact same toy for both boys. My rationale was that in real-world situations, it would be highly unlikely for them to enter a classroom, for example, in which there were exactly sixteen red guitars with the Wiggles on them. I didn't believe that it did anyone any good to create a world in which there was enough of any one thing to go around all of the time.

Mollie, on the other hand, believed exactly the opposite. She believed that as long as each boy had his own toy, which was exactly the same as his brother's, there would be no room for fighting.

To some degree, we were both wrong.

If you buy toys that are completely different, one kid always wants the one the other has. If you buy toys that are mostly alike, one kid always wants the one the other has. If you buy toys that are exactly alike, one kid always wants the one the other has. It never fails. In fact, one child can find a toy at the very bottom of a toy box that no one has cared about or played with for eight months, and suddenly, everyone in the house, including the much older sibling, is fighting over that toy. Kids truly epitomize the theory that forbidden fruit tastes sweeter (a philosophy that adults can also subscribe to, illustrated by the fact that when I was pregnant with the boys, all I wanted was beer, and I *despised* beer—until the boys were two and it became a necessity). Even if two kids are holding a yellow Fisher-Price school bus, each is convinced that the other kid's is better. If, out of frustration, you swap the exact same school buses for one another, you'll roll your eyes endlessly as the crying ceases because your children are convinced, for the moment, that they've each got the "better" yellow Fisher-Price school bus. It's absurd.

Mollie had one other strategy in addition to buying her boys the exact same toys in the exact same colors. She labeled everything. And I mean everything. All of Kevin's toys had a "K" on them and all of Tommy's had a "T." She took this all the way down to puzzle pieces. If she bought the boys the same Elmo twenty-four-piece puzzle, each of Tommy's twenty-four pieces had a "T" on the back of it. There was simply no debating whose toy (or puzzle piece) was whose because the owner's letter was on it. While they didn't learn what letter the symbols represented until much later, they learned what "their letter" looked like quite early on (before they were two, according to Mollie).

When Tommy and Kevin turned four, David and I gave them Elmo toys that are sort of like Mr. Potato Heads but instead of a potato, the main piece is an Elmo. Each one came with about twenty-five different appendages that could be stuck on to make Elmo look silly. As somewhat of a joke, I labeled each and every piece with a "K" or a "T." But I was pretty well put in my place when, four minutes into playing with their new toys, there was an ownership dispute over the elephant trunk Kevin was holding. Kevin looked at it, saw a "T" and gave it to Tommy. Well, he sort of threw it at Tommy in disgust, but he knew it belonged to him and that there was no getting around it.

Barb and Tim took an approach somewhere between mine and Mollie's. If the girls got any kind of a "big gift," such as a keyboard or a large kitchen set, it was given to them as a joint gift and they just had to figure out how to share it. Early on, Olivia adopted the color purple and Kambria the color pink. If the girls were given, say, play telephones available in purple and/or pink, life was easy because Olivia wanted nothing to do with any color other than purple and Kambria felt the same way about pink. If the girls received generic gifts that were not available in purple or pink, Barb and Tim put their initials on them to make it clear to whom the toys belonged.

One school of thought dictates that this sort of irrational competition is indicative of twins trying to claim their own territory, to establish their own identities separate from one another. I'm not sure how I feel about that. I think all kids compete for toys, and that young kids especially want what they want when they want it, plain and simple. It doesn't necessarily make any sense to the adults nearby or, most likely, to the kids either. It's likely primal in origin and, therefore, probably best to work through however you can until they are old enough to handle it peacefully on their own (which, I apologize for informing you, does not appear to be a solidified skill even by the time kids turn four).

So, take any approach you'd like on this front. Buy two of everything (and label them—or not), buy the same toy in different "varieties," or buy two completely different toys. In the end, kids have to learn to share, to ask for a turn, and to accept that sometimes their sibling (or another child) is going to say "No." It's frustrating, and it's a fact of life.

GOT MILK?

Opie, you haven't finished your milk. We can't put it back in the cow, you know.
        —Aunt Bee Taylor, *The Andy Griffith Show*

One challenge that may appear during the second year involves the introduction of milk. I have heard many moms complain that they believe they could put nearly anything, sewer sludge possibly, into a sippy cup and their child would drink it. But not milk. Put it into a bottle, she'll drink it. Put it into a sippy cup, forget about it. Let me stop for one moment to assure you that this is but one of the first ways in which this young child is going to attempt to manipulate the system.

Some parents do put milk into a bottle, while others use this changeover as an opportunity to transition their children to sippy cups. My personal cutoff point for bottles has always been one year, and I've always done it cold turkey. It was an easier approach for us because I believe it's too difficult on a child to be expected to understand that he can have a bottle sometimes but must use a sippy cup at other times. If he realizes that bottles are gone, he won't ever request one (after the first long, loud day of protest), and you won't ever have to deny him one.

I actually have no idea why kids sometimes boycott milk if it's served in a sippy cup. If this happens to you, you can check with your pediatrician for suggestions, or you can simply continue to offer milk in a sippy cup and hope that at some point in the near future, the child will accept that the bottles are gone, she's thirsty, milk happens to be in the cup, and she's going to drink it. Barb has a friend whose pediatrician advised exactly this. She assured the mom that ultimately, her child would be thirsty enough that the desire to drink something would overpower the desire to drink that something out of a bottle. And it did.

SLEEPING THROUGH THE NIGHT NO MORE

Arrange whatever pieces come your way.

—Virginia Wolf

It rarely fails. You've finally got both babies sleeping well through the night when one (or both) of them begin waking again for no apparent reason. When the babies had their crying spells as newborns, you probably spent many hours wondering "Is he hungry?" "Does he have gas?" "Is it possible that this child is deliberately and happily manipulating me even though he's only eleven days old?"

When they are toddlers and screaming like mad at 10:00 p.m., you may again spend time wondering, "Is she teething?" "Is she hungry? Did she get enough of a snack before bed?" or "Does she just want my company?"

There are myriad reasons why children begin waking again throughout the night after they turn one. Whole books have been penned on this phenomenon, and as I did in *Ready or Not . . . Here We Come!*, I will refer you to *Healthy Sleep Habits, Happy Baby* by Marc Weissbluth. This book does an excellent job of explaining the reasons—both physiological and emotional—behind night waking at all ages. As a pediatrician, Weissbluth has spent years assisting parents who are desperate to establish healthy sleep habits for their children. In this book, he helps parents to decipher with confidence whether or not the kid really needs something beyond another fifteen minutes with his new dump truck. Because Dr. Weissbluth is a far more knowledgeable expert on this topic than I am, and because he provides far more strategies on it than I ever could, if you are experiencing this challenge I would encourage you to pick up a copy of this book at your local bookstore or library.

Another great resource is Kim West, author of *Good Night, Sleep Tight*. West, also known as The Sleep Lady, has coached thousands of exhausted parents. Not only does Kim educate parents through her book, she also provides one-on-one coaching to sleep-deprived parents. My friend, Deana, solicited Kim's help when her one-year-old twin girls were still unable to sleep through the night or nap simultaneously during the day (for more than fifteen minutes). After filling out a questionnaire for each girl, discussing the situation in depth with Kim via phone, and receiving a customized action plan, Deana and her husband embarked on a mission to get the girls sleeping. After one week, things turned around. The girls were able to sleep for twelve hours straight at night and took one-hour naps—simultaneously. According to Deana, it was the best money they've ever spent. If you'd like to find out more about Kim West's philosophy and services, visit her website at http://www.sleeplady.com.

COMPETITION BETWEEN PARENTS: THE WORRY FACTOR

Normal is just a cycle on the washing machine.
—Whoopi Goldberg

During the second year, children experience considerable cognitive development as well as significant progression of gross and fine motor skills. They often go from crawling to running, and they go from few (if any) words to two- to three-word sentences. It's a time of incredible, obvious growth.

If you have older children, or have spent significant time with others who have a singleton, you're likely aware of the little dance parents do with one another around what their child has accomplished versus what their friend's child has accomplished. This dance starts as a waltz, slowly progresses to a tango, and within twenty minutes or so is a full-out quick-step, with at least one parent almost hysterically convinced that her child is extraordinarily far behind and will probably never catch up. This poor parent suddenly becomes unhealthily anxious to get home and get on the Internet to determine exactly what's wrong with her child that's caused her not to be able to consistently discern the difference between the number 6 and the number 9—as a two-year-old.

Parents with twins get to take this dance to a different level because they are often doing it not only with friends but with themselves since their own home provides two children who are the exact same age and, therefore, logically should be able to be compared. This can be very, very dangerous.

All children develop at different rates. Some children

display fine or gross motor skills early, while others begin to exhibit cognitive skills. There is a wide range of "normal" in this age group with regard to the development of nearly all milestones—both physiological and cognitive. It's easy to get stuck in a rut, spending an unhealthy amount of time focusing on the fact that a friend's twins are walking, while yours are barely crawling. Or you may incessantly ponder the fact that your friend's twins say four words, while your twins don't even appear to understand the word "Mama." However, if you approach the situation with a more well-rounded perspective, you'll quickly learn that there are plenty of things your children are doing that your friend's children are not. Or, twenty-four hours later, your children will suddenly be running around screaming, "Gimme that truck now!"

Points to Remember Regarding Developmental Milestones

If Not Today, Maybe Tomorrow

Skills develop very quickly in children within this age group. Some children begin at an earlier age to work their way up to walking confidently; they might take two steps and then fall, but according to their parents they are "absolutely walking." Others take their time and wait until they are sure they can do it—and then proceed to stand up one day and walk around the house, not falling once. In the end, they both might be able to confidently take fifty consecutive steps by the same date; they just had different approaches to get to that point. Or, as we've found, the child who starts working on a skill much later than another actually might master it earlier.

Gestational Age at Birth

When dealing with multiples, remember that you may not know at what gestational age another set of twins was born. So, while two sets of twins are both fourteen months old, the set that is walking may have been born at thirty-eight weeks, while the one that is not might have been born at thirty-two weeks.

Don't Believe Everything You Hear

Remember that some parents lie. Sorry, there's really no subtle way to say that. My mom had a friend who drove her nuts because she was always talking about how "gifted" one of her children was. One day, my mom ran into her and this child in a store. The little boy, who was then six or seven, was introduced by his mom as "my gifted one." His mom then proceeded to bend down and tie his shoes.

A mom who claims her daughter is walking may merely be nervous that if her daughter is *not* walking, there's something wrong. Observe the child the next time her mom puts her down in public and you may realize that a) she doesn't walk at all, or b) she pulls herself up on something and takes one step, but it's not walking as Webster's Dictionary or any pediatrician would define the achievement.

The only person you should rely on with regard to whether or not your children are on track developmentally is your children's doctor. If you have concerns, make an appointment to discuss them. Request an evaluation by a specialist if it would further allay your fears.

ANYTHING YOU CAN DO, I CAN DO BETTER (OR AT LEAST TRY TO DO BETTER)

The only competition worthy of a wise man is with himself.
—Washington Allston

As twins go through this period of rapid development, you may encounter what appears to be a wee bit of competition between them, frustration on the part of one who hasn't yet mastered a particular skill, or regression (or what appears to be regression) by one because his sibling hasn't yet mastered a particular ability.

In our house, Jack has always been Henry's savior. Even in the neonatal intensive care unit, when Henry needed something and the nurses didn't respond to his cries in less than thirteen seconds, Jack would cry at the top of his lungs until someone came over and tended to Henry, and then he'd stop. It seemed most bizarre, but having watched them over the last four years, it's become clear that a certain pattern of assistance began quite early.

Henry was quite late with his gross motor development. He was born with very low tone. He was also born with very low motivation. He quickly learned that he didn't need to learn to crawl, or walk, or do anything because as long as he made a noise that Jack understood (usually the same "Uh" that apparently has meaning only to those under the age of two), Jack would do just about anything for him. He'd retrieve his pacifier, bring him a toy, feed him off of his spoon, anything.

Jack started walking at about nineteen months. Henry wasn't ready yet. Jack liked to walk, but he never wanted to leave Henry. So he'd sometimes walk to get a toy, but otherwise, he didn't seem to see it as fun because he had to leave Henry behind. I had hoped that this might motivate Henry, but alas, it did not.

I worried that this was bad for Jack, but I was encouraged by all practitioners involved that it was fine. Instead of worrying so much about Jack's physical development being stunted in some way, they said we should focus on what a wonderful emotional relationship they were developing.

But Henry did get frustrated at times. Unfortunately, the frustration (and temporary motivation that came with it) at not being able to do what Jack was doing often was not enough to bring about his desired results. He needed time and therapy, which he got. It was fun to watch them together at Henry's therapy sessions, as Jack was often the only one who could get Henry to follow directions!

Young twins often compete with each other for their parents' attention. I had a mom tell me that she was losing her mind because she'd sit on the floor, one kid would come over and sit on her lap, and then the other would see this and insist on sitting there as well. She'd offer each a knee, but that was not sufficient. They both wanted sole attention and nothing less. She asked, "What do I do?" I told her to inform them that one could have the left knee and one could have the right. If one or both chose to accept that, great. If not, maybe she'd just have to get up and go fold laundry while they duked it out. Not every challenge can be a learning experience because many times you'll just be too tired to deal with it. In those instances, your best bet is to walk away for a while and take your own time-out. Honestly, when toddlers are in this mode, even if they do acquiesce and pick a knee, they'll then start fighting over where your hands are and the fact that one's big toe touched the other's big toe, and on and on.

Note: twin toddlers can be fighting to the death one minute and laughing and hugging each other the next, so don't worry too much about them "not getting along." This flip-flopping is completely normal and, frankly, to be expected.

SLEEP ISSUES

I love sleep. My life has a tendency to fall apart when I'm awake, you know?

—Ernest Hemingway

Historically, I've advised that if parents are going to split their twins into separate rooms, they should do it before the babies are four months old since after that point, they not only are aware of their sibling's presence, but are also able to vocalize (read: scream) that they are aware of their sibling's absence.

Having experienced the toddler years, however, I'm now advising a bit differently. Should you, at any point, be able to separate your children into different rooms and believe on any level that it might be the best thing to do, *do it!*

I saw a game in Costco a few weeks back called Lights Out, Game On. It was some sort of glow-in-the-dark basketball game. What parent in her right mind would buy such a thing? For heaven's sake, who needs a glow-in-the-dark game? When you have twins sharing a room—specifically twin boys—the lights go out and the game is on, athletic equipment handy or not. Of course, I should note that the answer to the question, "What parent in her right mind would buy such a thing?" is: your husband. No parent in *her* right mind would buy it, but almost every parent clearly *out* of *his* mind would. On one of our recent family trips to Costco, David walked by this game and proclaimed, "Hey, Cool!" He tried to convince me that we should buy it, and I don't know how the floor or toy boxes or other shoppers responded to his arguments for purchasing the game because I was already three aisles away.

When Jack and Henry were born, I thought, "Oh, it will be so cute for them to share a bedroom. They'll bond so nicely and read to each other at night and comfort each other during nightmares." This vision I had was what psychologists like to call a fantasy. Everything was groovy until Jack and Henry moved into their big-kid beds (which happened before they turned two) and then it all went South—quickly.

Many of us in the sorority who kept our children in the same room rethought that approach later. Some of us could do something about it and others could not. I happened to fit into the "could not" category. When Jack and Henry were thirteen months old, we built a new house. We constructed this house specifically to provide a room large enough to house the two of them through their high school years. And what a blow it was when, six months later, we realized that we had made a horrendous and irrevocable error.

Within a year, their bedroom was destroyed in ways I

could never have imagined. We had to bolt their floor vent down because they were stuffing everything under the sun into it. In fact, when we ultimately unscrewed the vent, having determined that they were mature enough not to stuff anything down there again (they were almost four when we made this determination), we reached in to find no fewer than eighty-six puzzle pieces, four golf-sized balls, one much larger ball, Henry's therapy ball that was about seven inches in diameter, and a Pluto stuffed animal that was about the size of my forearm. I guess that in our haste to bolt the vent down, we neglected to pull out its contents first. It's no wonder we were baffled as to why it didn't seem to get very cool in there in the summer or warm in the winter. We're lucky the contents of the vent didn't catch fire sometime between November and March!

When I finally determined with ninety-nine percent certainty that the boys were finished using their books as hammers on the walls, I spackled between six hundred and one thousand dents. We could not figure out how handprints were showing up above their window since the top of the window is about eight feet off the ground. I was also concerned that their windowsill was starting to separate from the window trim. One afternoon, David didn't feel great about what was going on in there during "rest time" and snuck in to find Henry, the less proficient twin in the gross-motor department, standing on the windowsill that is ordinarily at the height of his shoulders. So, out came the caulk gun. Their ceiling fan blades were chipped from the books that had been thrown up into them. And if you're wondering why I didn't remove all toys from their room, I did. More than a few times. I am still thanking the Lord that I didn't spend our first few weeks in our new home painting a mural on their wall as I had intended so that their room would resemble the lakeside retreat that David had dreamed of having in there. Frankly, perhaps I should have done that. I bet David would have moved right in there with them and then none of this would have happened.

The bottom line is that twins have plenty of time to bond. Naptime and nighttime are times to *sleep*, not bond. And furthermore, the bonding that goes on behind closed doors when more than one young child is involved is often not the kind of bonding a parent dreams about. So, make your own choice on this one. Take it a day at a time. I know, you look at those adorable one-year-olds and you think, "You'd never do anything like that, would you?" Keep believing. But, when you see the symptoms beginning to present themselves, when you feel the inkling to turn your craft room or your guest room or your walk-in closet that was just redone by California Closets into an additional bedroom, I'd advise you to contemplate it for not another second. As Nike has advised for years, Just Do It.

Dropping the Morning Nap

Sometime during this year, your children will likely drop their morning nap. In the beginning, you may find that there are days when, should you need to, you can force them to skip their nap and they'll do fine. You'll quickly learn for how many days in a row you can do this, as well as how late they will need to wake up first thing in the morning in order for you to attempt it.

Exactly when your babies will no longer need their morning nap is impossible to say. As with much else, it will have a good bit to do with their gestational age at birth and their personal need for sleep. If they were born only a few weeks early, it's not likely to affect the timing as much as if they were born two to three months early. Many babies drop their need for the morning nap between twelve and fifteen months. Even more take until they are fifteen to eighteen months to do so. I've known many moms whose children—twins or not—were still napping in the morning at twenty months. If this is the case for you, find a way to make that time positive; use it to get some housework done or spend quality alone-time with the baby who has outgrown the need to slumber in the a.m.

As they are transitioning to one nap per day, the number of days children can go each week without a morning nap will gradually increase (and may frankly jump to seven all of a sudden after you put them in their cribs one morning and realize they are spending the entire hour playing).

With a singleton, this is a pretty easy transition (or at least to us moms of twins it is). With twins, it can be a bit trickier because it's highly possible that both babies won't drop their need for the morning nap on precisely the same day. You may spend many days thinking, "If only Jason didn't have to nap this morning, we could get the grocery shopping done." As frustrating as it may be, it will be a whole lot less stressful to go grocery shopping in the afternoon or evening than to do it with an overtired baby. As with sleeping through the night, the amount of time you are likely to spend in limbo with one baby napping in the a.m. and the other not is not terribly long in the greater scheme of life.

Once a baby has dropped his morning nap, it's likely that at least initially, you'll need to push the afternoon nap up by thirty minutes or so. While a baby used to be able to go until one o'clock before going down for her afternoon nap, she may begin to fade right into her lunch tray if you try to stretch her out too long. And do not assume that the longer you stretch her, the longer she'll sleep. For the scientific reasons behind this, I will again refer you to *Healthy Sleep Habits, Happy Baby*.

If you are having a lot of problems weaning *yourself* off of your babies' need for a morning nap, don't forget that you can gate them into a play area and clean, do laundry, etc. It's good for the babies to spend some time without you constantly interacting with them. Provided they are in a safe area, they'll learn to play more independently, and they'll develop the confidence (if they haven't already) that you aren't going anywhere without them.

ONWARD AND UPWARD:
THE TRANSITION TO BIG-KID BEDS

Accept challenges, so that you may feel the exhilaration of victory.
—George S. Patton

Some parents move their children to big-kid beds sometime toward the end of the second year, while others wait until their children are closer to three or even older. In all honesty, I truly wish I could have waited until the boys were closer to eight!

Many pediatricians recommend moving a child out of her crib once she's begun trying to climb over the side rails. Jack was doing this at seventeen months, and since there was no way I could move one kid out of his crib and leave the other in his (since they shared a room), I was forced to move both of them.

Many people worry about how their children will react to a big-kid bed. Will they be afraid? Will they fall out? Will they walk around the house at 3:00 a.m.? Knowing my children as I did, my main concern involved how much time it would take before they realized that they were free—and began plotting.

There are a multitude of strategies parents can employ when moving their children out of cribs. One is to convert the cribs to toddler beds if that is an option; another is to purchase true toddler beds, which generally utilize a crib mattress; a third is to go right to twin (or full-sized) beds. Should you choose the third option, you can purchase actual bed frames, or you can put the mattresses right on the floor.

Hoping to make this transition as seamless as possible and alleviate the possibility of the boys falling out of bed (or realizing that they could play Superman and jump off of it), we left their mattresses on the floor for quite some time.

Strategies for Moving Twins to Big-Kid Beds

- Convert cribs into toddler beds (if possible) to provide a gradual transition to a freer world—and later a bigger bed.

- Buy an actual toddler bed (many avoid this simply because it's an extra purchase, times two, that will be used for only a very short period of time).

- Put crib, twin, or full-size mattresses on the floor.

- Put your children directly into twin or full size beds with bed frames.

Once you decide where the children will sleep, you must also decide how the transition process will work. Many parents of singletons set up the child's big-kid bed in the same room as the crib so that the child can get used to it. They sometimes let the child nap in the big-kid bed but spend nights in the crib until she's more comfortable with the big-kid bed. They then remove the crib. Some have noted later that the ultimate removal of the crib was perhaps more traumatic for their child than just switching them cold turkey to the big-kid bed, removing the crib at the same time.

With twins who share a room, it's quite possible that there is not nearly enough space in their room for two cribs and two beds. In this case, many parents have enthusiastically talked up the big-kid beds for a week or so, and then on a Saturday morning taken down the cribs and set up the big-kid beds (it's a good idea to make this transition on a weekend so that your ability to sleep-in or nap—should the transition go poorly—will be greater than if you did it on a Wednesday night). For naptime the first day, allow the kids to "explore" their new room. Inform them of the rules (no jumping on or off the beds, etc.), but don't expect them to actually sleep (or follow the rules).

Having done this three times, I'm a big proponent of the quick-switch approach. As you've probably noticed, I tend to prefer the cold-turkey method because whenever you try to do something gradually, the effort gets stretched out and stretched out and stretched out some more, and you start to wonder who's in control of the whole process. I'm not suggesting that a modified gradual approach isn't beneficial—my attempts at gradual usually involve talking about what will happen for a while, talking about when it will happen, and then just doing it. I've yet to have a child completely lose it over the loss of his or her crib, though I realize I do still have one child to get over that hurdle.

In all honesty, whether your twins share a room or not, it could be some time before they actually nap *in* their new beds. They will likely be so fascinated by the fact that they are free that they'll play, come in and out of their room, build a fort, and then hide in the closet (where they'll fall asleep).

Did you catch the potential activity after random playing and before building a fort? Your first challenge will probably involve keeping them in their room.

Strategies for Keeping Children in Their Room at Nap/Bedtime

- Put a gate at their door. Early on at least, they probably won't be able to climb over it.

- Once they learn how to climb over the gate, should they insist on doing it even after you explain that they are to stay in their room, explain that you'll have to close the door if they can't stay in their room.

- Once they can work the doorknob (or tear off the doorknob protector), if they refuse to stay behind the gate and refuse to keep the door closed, you can choose to turn the lock around so that you can lock the door from the outside. You'd give them plenty of warnings, but if they refused to follow the rules, this would be an option you could exercise to ensure that they stayed in their room.

Nighttime Issues

One of the biggest nighttime challenges parents face with mobile toddlers is their resistance to staying in their rooms once they are out of a crib (or, if they are still in their cribs, their need to express their displeasure at being in their crib and not downstairs watching *Rolie Polie Olie*). Kids roaming the house during naptime is frustrating, yes, but kids roaming the house at 4:00 a.m. is just not acceptable. When kids figure out that the party doesn't stop the minute they go to bed, they often fight like mad for the right to be part of the festivities.

No matter how tired they were, regardless of the fact that they were in a room together, even if we bought them the most exciting books on earth, Jack and Henry saw no reason to stay in their room if David and I weren't in ours. And many nights, even if we *were* in ours, Jack and Henry apparently felt as though they should be in there with us.

Tommy and Kevin apparently operated under the same mindset. After the boys transitioned to big-kid beds, Mollie and Gary woke up almost every night with at least one kid, if not two, in bed with them. Either Mollie or Gary would get out of bed and sleepily guide the child (or children) back to his bed. Thankfully, they found themselves providing this sleepwalking escort service only once a night. But as tired as they were, they were not willing to start a habit of allowing the boys in bed with them because they knew that before long, they would have to upgrade to a Shaquille O'Neal–sized bed to accommodate all of them every single night of the year.

Tommy and Kevin also developed a habit of climbing into each *other's* bed in the middle of the night, much to the dismay of the owner of the bed being climbed into. They typically duked it out on their own until Mollie decided they needed a little assistance and went in to inform them that they needed to be in their own beds.

Mollie wanted to close their door at night, but chose not to because she and Gary wanted to be able to hear the boys if they needed something. Using a monitor caused problems because there was so much interference with neighbors' monitors (and Mollie was a little bit afraid of what the neighbors might hear!).

At one point when the boys were between two and a half and three years old, Mollie told them that if they stayed in their room all night, they would get a sticker. Once they got three stickers, they would get a prize at the dollar store.

They never got three stickers.

Then the rule was that they could come out when they heard Gary in the shower in the morning. They finally achieved consistent success with this rule when the boys were close to four years of age.

Jack and Henry also chose to leave their room on occasion at night. Thankfully, we didn't have visitors in the middle of the night very often, but now and then at 11:00 p.m. or so as David and I sat downstairs watching reruns of our favorite sitcoms, we'd hear Ted Koppel upstairs. Because we were fairly sure that Ted was not broadcasting live from our bedroom, we'd go up to determine exactly what was going on. What we discovered was that the boys had seemingly decided that they needed to ascertain the current status of world events, and were therefore sitting in our bed watching *Nightline*. They were escorted back to their room and told not to come out again (many times they apparently turned their ears off just before we delivered this message).

They actually insisted on sleeping together for months after they graduated to their big beds. This was fine except that Jack hated to be touched and Henry was a cuddly sleeper. Jack would get royally annoyed when Henry would try to "spoon" him in the middle of the night. When we moved Jack to his own bed, Henry would cry because he had no one to cuddle with. We ultimately unknowingly alleviated this problem when we let them "decorate" their own beds with stuffed animals, books, and anything else that would entice them to sleep in their custom cocoons two feet from each other, but not on top of each other.

Unfortunately, we did reach a point at which we had to turn their door lock around. They refused to stay in their room at night (Jack could climb the gate in a single bound), they refused to stay in there during rest time, and they refused to stay in there when one was told to go up and spend some time apart from his siblings since he clearly was having trouble occupying the same floor without whacking someone.

Opinions abound regarding whether or not it's a good idea to turn a door lock around. I know that in many cases, it seems there are no other options. I believe that it's important that kids be given a warning before the door is closed and locked, but in the end, he or she should clearly understand cause and effect and learn to choose to play quietly or sleep. I just don't understand toddlers on so many levels. I mean, can someone please explain to me why *anyone* would turn down the offer to climb into bed and sleep as long as he'd like, after which point someone would make him a snack?

Olivia and Kambria had separate bedrooms from the get-go. A couple of months after they turned two, Barb and Tim put the girls' crib mattresses on the floor and they slept on those for some time. Barb thought it would be the hardest transition on earth, but she was pleasantly surprised to find that it was easy as pie. The girls thought those mattresses on the floor were awesome—and they didn't seem to comprehend their freedom. Barb remembers that, amazingly, it was a good six months before they realized that when they went to bed, the rest of the world did *not* go to bed. Once they became aware of that fact, and especially as it got closer to summertime and the sun set later and later, they felt that it was complete and utter abuse to be put to bed if their parents were going to stay up and clean, talk, or—heaven forbid—watch a movie.

They began to fight being confined to their rooms at bedtime. Shortly thereafter, they put two and two together to realize that during naptime as well, there was an adult downstairs doing something other than sleeping (even if Barb did sneak in a little nap, she was not in her bed, so Olivia and Kambria didn't understand in the least why they had to be in theirs). The first phase when they simply could not stand being in their rooms for any reason whatsoever eventually abated. But it restarted multiple times over the next couple of years.

Barb and Tim used gates at their doors to prevent them from escaping, but Kambria would scream so loudly that they'd end up having to close her door. Of course, she knew how to open her door (Barb's doors have French handles and they hadn't yet come out with a childproof apparatus for those). Therefore, Tim spent an hour on a Saturday reversing the lock on Kambria's door. Sadly, Kambria helped him do it because she had no idea what the result of that little exercise would be! At naptime and nighttime when Kambria escaped, Barb and Tim told her that if she came out of her room, they'd have to put up the gate. If they put up the gate and she screamed, they told her that they'd have to close the door. She had warnings, but in the end, if she couldn't stay in her room, or if she couldn't stay in her room somewhat quietly, they locked the door from the outside. This wasn't done as a punishment; they knew these outbursts were more a result of her being exhausted than anything else. Nonetheless, they had to enforce the rules because they were in the best interest of everyone involved, most importantly Kambria. Fortunately, Kambria disliked having her door locked so much that within a short timeframe, she agreed to follow the nighttime rules. As the girls got older, the need to close (or lock) their doors slowly disappeared, but even today they keep the gates handy for those times when the girls refuse to stay in their rooms.

Be prepared for the fact that once the kids agree to actually stay in their room, they probably won't fall asleep in their beds. You'll find them at all hours conked out in the middle of their floor, behind the door, or in the closet. Once, I even found Henry sound asleep inside his lidless toy box.

BANISHING THE BINKIES: WHEN AND HOW TO GET RID OF THE PACIFIER

If you paint in your mind a picture of bright and happy expectations, you put yourself into a condition conducive to your goal.
—Norman Vincent Peale

If a child becomes attached to a pacifier and has not either weaned himself of it or found his thumb prior to his first birthday, his parents may try to find a way to coax him away from his obsession between his first and second birthdays.

Henry needed his pacifier almost constantly from day one, while Jack wanted nothing to do with it—until he turned one, that is. Seriously, on his first birthday (or within a few days of it), he grabbed one of Henry's pacifiers, shoved it into his own mouth, and never looked back.

Exactly when parents decide that the binky's gotta go is a personal decision. Heck, they manufacture pacifiers for kids up to age four or five these days. From an orthodontics standpoint, it's probably better to suck on one of those than one's thumb, but for some reason, thumb sucking seems to be more socially acceptable for longer than is the pacifier habit.

Whenever you decide it's time to bag the binky, here are a few strategies:

Strategies for Leaving the Binky Behind

Limit Its Use

If you are ready to begin weaning your child from her pacifier but firmly believe that she still needs it at night, relegate the pacifier to your child's crib. Allow her to use it at night, and decide how often (if at all) you're willing to go in to replace it when she spits it out. Many children at this point only need a pacifier to fall asleep; they may not wake up in the middle of the night and need the pacifier to go back to sleep.

Stop Cold Turkey

I'm sure it won't surprise you that my personal theory on pacifier elimination is that cold turkey is the way to go. When stopping the pacifier habit—just like switching from bottles to sippy cups—trying to encourage a child to gradually limit his need for it tends to take quite a while, and it's confusing for the child. She doesn't understand the rules around when she can have it and when she can't. Therefore, sometimes just getting rid of it all at once is a better choice. If they've gone into the trash, you won't be tempted to give in "just this once." And at this young age, within a few days most children will forget that the thing existed in the first place. The first day may not be fun, but the second will be a bit better, and so on. Don't expect your child to forget immediately, and yet don't expect him to still be flipping out a month later either.

"Break" It

Some parents I know have suggested cutting off the majority of the pacifier's nipple. The theory is that without the nipple, the stimulation the child receives is gone and therefore the child won't be interested in the pacifier any longer. This approach makes me nervous because I always wonder about the small remaining pieces of the nipple coming off in the child's mouth. Cutting the nipple may be a good choice as part of another approach however. If your child is a bit older (two years of age or more) when you determine it's time to leave the binkies behind, you could cut the nipple and simply show your child that the pacifier is "broken." He can explore it while you're supervising him, but it's probably not a good idea to let him out of your sight while he's in possession of a pacifier with a cut nipple.

Leave It for the "Pacifier Fairy"

A suggestion I received from my fabulous pediatrician, Dr. Liberty, applies to children who are a bit older when the pacifier habit needs to be broken. For kids ages three and older, Dr. Liberty suggests that parents use an approach similar to the Tooth Fairy. Place the pacifier under a pillow from which the "Pacifier Fairy" will retrieve it in the night. In exchange, she'll leave a gift for the child—something to occupy him and hopefully distract him a bit from his frustration that this item on which he's come to rely so strongly is gone.

No matter whether you decide to curb the pacifier habit when your child is one or three or five, his reaction may be challenging at least for a few days. Nighttime may be hardest. The older the child is when this process occurs, the longer the transition will likely take because he's been dependent on it for longer. But remember that your child will find something with which to replace the pacifier. It may be her thumb or another finger, or it may be a stuffed animal or other item that comforts her. Keep in mind that a pacifier can be thrown away, which is not the case with one of your child's five fingers! My daughter sucked her thumb until she was five years old. We tried everything, including the topical liquid that is supposed to taste awful—but which she thought tasted like chocolate—to no avail. There were many, many days when I wished I had an object that I could throw away or present to the Pacifier Fairy.

BATHING

We tried to transition the babies from tub seat to tub and they were terrified. I stripped down and climbed in with them, but one tried to climb out and the other clung to my chest for dear life.

—Aimee, mom of girl/boy twins

The babies are bigger now—and more mobile—and therefore bath time will involve different dynamics. The most challenging time period while making the switch from the infant tub to the big tub is when the babies aren't completely stable by themselves. Some parents bathe their twins separately or on different nights, but since bath time has never been a favorite activity of mine, I preferred to kill two birds with one stone, so to speak. For those who choose to bathe the kids separately, you have a few choices.

Strategies for Bathing Kids Separately

- Bathe the kids on different nights.

- Bathe them one after the other. Put the one who's finished his bath in his crib, in a Pack 'n Play, or in a safe, gated room to play while you bathe the other.

- Bathe one, and then have your husband bathe the other.

- A combination of any of the above.

Should you believe that you cannot feel as though you're spending forty-seven percent of your life bathing someone (if you have any other children, you've got to work them into the rotation as well), there are a few other strategies to ensure that everyone gets clean and stays safe while doing so.

Strategies for Bathing Kids Together

Use Bathtub Rings
Until the babies were stable, bathtub rings came in handy for a few of us. I used them quite a bit and had good luck with them. If placed farther apart, they prevent your children

from being able to hit each other over the head with toys, or stand up in the middle of their bath. Two warnings, the first more important than the second: First, *Do not* leave a child unsupervised for even one second in the bath rings. There have been reports of the suction cups on the bottom coming loose and causing the ring to flip over backward, which could cause a child to drown. Second, babies with thick thighs, "Michelin Man thighs" as Barb refers to them, are often difficult to get out of these rings. Their legs get sort of stuck in the holes. It's not dangerous, but it might strain your back as you pull the kid out and have to hold her as you try to free her legs from the holes.

Bathe Them Together Without Bathtub Rings
Once they are more stable, you can put the kids into the tub next to each other (without using bathtub rings). Some of the common challenges with this approach include: they fight over toys; they stand up mid-bath; they hit each other with toys; they become fascinated with the faucet whether or not you have a cute rubber ducky or elephant attached to it.

Once many kids are able to be "free" in the tub, they realize how much fun can be had by standing in it, not to mention throwing water, toys, and anything else in sight. One option is to take their toys away if they won't stay seated. Another option is to consistently sit them down and explain that we don't stand, we don't throw water, and we don't hurl bath toys at anyone's head. A final option is to call an end to that particular bath! When we started putting Jack and Henry together in the tub, I swear their baths lasted twenty-three seconds. That was as long as they could last without misbehaving. I am one of the fastest child washers in America, I'm sure.

Use the Kitchen Sink
If the kids are stable in the tub, but you don't want to bathe them at the same time, another option is to bathe them in the kitchen sink one after the other. This only works if you

have a pretty deep kitchen sink, but I bathed the boys in mine (one at a time) until they were about eighteen months old. The sink is at chest height (or so) which was easy on my back, and I often gave them haircuts as they played with their toys. They were so involved with playing (or pouring water as I shouted, "Keep it in the sink!") that they didn't realize they were getting a haircut.

UTENSILS, ANYONE?

One must learn by doing the thing, for though you think you know it, you have no certainty until you try.

—Aristotle

At some point before they are two, most children begin practicing with child-sized utensils. It will take time for them to become proficient, and it's a messy learning experience, but the more they are allowed to practice, the more skilled they will become (and simultaneously less interested in how much mischief they can get into with a spoon).

As with adults, necessity is sometimes the mother of invention when it comes to children developing new skills. That was the case in my house. Jack and Henry didn't want anything to do with spoons because it required that they "work" and, in their opinion, did not allow them to get the food fast enough. One day, my sister called in need of some information just as I was sitting down to feed the boys. I handed them each a spoon and told them that I was going to be a second and if they couldn't wait they could use the spoons. They looked at me like I was nuts. They looked at each other like, "What the heck is she doing?" Within four minutes, they were using the spoons. Now, they were not using them well; there was food everywhere. But they were having a great time trying. It was at that point that they realized that they could not only eat with the spoons, but also fling food onto the walls, onto each other, and onto the floor.

That's when we began the I-feed-myself era. They refused to eat anything unless they were allowed to feed themselves (though many times, after five seconds of trying, Henry gave the "Uh" command and Jack began feeding him as well).

In this process, Point A is the place where the kids have no clue how to use a spoon. Point B is the place where they know how to use it and use it well. You cannot get from Point A to Point B without many messes and a ton of patience. Don't give them spoons at every meal if you are having anxiety attacks at the thought of cleaning yogurt off of the couch . . . again. Offer the spoon at one meal per day, or at a snack. Go into that meal expecting the worst mess on earth. That way, no matter how bad it ends up, you expected it. More often than not, it won't be as bad as you anticipate. Another good idea: strip them down to their diapers for these adventures and have a lot of wet paper towels on hand (or plan to give them their bath directly after that meal).

By the way, at about the same time that you begin allowing your toddlers to practice feeding themselves with spoons, you may also begin to get frustrated with their feeding seat if it's attached to a not-altogether stable chair. Unless the chairs on which your feeding seats are strapped are extremely heavy and sturdy, your child may be able to easily rock the entire apparatus by throwing his body forward and backward or side to side. Catalysts for this type of behavior include—but are not limited to—wanting to get down, wanting the food to reach his mouth more quickly, needing more milk, or wanting to dance as crazily as possible to "I Like to Move It" from the movie *Madagascar*, which is playing in the adjoining room.

Should you decide that your child is not yet ready to sit in an adult chair by herself, but is also at high risk of tipping backward, over, or forward by rocking too hard in the feeding seat strapped to another chair, an option is to purchase the restaurant-style highchairs. You know, the wooden highchairs with just a square opening at the top in which the kid sits? I've never seen these in a baby store or the baby section of a store so the idea didn't hit me right away. However, these chairs are sold in high volume on eBay. You can find them by doing a search on "restaurant highchair." Parents of twins are in luck because the chairs are often sold as a two-pack for around $50 total (plus shipping, I'm sure). Another benefit of these chairs is that they are easier to clean than the feeding seats. One could feed the entire rhino section of a zoo with the meal remnants stuck in the cracks of the feeding seats at the end of each week! Finally, if your child is no longer using the tray on his feeding seat, but is able to get his feet up onto the chair onto which the feeding seat is strapped (no matter how tightly you strap him in, it may seem) and proceed to practically stand up, know that they'll have more difficulty accomplishing this in the restaurant-style highchairs because they'll have to get their legs through the leg-holes, much the same way you'll have to pry them out of bath rings.

Another option during this time is to let the kids sit at a child-size plastic picnic table for meals. We used the kind of small plastic picnic table that you'd typically put outside. The boys used it not only for meals, but to color or play with Play-Doh (both activities were heavily supervised, I can assure you). At times, the boys would take one bite of food and then get up and run around the house which wasn't acceptable. So, we began implementing the rule that once someone leaves the table, his meal is finished.

TRAVELING WITH TWIN TODDLERS

During takeoff, landing and turbulence, adults are required to be buckled up, baggage and coffee pots are stowed, computers are turned off and put away, yet infants and toddlers need not be restrained.
—Mark Rosenker

Regardless of whether it's for the first or the fifty-first time, one can't help but laugh while watching Clark Griswold and his family endlessly and hopelessly circle Big Ben and

Parliament, unable to "get left," in *European Vacation*. However, when imagining their own crew in the same situation, most parents' laughter quickly turns to nauseating anxiety.

Traveling domestically or internationally with twin toddlers can seem a daunting proposition at first. In fact, after thirty or so seconds of consideration, many parents likely decide to simplify their adventures by heading for the shores of the continent on which they reside. However, traveling with twin toddlers is absolutely doable. It takes only careful planning and the right attitude.

Whether heading for the local lake or the Louvre, the importance of effective preparation cannot be overlooked. It can undeniably set the stage for a wonderful experience or a Never Again nightmare.

Strategies for Successful Travel with Twin Toddlers

Plan for Possible Pitfalls

A valid concern for families considering a trip with young children is the potential for a child (or two) to fall ill days prior to departure. Be sure to purchase travel insurance (which can be done easily over the Internet) to cover money that may be lost due to trip changes and cancellations. Also, check your medical insurance plan to ensure that you fully understand what it covers while you're traveling, whether domestically or internationally.

Pack Properly

With four children under the age of six, the number of items my husband and I are likely to leave behind inadvertently when embarking on any trip is astounding. My mantra has become: as long as I have my driver's license and my credit card, anything else can be purchased en route. For the kids, however, you need to ensure that you have supplies to keep them occupied in the car or the plane.

There's nothing worse than setting off on a much-anticipated adventure with children only to have them begin complaining before the pilot has had a chance to welcome you on board. Choose the contents of your carry-on bags carefully. Doing so will go a long way toward avoiding the type of meltdown that might have you wondering when the flight attendants will begin serving "adult beverages."

My friend Sarah frequently travels to England with her two young sons. She suggests having a backpack for each child. Include small, wrapped activities such as crayons and stickers that they can open at certain milestones along the way. Stash snacks in each bag in the event of an unforeseen delay. Finally, put all sippy cups and liquids in their own Ziploc bag with a paper towel. This way if something spills or leaks due to pressure changes, clothing and other items aren't ruined.

Leave Car Seats Behind

When flying to their destination, many parents wonder whether to take their children's car seats on the plane or check them. Given that you'll have two rather large car seats until the kids are old enough to be in booster seats, it makes a good bit of sense to rent the car seats at your destination from the car rental agency, if you are using one. If you are traveling to see family who will pick you up at the airport, inquire as to whether they might have any friends in the area who have reliable car seats you could borrow for a few days. They may have friends who keep a car seat on hand for their grandchild.

If you feel strongly about taking your own car seats with you, there are all kinds of backpacks or rolling carry-on bags designed to hold a car seat.

Anticipate Schedule Modifications

Whether or not your trip involves a change in time zones, be prepared for your kids' schedules to be impacted. For one thing, they will be sleeping in a new place. Additionally, they will be excited over this new place and all there is to explore there. This means one thing: excessive stimulation. Your kids might fall asleep later than usual for one reason or another, and they may miss their naps either because you choose to attend an event or because they aren't able to get comfortable in their new surroundings.

Consider the effect of these changes if your children start to behave in ways that have you convinced that you left the airport with the wrong children. Do your best to keep their schedules as similar as possible to those they have at home. An afternoon without a nap now and then probably won't have horrible long-term consequences, but a week or more with no afternoon nap and late bedtimes will leave you wondering if you can travel home on one plane while your children travel on another.

Mentally Prepare for the Return Home

In all likelihood, you will not notice the effect of the change in schedules while on the trip—at least not until the end—which is a good thing. On the other hand, you will notice the effect the moment you return home, after which your children spend the next five days or so melting down almost constantly.

We took Grace, Jack, and Henry to Florida over the boys' second birthday. Schedule changes and all, they were extremely well-behaved while we were there. However, the minute we boarded the aircraft to return home, Henry's body suddenly went over the edge of exhaustion. He screamed, and I mean screamed, for the entire two-and-a-half-hour flight home. It was extraordinarily awkward, especially when the woman sitting in front of us with two young children of her own wondered aloud, "What is wrong with that kid? Can't they just give him some Benadryl or something to shut him up?" (I should have asked her what her secret was since, clearly, her children had never had a meltdown in all of their lives.) He finally conked out—just as we were pulling up to the gate in Chicago.

While parents will likely fall with a long sigh of relief into their own beds after returning home, they shouldn't necessarily expect their children to have exactly the same reaction. Do your best to get them back to their regular routine as quickly as possible, and know that in a few days their exhaustion and the related behavioral issues will subside. At that point you can begin planning your next vacation!

THE CELEBRITY FACTOR DISAPPEARS

Do people ever stop noticing that you have twins?
—Bari, mom of boy/girl twins

I read a pretty funny book by a guy named Bruce Stockler called *I Sleep at Red Lights: A True Story of Life After Triplets.* Bruce is the primary caregiver for his son and younger triplets. At one point in the book, he talks about the fact that somewhere along the line, the general public seems to stop noticing that you have multiples, and much of the attention that you received—albeit complained about from time to time—disappears.

The reality is that as much as it does annoy moms of twins to have people constantly asking questions, making suggestions, and the like, having that attention—however negative it may feel at times—is a huge part of having multiples. Many parents of multiples don't realize this until it suddenly dawns on them that no one is stopping them to ask about the kids anymore! They may even find themselves missing the attention on some level.

My friend Bari worried that her sudden sadness at not having anyone ask much about whether her kids were twins, or how many weeks early they were born, or how much weight she gained while she was pregnant, or whether her husband was the father of both babies was slightly egocentric. In my opinion, it's nothing of the sort. As we learn from our toddlers, negative attention is attention nonetheless. But we've found that the majority of the attention you'll lose is from the folks who didn't have anything terribly kind or encouraging to say anyway—the folks who weren't really interested in you or your kids, but were merely trying to find a juicy discussion topic for their ride home.

I'll never forget the day I realized I was completely over the need for people to know that Jack and Henry were twins. I had stopped into a little children's boutique in town while Grace was at an art class. I had an hour all to myself and I just wanted a quiet sixty minutes of browsing.

I happened upon a toy that I remembered playing with when I was little. I got so excited—I seriously could not believe I was staring at this thing. I decided to get one for Jack and one for Henry for a road trip we were taking a few weeks later. I knew that in this instance, it was probably best to just go ahead and get them the same one. However, there was only one of the variety I wanted on the shelf.

I asked the owner if she had another one. She was mid-conversation with some guy whom she clearly knew personally, and she didn't seem to understand why I might need two of the same toy. I informed her that I had twins.

Not a wise choice.

Mind you, *she* could not have cared less. But this man she had been talking to could not have cared more. He very excitedly informed me that he, in fact, was a twin. He went on and on about his twin sister and how fun it was to be a twin, yadda yadda yadda. Finally, he said, "So, you're really getting them the exact same toy?" I told him that yes, I was, because I didn't feel like listening to all the screaming in the back seat for eight hours due to one boy's conviction that one of these toys was absolutely better than the other. He then said to me, as though he had the insight of Bill Cosby (I can assure you, he did not), "That's not the best way to teach them to share, is it?"

I did not miss a beat (finally, I was ready for one of these people!). I said, "Sir, I'm not worried about teaching them to share on this trip. I'm worried about staying sane."

He just would not stop. He went on and on, and the grand finale came when he said, "So, does one cry when you spank the other?" Now that I was not prepared for. I said, "Excuse me?" and he said, "Whenever my mom spanked me, my sister cried and cried and cried. It was so cute. Oh, but you probably don't spank them, do you?"

"No, I do not," I responded.

He launched into some spiel about the fact that moms today are too lenient and the kids are spoiled and blah blah blah, and I was just throwing money at the owner in order to get the heck out of there. She was trying to put the toys in a bag and I said, "Don't need a bag. Just the toys." If I'd known these things were available anywhere else in town, I would have made an exit long before this point, I promise you.

So, I don't get a lot of questions anymore. I don't get a lot of concern over how much amniotic fluid a woman carrying twins actually manufactures or if they make a bra big enough to fit a woman breastfeeding twins. I did notice the shift, and for a little while I can honestly say that I was sort of saddened by it. It was the end of an era in my world of raising multiples. But after this exchange with Mr. I-Just-Can't-Shut-My-Mouth, I realized I was just fine putting that part of this experience behind me.

I was also pleased to recognize that the people who were genuinely intrigued, or impressed, or awed still made comments. They still asked me how I did it, or proclaimed that they had no *idea* how I did it. They asked Jack and Henry directly if they were indeed twins instead of asking me (the answers to this question got relatively humorous). They asked my kids how old they were and what their names were (and I guarantee you that at least once, your kids will take each other's names when introducing themselves, which proves most difficult when they are identical to begin with). So the attention overall will wane, but the positive attention will remain, and that's a good thing.

THE THIRD YEAR
(TWO- TO THREE-YEAR-OLDS)

I try to take it one day at a time,
but sometimes several days attack me at once.
— Jennifer Unlimited

Ten Signs You Are a "Normal" Parent of Toddlers

---

10. You have stealthily stolen a swig from one of the kids' sippy cups because you left the house without the drink you specifically set by your keys.

9. Your day is moving so quickly that you rush to the computer to check your e-mail, and suddenly have difficulty typing your password because you are still wearing the oven mitt used to retrieve fish sticks from the oven.

8.	You wear t-shirts in the middle of January because you're always sweating.

7.	You jump at an opportunity to clean the entire upstairs because it's quiet up there and you can do it uninterrupted.

6.	You can't find the phone, and you don't feel like wasting time searching for it, so you simply buy a new one. This is a *very* rational solution in my opinion.

5.	You find yourself driving down the road happily singing to a VeggieTales or Sesame Street CD, and then you realize there are no children in the car.

4.	You inadvertently adopt toddlerese when referring to certain items. For example, one day while searching my purse for my notepad, I informed my kids that I could not find my Handy Dandy Notebook (a *Blue's Clues* reference for those of you not yet shoulder-deep in Nick Jr.).

3.	You sport Sesame Street or Barbie Band-Aids whenever you get a boo-boo.

2.	You are fluent in the language of spelling, and can speak it so quickly with your girlfriends that the men in the room are as clueless as the kids.

1.	You relish the idea of going to the dentist (for a root canal), the gynecologist (for an invasive exam), or even the salon for a bikini wax (Brazilian-style) merely because each procedure requires that you go sans children—and lie down for the procedure.

For all of the *Desperate Housewives* fans reading this (those of you who aren't fans are either terribly sick of these references or you've decided to become fans just to understand them all), do you remember the episode in the first season when Lynette—who was so frustrated by her twins' refusal to behave in the car—was counseled by a much older, more "experienced" mom to simply leave the boys by the side of the road when they refused to follow the rules? First, Lynette was horrified. Next, she somewhat guiltily contemplated the suggestion. Then, she did it. Of course, it didn't work out all that well for Lynette, as a neighbor saw what she did and, while Lynette waited the requisite two minutes in a driveway at the end of the street, brought the boys inside for cookies and later threatened to call child protective services.

I have absolutely, unconditionally, *not* stopped the car and informed the boys that if they couldn't behave they couldn't ride. But believe me, the idea appealed to me on more than one occasion during the two- to three-year timeframe, and I fantasized about employing the strategy at more than a few stoplights.

Raising two- to three-year-old twins is pretty hilarious and pretty exhausting—sometimes both in the same ten-minute stretch. During this timeframe, the kids are going to begin to figure out precisely what they think about all kinds of stuff, and then they're going to find all kinds of ways to express those feelings. This is the year when the most hysterical things will start coming out of their mouths. And it's the period when you're going to be busy enough that you're going to forget to write half of them down. (Refer to the aforementioned solution of scribbling them on paper and tossing them in a box in the cabinet for safe keeping until a later date.)

CONVERTING AGE FROM MONTHS TO YEARS

This is my daughter, Lucy. She's sixty-two months old.
   —I made up this quote. Hopefully it's never been uttered.

I don't know about you, but I have a strange reaction when I ask someone how old her baby is and she responds, "He's twenty-nine months." Part of me wants to laugh, but that part is quickly overshadowed by the part that's doing the math. Since math has never been my strong suit, I'm pleased to report that I've never been informed that anyone's child is sixty-two or seventy-three or 154 months old. I think the reason we ultimately convert is that as the number gets bigger, we feel older and/or realize our children are getting older. Saying your child is three years old sounds younger than saying he's thirty-six months old. Saying I'm thirty-three years old sounds *far* better than saying I'm 396 months old. Good God, the latter makes me want to make an appointment for full-body Botox immediately.

A good rule of thumb: once your children turn two, stop using months to communicate their age. There is a big difference between a two-month-old and a seven-month-old developmentally, but the gap narrows as kids age. A two-year-old is a two-year-old. A two-and-a-half-year-old is a two-and-a-half-year-old. Most kids in those six-month spans are functioning in relatively similar ways. If you feel the need to be more specific, tell strangers that your children *just* turned two, or are *almost* three. Frankly, announce that your kids are two and everyone understands the reality of your world immediately. Tell someone your child is six months old and she'll ask, "Oh, does she crawl yet?" Tell someone your child is thirteen months old and she'll ask, "Oh my, is she walking yet?" Tell someone your child is two and she'll simply respond with something like, "Ohhhh, I see. So, how are *you* doing these days?"

HAVING ANOTHER BABY

If evolution really works, how come mothers only have two hands?
—Milton Berle

One of the most frequent questions I receive from women whose twins have recently turned one is not necessarily what you'd expect. Instead of "When will they start walking?" or "What do you do when they are going in different directions?" I hear, "What if we have another baby? How do you juggle a new baby when you already have young twins?"

Many moms start thinking about whether or not to have another baby when their youngest child (or children) is between one and two years old. I hear time and time again prior to twins turning one, "I am so done. These are absolutely our last children," only to have the tune change to "Weeell, I don't know. We might think about it." Should they do more than just think about it, a new baby may arrive when the twins are between two and three years of age. Just for you, my friends, I put the questions and concerns to the test. And I'm ready to weigh in.

Up until Jack and Henry were about twenty-two months old (which is under two, so according to my rules, I can qualify their age in months), I professed that only by an act of God would I have another baby. I had three children under the age of four, and I felt pretty confident that that was all my mental state could handle. Apparently God felt differently.

There was a two- or three-month window when Jack and Henry were so well-behaved on a consistent basis that David and I thought, "Should we try for one more?" I occasionally joke that we decided to have one more merely so that I'd have the answer for the many moms who asked how to manage a new baby with twin toddlers. But in all seriousness, as much as I love my children, as much joy as they've brought to my life, and as much as I believed another child would bring just as much joy, I truly wasn't convinced that I had caught up on sleep to a point where I could make a coherent decision on whether or not to bring another child into this world. I wasn't particularly worried about whether or not I *could* do it—at least in terms of the hour-by-hour minutiae that is child-rearing—I was worried about whether or not I *should* do it. I felt confident that I could put one foot in front of the other on a daily basis, but I wasn't sure that I could maintain my long-term sanity in the process. I figured that an insane mother probably wasn't in the best interests of the three kids I already did have. So I decided that I would not actively try to conceive a baby, but I also would not actively try *not* to. I was comfortable leaving the ultimate reality completely in the hands of the powers that be.

With my obstetrician's blessing, I gave up birth control thinking there was no way, after two pregnancies that required a bit of extra help, that conception would be immediate or easy. "Maybe someday we'll be pleasantly surprised," I thought. And that someday occurred twenty-nine days later. One shot (literally).

Never having had a regular cycle, I wasn't exactly waiting for a specific day on which to expect my period. Time went by and I thought, "Well, clearly in a few months I'm going to have to go to the doctor to take whatever drug they prescribe nowadays for a woman who hasn't had her period in six months."

Then one Sunday at church some friends had their newborn baby baptized. As the pastor was walking around the church introducing the baby to the congregation and talking about what a blessing children are, I felt ready to break down like Nathan Lane in *The Birdcage* when Robin Williams asks him to disappear during an important dinner. Being the more or less unemotional person that I am (especially in public), I found this reaction completely bizarre. Then, that same evening, as I lay down on my stomach to go to sleep, I could not get over the fact that it felt as though I was dragging my nipples over fifty-grit sandpaper every time I moved. Suddenly, my eyes shot wide open in what I imagine must have been a pretty solid imitation of one of Joey Tribbiani's many moments of surprise on *Friends* as I realized the possible reason for this discomfort.

I didn't say anything to David because I truly did not believe there was any way it could be so easy. The next day, I took the kids on a little shopping trip to Target and tossed a pregnancy test into the cart (and hid it under a pile of diapers and Tylenol lest I bump into anyone I knew). During naptime, I began the science experiment.

After the requisite minutes of waiting, I looked at the test strip. There was a minus sign in the first window and a plus sign in the second. I consulted the back of the box, which explained that the first window was the control window and the second was the test window. I could not wrap my mind around what appeared to be the test result, and I quickly became convinced that the directions were printed incorrectly and that the first window indicated my actual result—negative. The longer the minutes ticked by (and I could hear them ticking loud and clear), the more confused I got. So I called Barb.

"Dude, are you freaking kidding me?" she asked.

"Well, maybe," I said. "I don't know if I'm reading this thing right!"

I then called Mollie.

"You are *not* serious," she yelled (and she was yelling).

"Well, I feel like an idiot because I'm not sure if I'm reading this properly."

And then Mollie asked the one question she'll always ask in any sort of emergency—including a moment when you're not sure if you can use butter in place of margarine for a specific recipe—"Is there an 800 number on the back of the box?"

I tasked her with calling the pregnancy test people while I called my obstetrician's office, told the receptionist it was a medical emergency, and demanded to speak with a nurse immediately.

"Oh honey," consoled the nurse after I finished my spiel, "there's no need to be embarrassed; most first-time moms get confused by the results on the test strip."

"I don't think you understand," I practically yelled at her. "I have *three* children at home, the oldest of whom is *four*. I have never ovulated on my own in my entire *life*. My husband and I have had *one* romantic encounter in the last two months, and I have got to know *today* if this test is accurate or defective or what the hell is going on!" (and I think I did use the word "hell"—my apologies, Val).

God bless nurse Val because she told me to come in at 5:20. And I did. And I did not allow myself to go to the bathroom once until that appointment so my urine would be as concentrated as possible. With a nearly exploding bladder, I filled that cup and put it into the secret cubby between the bathroom and the lab area. I swear, before I had even pulled up my pants, I heard, "Okay, so your due date is . . . "

"Due date? What due date? You mean I'm *pregnant?*"

"Oh, honey, this test was positive the second the urine hit it."

I don't think I heard anything else that was said for at least six minutes. I was dumbfounded. Elated. Ecstatic. And then again paralyzed with sheer terror.

"Uh, nurse? How long before I can find out how many are in there?" I asked.

"How many what?"

(pause)

"*Babies*! How many *babies*!"

"Well, it'll probably be a couple of weeks until . . . "

"*Oh* no. I'm going to have that ultrasound today."

"Well, we can't do it today. The doctor is already gone, and . . . "

"Nurse, I've had twins. I've had more ultrasounds than you can imagine. I could work that machine with my eyes closed. I can probably do an internal exam on myself right this very second for crying out loud and tell you if I'm dilated yet or not. Just put me in there with that machine for five minutes. Four will suffice. I promise, I won't tell a soul."

Needless to say, my date with the ultrasound machine had to wait—for two interminable weeks. And when that day finally arrived, at the precise onset of my first official appointment, the doctor walked into the room and, after extending his hand in offertory congratulations, was met with, "We *are* going to do an ultrasound today, right? Because I'm *not* leaving without an ultrasound."

I chose this obstetrical practice for many reasons, not the least of which is that its doctors are far from stupid. Within four minutes, I was lying on that ultrasound table. I made him check and recheck about seventeen times. I felt very Hollywood as I lay there with my feet in the stirrups, the internal ultrasound wand doing its thing, and my cell phone clutched to my left ear as David could be heard by the innocent bystanders in the parking lot loudly persisting, "Is he sure? Did he check everywhere? Is there *any chance* that one is hiding? Because if he says there aren't two, and there end up being two, is he aware that he's taking one home with him?"

George David was born seven months later—neither preceded nor followed by anyone—and not a minute too soon as I could barely walk because my pelvis was so out of whack. The anesthesiologist could barely get the epidural in due to the fact that my vertebrae were so compressed (or something to that effect). Dr. Feel Good got almost as dire a lecture as the OB nurse had early on as I informed him that I would *not* be delivering without anesthesia, so he'd better keep trying. After three attempts, the sweet sensation of numbness crept into my lower half, and I breathed an enormous sigh of relief before perusing what would be the last issue of *People* to cross my path for quite some time.

For months, everyone told me that George would be totally laid-back because he'd have no choice. He'd be carted around all day, woken from naps prematurely, and forced to sleep in a car seat far more often than the experts profess acceptable.

And once again, everyone was wrong.

George made absolutely sure that we never forgot he was here. He was what I like to call a "high maintenance" baby. He cried almost constantly, and ate even more often. However, I was fully able to relish how easy it truly was to have only one baby. The older kids—even the twins—were extremely helpful. I was able to breastfeed him exclusively until he was ten months old since, thanks to a few new hero friends of mine who breastfed their twins exclusively for a year, I had the necessary support system in place to bulldoze me with strategy after strategy and, on multiple occasions, talk me down off the I-don't-think-I-can-pull-over-and-nurse-this-kid-in-the-front-seat-of-the-car-again rooftop.

There were days when a delivery guy was dumb enough to ring the doorbell two or three times in a row, and in order to educate him on the reasons he should stop at one (especially since I had a PLEASE KNOCK sign posted directly over the doorbell), I'd answer the door with George on a breast, an ear-to-ear grin, and an unnaturally enthusiastic "Thank you so much! Have a great day!" I was on a mission to prove that I could do this on my terms, and no one, not even UPS, was going to stop me. So, What Can Brown Do for You? I'll tell you: they can follow the rules posted on the front door! That's the only way the machine stays up and running—everyone must follow the rules.

It was a lot of work in those early months, but I knew he was the last (truly people, he is the last—I'm pretty sure), and I loved every minute with him—screaming or not. I loved the ability to cuddle one baby at night, to focus on his newborn needs exclusively, and to watch developmental milestones that—because Jack and Henry were born a bit prematurely—I had become (admittedly somewhat neurotically) positively fascinated with.

I had a singleton first, and because I'd never had a baby before her, I perceived the art of parenting her as most challenging. Then the twins were born and I wondered what was wrong with me to think that having one baby was difficult! So to finish up with one was really special because my perspective was so in check.

The first four months were absolutely the hardest. Getting on a feeding schedule—or any schedule, given that I had to shuttle Grace to and from school every day and take the boys to their Parents' Day Out program once a week—was tiresome. I won't even discuss a sleeping schedule because George did not sleep through the night until he was one. Not kidding. I'm all for letting a baby cry when he's old enough and eating well enough to sleep for more than two hours at a stretch. George cried—screamed, rather—for between two and three hours straight, day and night. At one point, while driving around hoping to lull him into sleep, I needed a distraction from his screaming and called my mom. The call provided a distraction for me but his tirade provided a different kind of distraction for my mother, who was thoroughly convinced that I needed to get him to the doctor immediately. I assured her that this was simply "normal" at this point in his young life. She wondered how, with my lack of medical training, I could know with such certainty that he was okay. I pulled over, turned off the car, opened his door, and took him out of his car seat, at which point the screaming ceased altogether.

"Oh!" she exclaimed. "That's refreshing! What did you do?"

"I picked him up."

"Oh dear," she answered. "Well . . . Oh dear. That's not great."

No kidding.

Needless to say, I carried him a lot during the day. The BabyBjörn was my best friend. I inserted earplugs at night and then sandwiched my head between two pillows—and I could still hear him. On a few occasions, David sent me to the basement to sleep (it's furnished, don't call law enforcement) and I still could not get away from his hysteria because it traveled through the vents.

When George was nearly four months old, I had to admit that something needed to change temporarily. The boys had entered another "challenging" phase, I was getting no sleep, and my saving Grace (literally) was in school all morning. We found a fantastic program in which we enrolled Jack and Henry two days per week. They had a great time; learned the word for "blue" in Spanish; did art, music, and gym; and were completely exhausted by the end of the day. We kept them enrolled for four months. During those months, I had two somewhat sane days per week. I was still teetering on the edge much of the time, but this little respite kept me from falling off of it. After these four months, winter in Chicago had passed; George was sleeping for a whopping five hours straight per night (beginning at 7:00 p.m., so we were still muddling through the crying fits that ensued at midnight and then again around 3:00 a.m.); and I had a system whereby I could nurse George at 6:00 a.m., chug caffeine, and then nurse him again at around ten o'clock with no adverse effects. In many ways, it was sort of a sitcom. But although I was exhausted, I loved it. I knew we'd do what we needed to do to make it work a day at a time. And we did.

After those few months, the most difficult aspect of having a baby with toddler twins in the house—at least in my experience—is illustrated in the following tale. You see, having an eleven-month-old when twins are three works pretty well, most of the time. The boys loved him to pieces (sometimes a little too much), helped to feed him, got his clothes, found his toys, and comforted him when he was sad (which, as I mentioned, was a constant reality). The additional reality was that there were older kids in the house and, hence, toys meant for older kids as well as the remnants of the older kids' breakfasts, craft projects, and dress-up box contents lying around despite all my efforts.

One morning, I apparently missed something during my hourly pick-up-anything-dangerous routine. I'll never know what it was, but George got hold of it before I could notice and ingested it. Before it began its descent into his stomach, it caused George to choke like I've never seen any of my kids choke.

Thankfully, my friend Bari was over. I was trying to manage the situation because even though I have a panic attack over whether or not the grocery delivery will be on time, when it comes to medical issues I'm surprisingly calm.

"Do you want to call 9-1-1?" Bari asked.

"I don't know. Should I?" I responded.

"Um, yes. *Now.*"

Seven minutes later, an ambulance and a fire truck pulled up outside my house. Of course, I was still in my pajamas (remember, you need friends who care not what condition you or your home are in when they come over). I had not even put a bra on yet (and let's remember, folks, that I've had four children, the last of whom I breastfed about eighty-six times a day for ten months). So, up my front lawn run *nine* strapping firefighters/EMT personnel. And by that point, George was in my arms, smiling and happy as could be having completely swallowed whatever it was that he was choking on. Four kids in five years and this was the first time I had to call 9-1-1. I felt a bit silly, and a lot underdressed.

The lesson learned on this one was clear and simple: heed my previous suggestion, and please take a CPR class. Vow to do it again every two years as recommended by the American Red Cross. I remembered the basics from the course I had taken nearly six years earlier, but because an eleven-month-old is neither a newborn nor a toddler, I did spend a fraction of a second worrying about the fact that if I had needed to do something on that morning, I wasn't sure exactly which strategy was safest—the one for infants or the one for older children. It's easy to think either, "I'll do it someday," or "I always watch the kids. This will never happen to me." It can happen to anyone, so pray it won't happen to you, and by all means ensure that you're prepared in case it does. Oh, and put on a bra before going downstairs in the morning.

One positive that came out of this experience was that the kids truly did learn that many of the things they can eat and play with are not permissible for George. For at least six months after this incident, Henry announced not only in our home, but in overcrowded, public places, "George cannot have this (or eat this, or whatever) because he might choke. And we do not want the firemen coming again." Another positive was my newfound realization that we only *think* people aren't paying attention to our conversations in public. The reality is that the minute a kid utters a comment like Henry's, every head within a twenty-foot radius turns in your direction, as though the room is filled with undercover CIA operatives.

Beyond that, the whole new baby thing was pretty uneventful. We didn't have family living nearby when we had Grace or Jack and Henry, and nothing could be more challenging than newborn twins (except newborn triplets, quads, quints, etc.), so we weren't terribly fazed by that lack of assistance. We knew to have the supply of take-out menus stocked, and I knew to freeze a few meals in advance of George's birth. One truly does develop amnesia regarding the challenges involved with getting little to no sleep and then being responsible for caring for not only a newborn, but other children in addition, but we just muddled through.

Another concern many parents have when expecting a new baby is how to ensure that an older child does not feel displaced by the new arrival. In the case of twins, you're dealing with kids who have never been the sole focus of a parent's attention (at least not for more than a few hours at a time). Therefore, you're far less likely to have to contend with your twins' feeling left out than you might with a singleton. At almost three years of age, Jack stood protectively over

George's little bassinet in the hospital while the pediatrician examined him, terrified that the doctor was hurting his baby brother. He's been that protective of George ever since.

Henry sat in the chair on the other side of the room asking when he could go home. He could not have cared less one way or the other that there was a new baby around. His attitude could be summed up as follows: "Okay, there's one more of us around here now. And the big deal is . . . ?" He, too, has been like that ever since (except when he's concerned about the firemen coming again).

Grace, while not at all pleased that George wasn't a Georgia, sat patiently waiting to hold him and begin her role as Assistant Mother. She asks weekly when I'm going to give her a little sister. My answer remains the same: it's not going to happen.

Mothers of twins, as you know, have no idea precisely how they get through those more challenging first few weeks or months. They just do it. When you have another baby after twins, you maintain that perspective. David asked me recently, "How *did* you get through those ten months without any caffeine?" and I didn't have an answer other than "I just did." That was my secret. Very profound, I know. And yet thankfully, you guys are the ones I don't have to explain it to in any more detail than that because you understand how one "just does it" better than just about anyone! The strategies that got you through the first few months with twins will get you through the first few months with a new baby. They'll get you through almost anything (though a continuous IV drip of my Starbucks drink of choice—an iced, nonfat latte with two Splenda—would have been a nice addition to my arsenal of tools).

So, for all of you who've asked, I can tell you without reservation that having another baby after twins is doable. If you do have family nearby, regular cleaning help, a live-in chef, a live-in nanny, and/or a driver, it will be less challenging (or, perhaps I should say, challenging in different ways) than it was for us. We did it without any of these things, and I would not trade it for anything (and I can complain with the best of them should I desire!). A few additional thoughts to make the road a bit smoother:

Strategies for Welcoming a New Baby

Obtain an "Extra Set of Hands"

Have a BabyBjörn or other baby carrier on hand. When the baby needs to be near you, or more importantly, when it's not safe for her to be anywhere else because you're terrified that the twins playing tag in the living room may inadvertently knock over the bassinet or crash onto the bouncy seat, you can strap the baby to you and continue to clean while you soothe the baby or otherwise multitask by holding a copy of *Healthy Sleep Habits, Happy Baby* in one hand and a copy of Vicki Iovine's *Girlfriends' Guide to Getting Your Groove Back* (because at this point, you'll really want to) in the other.

Note: one activity to avoid while carrying a baby in a BabyBjörn, sling, or other such apparatus is cooking with heat. Grease from a frying pan could splatter, or a hot oven door could come into contact with the baby's legs as you open it to retrieve a cooked casserole.

Establish Napping Quarters

In the early weeks, have a Pack 'n Play or other "safe" place nearby where the baby can nap. Since newborns can sleep through nearly everything and often don't sleep for long, this will save you from going back and forth to her room each time she falls asleep.

Arrange for Help

If your budget can accommodate a weekly or bi-weekly cleaning service, even just for a couple of months, schedule one. Not much else (beyond the obvious lack of sleep) makes a new mom feel more tired and cluttered than a cluttered, dusty house. Having your entire house cleaned—by someone else—in one day will make you feel as good as a shower did after you gave birth. If you are able to arrange help to take your older kids to school, do so. The less often you have to get out of pajamas first thing in the morning, the better. This wasn't an option for me, but you have no idea how many times I drove Grace to school in my pajamas and slippers—and picked her up that way at three-thirty in the afternoon.

If a grocery delivery service is available in your area, utilize it for the first few weeks or months after the new baby is born. You may pay a little bit more overall, but the convenience of not having a long grocery errand looming over your head each week will be worth it.

Beyond juggling the new baby, you may find yourself in a position where you need to juggle your older kids' needs a bit as well. Again, they aren't likely to feel as displaced as a singleton might; however, they may need some reassurance now and then or something to do while you tend to the new baby.

Strategies for Prepping Older Children for the Arrival of a New Baby

---

Choose Your Words Carefully

Refer to the new baby as "our baby" instead of "mommy's baby." This way, your older children will view the new baby as an addition to the family instead of someone who belongs only to mom.

Let Them Be Moms Too

If your twins are under three or four years of age, purchase a baby doll for each of your children (a new one if necessary) and have a "naming party" to officially name the dolls, even make birth certificates and put mock hospital bracelets on their arms. Put together supply baskets for their new "babies" consisting of a bottle, blanket, onesie, and any other supplies you feel are appropriate. While you are taking care of the new baby, your older children can care for their babies as well. In their minds, you'll be doing something together as opposed to their feeling as though you've left them to care for their new sibling.

Involve Them in the Baby's Development

Purchase a book that tells you each day about the baby's development in utero. Read it aloud to your children. Kids often find such excitement in knowing that the baby now has ears or toenails.

Introduce Them to the Baby

Once the baby starts kicking, let your children feel their new brother or sister moving around inside your belly. Tell them their little brother or sister is already trying to play with them. This may encourage the bonding process between your older children and your unborn baby, and may increase their excitement over the baby's entrance into the world.

Help Them Bond with the Baby

Take your kids with you to pick out a special toy for the toy room or blanket for the crib. Smaller children can help select pacifier colors or bottle patterns. What's important is that you involve your children in the process in some way.

Be a Little Crazy

Another fun activity (which may be more trouble than it's worth for children under the age of three or four) is creating a belly cast. These kits, meant to be used toward the end of your pregnancy, allow you to put papier-mâché strips from your thighs to your neck in order to create a permanent mold of your body's shape during this incredible time. Once dried, your children can help you paint or otherwise decorate the cast. Don't worry, you don't have to hang it front and center over the mantle. You don't even have to keep it forever. If nothing else, it's a fun family activity for a Friday night. Warning: follow to the letter the directions to apply copious amounts of Vaseline to the areas over which you'll apply the papier-mâché strips. Otherwise, your children will also get a lesson in the pain caused by waxing yourself where you didn't even know you grew hair.

Keep Distractions on Hand

Keep a few coloring books, mini Play-Doh containers, puzzles, matchbox cars, and/or mini Etch-A-Sketch games hidden in a secret—yet easily accessible—location. Each time you need to tend to the baby and you notice that your older children seem to be feeling a bit left out or needy, sneak a hand into the stash and pull out a surprise. This isn't meant to be a bribe to allow you to tend to the baby; it's merely a distraction (and with young children, it will likely be fun for only ten minutes anyway).

The reality is that no matter how prepared you are and how hard you try, there are going to be moments—whole days perhaps—when it doesn't seem like you can do enough to reassure your older children. You'll wonder with each whine or tantrum whether or not it would be happening if you hadn't had the new baby. Chances are, it would.

If you have a child who's older than your twins, be sure to address her unique needs as well. While possibly less vocal regarding her concerns about a new baby, she may feel more left out than anyone because it seems as though she's constantly being barraged by babies! Involve her in unique ways. She might be the perfect person to help you with a belly cast or come with you to your ultrasound appointments. I took Grace with me to have my ultrasound of George, and it made her feel really special because it was something she was allowed to do that the boys were not. It actually provided great benefit to me as well, as I cannot decipher an image on ultrasound to save myself. Grace correctly identified George's spleen within six seconds, I swear. She and the ultrasound tech were discussing this kid's development over my head half the time! Of course, the fun stopped when the tech announced that she caught a glimpse of what appeared to be a penis, but . . .

FOSTERING INDEPENDENCE

In the final analysis it is not what you do for your children but what you have taught them to do for themselves that will make them successful human beings.

—Ann Landers

A child's first steps and first words are momentous. They often blindside parents with the reality that their child is becoming a person with fewer needs for some types of assistance, yet a greater need for others in order to gain independence and self-confidence. There are many strategies you can utilize to ensure that your children will be able to forge their way in the world as autonomous, capable beings.

Strategies for Fostering Independence

Let Them Explore

I know firsthand that it's hard to live in what feels like one big crate of toys. David and I have been married for eight years, and the closest any of our wedding china or crystal has gotten to unveiling itself in a manner even remotely resembling a formal display is being crammed like sardines into our one glass-front display cabinet. Much as I wish it could be otherwise, I've accepted (temporarily) that children need to be able to safely explore their world in order to really gain a sense of it. They learn by exploration and experimentation. Exploring what lies in the depths of the toilet bowl and experimenting with what happens when you toss a sippy cup at a priceless work of art aren't exactly ideal methods of learning in the eyes of most parents.

If children are constantly told "No," or only permitted to enter two rooms of the house, they don't have much leeway to truly explore in a safe and positive way. There is so much to learn simply by walking around and determining how to get objects (safe objects) off of tables, how to get onto a couch, or how to climb stairs (while supervised, until they are proficient). These activities give children important reasoning and problem-solving skills, not to mention confidence. Teaching your children to "look with your eyes, not your hands" is important so that they respect that rule when in someone else's home. However, you'll be pulling your hair out if you're hearing crashes or otherwise concerned about safety all day long. So ensure there's an appropriate balance between your need to decorate with something other than Legos and their need to safely explore.

Teach Them to Be Comfortable with Separation

Beyond interacting in activities with you, children ultimately need to be able to be placed in the care of another loving, caring adult and know that they will be okay and that you will come back. Begin by ensuring that you have a good babysitter so that you can go out now and again, and your children can be comfortable with someone else in your home. From there, introduce your children to experiences in which they're safe and will learn to self-entertain or play with others. A church or gym nursery or a Mother's Day Out program are good options. Many children will initially not appear pleased with these activities, and it's natural to feel compelled to stay with them or remove them and change your plans. However, if you feel comfortable with the person in charge, let that person know how to reach you, say a quick goodbye, and head out. You'll probably be surprised to learn that after a few moments, the caregiver was able to distract your children and they ended up having a great time.

Start by leaving your children for only thirty to sixty minutes at a time and build from there. Start with fifteen minutes if you need to. If your children are extremely wary, it's likely a good idea to start even more slowly, leaving them with a close family friend or relative.

It's helpful to positively talk about the time when they will be cared for by someone other than yourself. Enthusiastically communicate to your children how much fun they are going to have while you're away. If you approach the separation with an attitude of concern or a lot of coddling, your toddlers will pick up on your anxiety and respond accordingly.

Don't propose the separation as though they have a choice in the matter, and don't suggest that you are looking for their approval. The message you need to send is that you *are* going to run a few errands, attend the church service, or go out to dinner. If you introduce the situation by asking your children whether or not it's okay for you to run to the grocery store, attend an exercise class, or go out to lunch with a friend, I can guarantee that the answer will be no on all counts.

However you approach it, it may take several attempts before your children consistently seem all right with your leaving them. It may happen sooner if they know that pitching a gigantic fit won't change the plans. If you allow them to, your children will become quite skilled at ensuring that you never leave them anywhere, which is good for neither you nor them.

Let Them Make Choices

One of the most critical skills we have as human beings is our ability to make choices. In many cases, the difference between one choice and another can mean the difference between seeing things positively or negatively, getting somewhere on time or not, even staying alive or not. The luxury to make our own choices day-in and day-out carries with it great power.

You can begin to empower your children to make their own choices at an early age. Begin by allowing them to choose between milk and juice, or show them different colored shorts and shirts and ask them to choose which they'd like to wear. The key is to ensure that either choice is acceptable by your standards (don't offer your two-year-olds the choice between water and cappuccino unless you're truly okay with the latter!).

From this point on, you'll be able to positively incorporate the power of choice into nearly every aspect of your children's lives (unless you're in my house and the six-year-old wants to be able to choose between leopard-print leather pants and fluorescent pink hair spray while selecting school necessities).

Encourage Self-Sufficiency

It won't be long before your toddlers begin to insist that they put on their own shoes, zip their own coats, or don their own gloves. "I do it!" is likely to become one of the most frequently used phrases in your home. Toddlers love to prove that they can do things on their own. It makes them feel proud, and they feed off of the excited response they receive from parents.

Nonetheless, it can be frustrating to endure the nine minutes it takes them to get an arm in a sleeve when you are twelve minutes late for an appointment. Logically, it would be far easier to just do it yourself. In the end, however, that doesn't help anyone. What your children will learn is that you don't believe they can do it, and worse in the long term, they won't learn how to do it for themselves. Of course, there will be times when you will have to endure the protests as you tie a shoe or button a pair of pants. However, when your children begin expressing an interest in doing things for themselves, alleviate the need to jump in any more often than necessary by building extra time into your schedule.

A few months ago I was in a clothes store with Jack and Henry. A young mother approached me and said, "Your son in the orange shirt has his shirt on backwards." I said, "Yes, he dressed himself today; isn't that great?" She responded with, "Well, I just thought you should know that he put his shirt on backwards." Honestly, I can't imagine anything worse than a mother saying to her child, "Honey, you did such a great job getting dressed all by yourself this morning! And you did it all wrong!" I can't tell you how many times we've left the house with clothes on backwards and/or inside out, and unless we're going to meet the president or have our picture taken for the cover of *In Style* magazine, I could not care less. I'm hopeful that by the time they are ten, they won't want their shirts buttoning up the back any more than the rest of us would.

Fostering independence in children can create a double-pronged emotional reaction in parents. Of course we want them to become capable and confident, and yet we realize that in doing so they are moving closer to the day when they'll walk out the door solo toward the world of limitless possibilities. As Lisa Earle McLeod notes in her book *Forget Perfect*—and I love this so much I mention it everywhere—it is your job as a parent to create "a functioning adult." The prize will come the day your children walk out the door with suitcases containing their diplomas from top universities. They'll confidently turn to thank you and hug you goodbye (and with any luck, won't ask you to bend down and tie their shoelaces).

EAT, BABIES, EAT!

Green Eggs and Ham *was the story of my life. I wouldn't eat a thing when I was a kid, but Dr. Seuss inspired me to try cauliflower.*
—Jim Carrey

When I was a young child, sugar-loaded cereals were an absolute no-no in our house. Any cereal that contained floating marshmallows or turned the milk a different color was off limits. Once I was old enough to pour my own cereal, however, I coated the top layer of it with so much sugar myself that in all honesty, I probably would have consumed less sugar overall had I just eaten a marshmallow-loaded, pink and blue concoction that turned the milk purple, but . . .

I didn't ever have tremendous difficulty with Grace in the food department. Of course she didn't love everything, but I could almost always come up with something healthy for each meal that she'd agree to eat—even if it was chased by seven handfuls of goldfish crackers. Not so with the boys.

I did my best. But once they turned three and a half, I admittedly maintained a constant supply of Apple Jacks, Fruit Loops, and marshmallow fluff in the pantry (the last is completely Mollie's fault; she started it). One of the most effective philosophies I've employed over the past few years when faced with a question over whether I impose a consequence for an inappropriate choice on someone's part, clean up the spilled milk or insist that the one who spilled it does the cleaning, or acquiesce regarding sugar-loaded cereal and fluffernutter sandwiches is to ask the question, "Will it matter in five years?" Because if it won't, I'm not going to get up in arms about it now. Frankly, the stress-induced damage I incur from constantly pleading for them to try just one bite of granola or chicken à la King *will* matter in five years!

Mealtime dilemmas seem to reach a new plateau during the two- to three-year timeframe. Kids' tastes again change (which can leave you wondering many days if your destiny is to be a short-order cook), they are more mobile (and interested in doing anything but sitting), and/or they suddenly decide to boycott every food in the grocery store besides donuts, ice cream, and french fries.

Many toddlers go through a phase in which they will eat only a few items such as SpaghettiOs or Cheerios. It's easy to become concerned about your children's eating habits and even to begin considering them picky eaters. Don't worry, kids go through food phases throughout their toddler years. One day they love bananas. The next day, bananas are the worst thing they've ever eaten. On Tuesday evening, broccoli is the best food ever. By Wednesday, they're gagging at the mere mention of it. It's frustrating, but it's perfectly normal.

Do your best to offer your kids a variety of easily prepared foods such as applesauce, yogurt, and bananas at each meal. This way, you won't spend too much time slaving over perfectly balanced quesadillas only to have the kids take one look at them and begin retching. Provide at least one food that you know (or feel extremely confident) that your children like. Then, let your children choose their side dish. This way, they have control of their choices, and you have control over the choices offered. It helps to eliminate a situation in which he's begging for ice cream next to his chicken (though frankly, if a kid in my house actually agreed to eat his or her chicken, I might be coerced into putting ice cream next to it).

For as long as I can remember, one of our nightly staples has been ketchup. Ketchup goes on things that I never imagined one would consider putting ketchup on. The most recent surprise beneficiary was broccoli. Whether ketchup does the trick or not, do *not* feel as though you need to become a short-order cook to keep your children happy and well-nourished.

Dr. Mark Gettleman, a pediatrician in Glendale, Arizona, notes, "I am very comfortable with a child missing a meal if [he or she] refuses to eat the prepared meal (or alternatively, if one other option is offered and refused)." He also proposes a power-struggle solution: "Parents decide what and when kids eat, and kids decide how much they eat."

New toys excite toddlers. New foods do not. The best thing you can do when your kids refuse or fuss about food is ignore it. Another approach is to add "today" or "right now" to the end of their sentence. "Oh, you don't like broccoli *today*?" This suggests the possibility that the next time that particular food is served, the reaction might be different.

Fortunately, parents don't need to be terribly concerned over the daily content of their children's diets. "While I would love for children to eat more fruits and vegetables and less fat, young kids (especially two- to five-year-olds) tend to prefer only two to three foods such as mac and cheese, chicken nuggets, and hot dogs," notes Dr. Gettleman. "I believe that nutrition should be judged over an extended period of time, not meal-to-meal or daily."

Pam Fierro, a mom of twins and the moderator for multiples.about.com, has great perspective. She said, "Sometimes, when I am overwhelmed with frustration, I think ahead to the time that my girls will be out on their own, not eating at our table any longer. Our time with them is so limited! There is plenty of time for quiet, elegant meals when they're grown. Give me my share of chaos, spilled milk, and giggles while I can get it!"

Even if your children appear pickier than most, it's easier to deal with when they are able to communicate the reasons why lima beans are a problem. It's also nicer when *you* are able to communicate that regardless of the issues with lima beans, they can choose either to try them or to look forward with great anticipation to apples for dessert.

Beyond the challenges faced by the changing tastes of young children, parents often face a challenge themselves: it's called the I-can't-bear-to-look-at-another-bowl-of-macaroni-and-cheese-or-butter-another-pancake-but-they-won't-eat-anything-else syndrome. While toddlers may see no reason not to subsist on hot dogs and pizza until they leave for college, their parents would fall apart on this diet day-in and day-out. Many parents get a bit of a "second wind" in the kitchen during the toddler years and vow to begin cooking healthy, easily prepared meals that the family can enjoy together. Oftentimes, however, only the parents enjoy the meal while the children cry in protest.

For many parents, the ability to cook a nice meal (or more than one paltry course) during the "witching hour" is often lacking. Thankfully, a few parents out there recognized this and started businesses to make our lives a *little* easier and our stomachs a *lot* thankful.

Many national chains have popped up around the concept of freezer cooking. Typically, you attend a two-hour session wherein you assemble between eight and twelve preselected frozen entrées. The beauty of this is that the owners slice, dice, and purée all of the ingredients. They provide the assembly instructions, the containers, and the cleanup. You come home with enough freezer-ready entrees to cover a large portion of the next month, should you opt to serve two or three per week. Oftentimes, you can split these meals with a friend, or you can divide them for yourself. So, if a particular entrée has six chicken breasts and you know that between you, your husband, and your children you'll only consume three of them, you can split the meal in half, and suddenly you have two meals. Additionally, if you have succumbed to the fact that the only way to nourish your children may just be to serve them macaroni each night, you can split the entrées so that you and your husband at least have a healthy meal while the kids load up on whatever makes dinnertime pleasant.

Some businesses offer side dishes, many offer suggestions for sides, and most offer desserts. Beyond the national chains, many privately owned freezer-cooking establishments exist, so check your local phone book.

Several online opportunities exist to streamline the dinner-making process as well. One of my favorites is Saving Dinner (www.savingdinner.com), owned by Leanne Ely, a certified nutritional consultant. The service offers subscribers a weekly Menu-Mailer that contains five or six recipes, the associated grocery lists (broken out into the appropriate grocery store section), and the nutritional information for each entrée. Also provided are suggested side dishes. There are six versions of the Menu Mailer from which to choose, including regular, low-carb, and crockpot meals.

Once everyone is seated at the table, and the kids have actually expressed mild interest in what's been placed before them, another set of challenges may present themselves.

Mollie's boys love to play—all the time. This proves challenging during the dinner hour because the minute one is finished eating, the other also has to get down to protect his toys and make sure his brother isn't having fun without him. It sometimes seems as though a meal is never finished.

Many kids jump down from the table only to return five minutes later intending to shove a handful of food into their mouth and run off again. Let them know that this isn't an option. Tell them that once they get up from the table, their meal is over, and food won't be served again until the next mealtime.

As hard as we might try, it can be tough to elicit a firm choice from a toddler, even when it's between only two cereals, two types of juice, or two pizza toppings. Furthermore, with more than one child picking and choosing, the fun doesn't always stop once the decision has been made. In many cases, as the Carpenters sang, "We've only just begun."

It's common for parents ultimately to surrender and accommodate each of their children's choices, if for no other reason than to make everyone happy enough that the parents themselves can sit down to eat. But it might not be more than four seconds before the poor parents hear Jimmy whining that he wants Johnny's sandwich and Johnny yelling that he wants Jimmy's drink.

If you are going to allow your children to choose something, such as what kind of sandwich they'd like or what kind of drink they prefer, it's important to inform them up front that they have the privilege to make a choice *one* time. Whatever they select is what they will be served. If a child complains once he's served, a parent may let him know that he can choose either to enjoy the item he picked or to be finished with his meal altogether.

If you have kids' plates, bowls, or forks that are different from each other in any way, twins will often use them as an opportunity to see how far they can push the control envelope. You would not believe how often I've seen children who were previously complaining that they were so hungry that they might just evaporate momentarily lose sight of that fact in order to bicker over who has the orange fork or the blue plate. It's insane. Even when the boys were three and Grace was five, they would argue over who got the Dora bowl and who got the Spiderman bowl for breakfast.

A firm and consistent approach is key, no matter how you choose to handle such rivalries. Assign each child a color and ensure that he or she always gets that color. Allow each child to pick a plate, fork, cup, whatever, before each meal and explain that they get to choose only once. Tell the kids that you will choose who gets what and they'll be fine with what they get. Take Mollie's approach and give each child "his" day to choose first (see the "Give Each Kid 'His' Day" segment of the "Strategies for Avoiding Competition" section for explanation of this approach in all its glory). Adopt whichever approach seems best, but be firm. That has always been Mollie's secret. She remains clearly and constantly in charge. The boys try to mess with her, but they know they won't get very far. I have no idea how she does it. But actually, sweet cherub that she is on the outside, I wouldn't mess with her either.

Playing musical chairs at the dinner table seems to be a much-loved pastime for multiples. A child chooses a seat only to decide he'd rather sit next to his sister, or his mother, or his father. Of course, his sibling must then change seats as well. In our house, children move in haste to a new seat many times during a meal either because they've suddenly decided they don't like their neighbor or to get as far away as possible from any fly that's taken up residence nearby.

There are several solutions to this challenge. One option is to assign seats by putting fun nametags or placemats at each seat. They can be changed weekly for variety, but at least you'll (hopefully) get seven days out of them. I've considered using Super Glue to adhere plates and cups to the table at the assigned seats, knowing my kids will go nowhere without their food, but I quickly realized this thought presented itself during yet another moment of fleeting insanity on my part.

In all honesty, this particular challenge may present a choice for *you*: let them dance around the table and ultimately eat, or force them to stay put and potentially refuse their meal. I happen to be partial to enforcing a you-stay-where-you-sat rule because otherwise the dinner hour turns into a circus act, but you can only enforce as much as your sanity will allow.

Mollie's boys have always had to sit in assigned seats. With two parents and two kids, each kid is always sitting next to both parents, which may contribute to the success over there. At our house, there's intense competition over who gets to sit next to David. Absolutely no one ever wants to sit next to me. Don't feel sad for me; by six o'clock at night, I'm perfectly fine with that reality.

FECAL FASCINATION

How about putting them to bed in a two-piece outfit and having them get the pants off, remove the diaper, poop in the bed, and then play in it? That one was a little gross. It was not fun to clean either.
— Karen, mother of twin boys

I have to admit, I was immeasurably pleased to receive this anecdote from Karen. Why? Because it confirmed that my twins were not the only ones who had engaged in an activity that I can only hope was a subconscious experiment to prove that we haven't evolved that much from our furry predecessors who still beat their chests and walk on all fours much of the time.

I cannot remember exactly when this phase started in our house. I know it was before the boys were two, but probably not by much. I will never understand why children are so fascinated with poop. My daughter went through a similar phase, but it caused far less damage and lasted for far less time than the one I went through with Jack and Henry.

It all started on a day similar to that which Karen described above. I was appalled. I cleaned their room with angry hands and my tongue bled from being bitten so hard. My mantra as I went forward and back, forward and back with the towel was, "Never. Again. Never. Again." (Even though the Queen of Clean admonishes anyone who scrubs the carpet, sorry Linda, but this was not a dab-dab-dab kind of job.)

Never Again was not to be.

A few days later, I heard Henry screaming wildly in the middle of what was supposed to be naptime. I raced upstairs to find my poor Henry at the door, crying and transformed from his previously milky white complexion to one of brown splotches. Jack was sitting proudly on the floor, hands covered in poop, proclaiming "I paint Henry!" And paint he did. Henry's hair was covered, as were his face, his arms, and his legs. I said nary a word. (The books do say that negative attention is attention nonetheless and one should avoid it during times such as this. Frankly, I don't think attention is what the boys were after. I think first place in a poop-painting contest was.) I carried Henry to the tub. I carried Jack to the tub. I scrubbed . . . and scrubbed . . . and scrubbed. I scrubbed their carpet, again sweating to the mantra, "Never.

Again. Never. Again." I scrubbed their walls (yes, their walls) and I washed their sheets. And then I rested.

A few months later, all of this was *still* going on. I might mention that at this point, I was newly pregnant with our little surprise baby. Olfactory senses heightened, my cleansing ritual was preceded and followed by the same old comment: "Poop goes in the potty or in your diaper, *not* on the carpet or on your brother." Honestly, I wasn't always this calm. A few times, I yelled that comment. I blamed it on the hormones. And truthfully, I would have found something to blame it on even if I wasn't pregnant.

I tried one-piece pajamas at night. They learned to unzip them.

I tried putting one-piece pajamas on backward at night. They unzipped each other's.

One night, I took Mollie's suggestion and duct taped their diapers. "No problem," they thought. "If we can't get them off the traditional way, we'll just go up through the legs." And they did. And the duct tape worked so well that David could not get Henry's diaper off one morning when I was out of town. I think David's Dad was visiting when this happened. David was livid, but he keeps his anger in check quite well. He said, "Henry, this is unacceptable. You do *not* put poop anywhere but in the potty or your diaper. Dad, get me a pair of scissors." I think his dad wondered what on earth David was going to do with those scissors! He pinned Henry to the floor and cut. The duct tape was, at that point, retired.

For naps, I put Jack and Henry in pants with belt loops and put the belts on backward. Jack figured out how to get his off, and Henry has such a little set of hips (he didn't get that from me) that he could just wiggle his off, much the same way Houdini got out of a straight jacket, I suppose.

One afternoon, all was quiet in their room, and I entered to find them sound asleep inside their closet, pants around their ankles (belts still in the loops and, in Henry's case, still buckled) and poop everywhere. I believe that on this day I called David at work and told him to get in his car, drive fast, go straight for the cleaning supplies upon entering the house, and come up with a plan if he wished for me to stick around.

Might I add that during this time, we still had our two Weimaraners, who were three or four months old and not even remotely house trained. As if that were not bad enough, they had a fascination with *eating* their feces. I swear, there were days when I'd look out into the backyard and see the dogs eating something I knew wasn't meant to be edible and simultaneously hear one of the boys shouting, "Mommy! Poopy everywhere!" I'm sure there was at least one day in there when I just sat on the kitchen floor and cried, letting them all wallow in their pleasure or misery for a few extra minutes.

One evening I thought that surely Yankee Candle had developed a new scent called Daisies and Dung because the whole house just reeked. I smelled like poop from being licked by the dogs that had just eaten it. Jack and Henry smelled like it because, well, I've explained already. The house smelled like it because all of us were living there (and some of us were embedding poop so far into the carpet that it was likely never going to come out). And even with my morning sickness (all-day sickness, actually), I could not vomit because there just wasn't time.

And that was it. I'd tried it all. I'd gone from backward belting my sons to running around the yard pouring hot sauce on the dogs' poop hoping that would deter them. I'd spent an hour reading about breaking this tendency in children and the next reading about breaking it in dogs. I'd put the dogs on prescription medication for just this ailment hoping that might help, changed their diet, and run around after them with a shovel, throwing away the stuff before they could get to it. I'd duct taped my children's diapers, lectured them about where poop goes, taken away all of their toys and books and animals and anything else they could (or did) contaminate. The absurdity of it all finally hit. I felt as though the boys were behaving like animals and David was so in love with the actual animals we owned that through his likely brown-colored glasses, they were almost like his fourth and fifth children. Either way, I had gone from having twins to having quads with an issue I was no longer able to deal with.

I thought about how nice it would be to have a pet just like Jinx in *Meet the Fockers*; he actually used the toilet. I briefly wondered how much I could get for the boys on eBay. I took a deep breath and accepted that ultimately, the boys would figure out that this hobby was disgusting and stop. I wasn't sure the dogs would. So the discussion about finding new homes for the dogs commenced.

I've blocked out many of the incidents, but suffice it to say there were many. The fecal fascination phase lasted for about eight months. One solution may have been to split the boys up for naptime and bedtime, but we didn't have a lot of options. They were out of cribs, but still young enough that putting one of them in Grace's room full of Polly Pocket pieces and stuffed animals that she considered her children was not going to work. Should they have become covered with even a millimeter of poop, it would have sent *her* packing. It was a huge accident waiting to happen, plain and simple. And I wasn't about to cater to this pastime of theirs by emptying out Grace's room every single afternoon just so one of them could nap in it. I'm sure there are experts out there who would swear that had I done that, all would have been well within 3.2 days. But we all have our limits, and that was mine.

The last event I can remember was a day when I was about six months pregnant and they had been in remission from this habit for so long that I had stopped putting their belts on backward for naps.

While I've forgotten many of the Poop Encounters, I remember this last incident as though it happened yesterday. My mother-in-law was visiting, and she had gone upstairs to get the boys up from their nap. I was standing at our kitchen counter going through mail. She came downstairs, slowly walked over to me, put her hands on her hips, and let out a sigh. The look on her face said it all.

I grabbed my Resolve carpet cleaner along with a pile of cleaning rags and headed upstairs. I cried as I cleaned their closet. Not an angry cry, just a sad one. I was so tired. And I think maybe the universe really heard my heart that day because there were no more incidents after that one. We had licked the poop issues (not literally, though I wouldn't have put it past them!).

And then we began to think seriously about potty training.

COMMUNICATION

Confusion is the welcome mat at the door of creativity.
—Michael J. Gelb

Though it may often appear otherwise, two- to three-year-olds should begin to understand the concept of taking turns and ought to be able to follow simple two-step commands. While it can be frustrating, it is also normal for them to repeat words or sounds in a sentence. "The most common description for the repetition of a single word is 'stuttering,'" notes speech-language pathologist Katherine Cook. "It isn't correct to refer to the speech pattern in this way. Young children have a lot to say, and their mouths simply aren't able to keep up with their brains at this age, which results in what speech-language pathologists define as age-appropriate non-fluency."

The best way to approach a child of this age is with short sentences, preferably of no more than five to seven words. Additionally, when you aren't too frazzled to think through your approach, try to use positive requests ("Please walk") instead of negative ones ("Don't run").

Finally, try not to use sentences that contain more than

two commands or requests. Asking your child to pat his head, rub his stomach, turn around, and then put his dishes in the sink will likely produce nothing more than a confused child who, in his frustration, *bangs* his head on the table and then hurls his dish of spaghetti across the room.

If, by three years of age, your child's speech is not approximately ninety percent intelligible or she is not pronouncing all vowels, discuss it with your child's doctor or a speech-language pathologist.

GUIDING YOUR
TWO- TO THREE-YEAR-OLD TWINS

A two-year-old is kind of like having a blender, but you don't have a top for it.

—Jerry Seinfeld

Are any of you yet familiar with the cartoon *Caillou*, which airs on PBS? If not, just wait; it's on the horizon. For those of you who are familiar, has it ever struck you as bizarre that Caillou's mom is able to maintain her cool in absolutely every situation? I personally cannot watch *Caillou* because Caillou himself whines his way through the day and I have enough of that going on here already. Plus, I don't understand his mother; she's so patient, has an answer for everything, and never, ever loses it. If she teaches a seminar anytime soon, I'm going to be first in line.

One of the greatest challenges of guiding two- to three-year-olds, twins or not, is the fact that despite all the behaviors you'll want to modify immediately, you'll have to choose one or two challenges to work on at a time. The analogy I often use to describe the difficulty faced when trying to tackle too many issues simultaneously is that of being taught golf by David. As I stand in position at the driving range poised to swing the driver, David's shouting out orders: "Chin closer to your chest. Move your left foot half an inch to the right. Back an eighth of an inch. Move your right thumb down a bit. That's a bit too much. Your chin's too far from your chest again. Drop your left shoulder. Okay, but don't bend your body into a half-moon . . . " I get so confused I don't know *what* to do! It would be far easier to spend each lesson focusing on one area. And so it is with guiding two- to three-year-olds.

There tend to be quite a large number of behavioral challenges that erupt during this year. If you feel the need to address each of them every single day, you'll spend your whole day again pivoting Ross Gellar–style as you demand, "Get off the chair. Please keep your hands to yourself. Let go of the cat. You may not eat the puzzle pieces. Please use a quiet voice. Please don't whine. Please get off of the dog; he's not a horse . . . "

At some point, when you're mentally pivoting so often and so quickly that you're downright dizzy and extraordinarily tired, do the following: First, sit down. Second, identify which behavior (whining, biting, hitting, etc.) is bothering you the most or causing the largest number of issues at this time. Don't worry about which behavior most bothers your mother or your neighbor or the person in the checkout line in the grocery store. Which one most bothers *you*? Once you have identified that behavior, identify a strategy to work on eliminating, or at least minimizing, it. An online search on the behavior will probably net no fewer than 683 pages of results and, with any luck, some good suggestions.

Talk to your friends about what approaches have worked for them. Refer to *Parent Talk* by Chick Moorman or *How to Talk So Kids Will Listen and Listen So Kids Will Talk* by Adele Faber and Elaine Mazlish. Try another book (this is a great time to become a loyal patron of your local library; you can snag thirty-four books simultaneously, pray that one has an approach you agree with, and keep your checking account intact). Once you feel as though that particular behavior is lessening and/or you're comfortable with the approach you're using to manage it, you can move on to the next-most-annoying behavior on the list. And so it goes.

Specific Approaches to Behavior Modification

Time-Outs

Even during the two- to three-year timeframe, it doesn't seem that much benefit is gained from time-outs done in the traditional way, where a child is placed in a designated time-out spot simply to sit and be punished for his or her actions. I certainly tried them and, again, many times found them a useful solution for simply moving the offending child to another part of the house for three minutes, but it rarely netted the long-term result I needed.

When the boys were almost four, I learned of another way to think about time-outs. I think it's brilliant, and as with so many other things, I wish I'd heard about it far earlier. In sports games, when teams ask for a time-out, its purpose is to allow the players time to regroup, gather their thoughts, and formulate a plan for proceeding in a more effective manner to garner the result they desire. Should any player not be able to follow the new plan once back on the court, he is benched.

This is a positive use of a time-out, and it is a wonderful application when dealing with toddlers (or older children). After all, simply sending a child to her room when she's misbehaved does not teach her why what she did wasn't acceptable or, more importantly, how to handle the situation more effectively the next time. Those should be the goals of any time-out—even though I understand all too well that at times, your one and only goal may truly be to remove the child from your presence for two to four minutes.

Following are some strategies for effective time-out sessions:

- Identify a time-out spot. When you identify a consistent time-out spot, your child understands where to go right away. Some parents choose a couch in a living room. Mollie created a V shape with her gate system. She put the child who had misbehaved into the corner with the gate surrounding him for two minutes. Mollie's boys actually knew on occasion that they had done something they shouldn't have, and went to the spot without even being asked!

- After an incident occurs, place your child in the time-out spot in order to give him a few minutes to calm down. (Use this time to calm down yourself, if necessary.) A common guideline for how long to leave a child in the time-out spot is one minute for each year of his life.

- Once your child has calmed down, take a few minutes to discuss the action that necessitated the time-out. Don't go on and on; your child will stop absorbing what you're saying pretty quickly. Pretend you have only as much time as a coach does when he calls a time-out in the middle of an important game. You need to get the most important points across in as few words as possible.

- Be sure to convey a more appropriate approach for the next time your child is frustrated, angry, or disappointed.

- If the action that resulted in the time-out involved a child hurting her sibling or another child, and if you're a proponent of children apologizing when they've physically or emotionally hurt someone else, guide your child in doing so.

- Many times, the sorority members found that at this age a time-out and/or discussion of the offending behavior did not stop the child from doing the exact same thing five seconds later. In Mollie's house, she found that she often had to go one step further than a time-out. If one of her boys hit the other with a toy, the hitter went to time-out and the toy was taken away for the rest of the day. Mollie's not entirely sure that the end result of this was worth the fits that ensued when the toys were taken away, but it seemed like a good approach at the time.

Counting

Counting to three wasn't typically effective when the kids were one, and we found that that fact didn't change much when they were two. Mollie tried it, and the boys would finish counting for her. They thought it was hilarious. She'd say, "One . . . Two . . . " and one of the boys would shout, "Three! Haaaa . . . " I tried it, and it was so futile that at one point, with no other strategy yet in hand, I started counting in different languages thinking that if they didn't know how to say "three" in Japanese, maybe they wouldn't chime in. Problem was, they didn't understand "one" or "two" either, so they just looked at me like I was from another planet.

Barb continued to count during this period, again more as a way to calm herself down than anything else. But she did begin to notice during this time that the girls seemed to understand what happened if she got to three. She observed them complying more quickly and frequently than they did when they were one.

Positive Reinforcement

Two-year-olds derive great pleasure from pleasing their parents. You will net far more positive results when you praise positive behavior than when you address negative behavior. When you see your child doing something positive—even if she's sharing nicely for only fourteen seconds—acknowledge how nicely she's sharing. When she comes to get her coat on when she's called, enthusiastically tell her how happy that makes you. It may not be vividly apparent, but they are absorbing this praise and, somewhat subconsciously perhaps, soaking up how good it feels. They'll realize over time that in many instances they'd rather get that positive response from you than the alternative. It won't turn your child into a princess overnight, but it will make her feel good about the choices she's made, and it will make you feel good about her choice to handle a situation in a manner that did not involve teeth.

COMPETITION BETWEEN TWIN TODDLERS

Parents are not interested in justice; they're interested in peace and quiet.
—Bill Cosby

When they are somewhere between two and three years of age, you are bound to notice your twins beginning to compete for . . . well . . . everything: your attention, the privilege of getting into the bathtub first, the color of their dinner plates, who gets the red socks and who gets the blue socks, and who gets her diaper changed first (and when this happens, you'll know it's all about competition because no toddler ever volunteers to get his diaper changed for any rational reason whatsoever).

This can be frustrating, and frankly, it's not going to end anytime soon. They're kids—put two young kids of any age in a house together and they'll compete for toys, the status of "winner," and the choice of cartoons. When you have playdates between singletons and experience this behavior, you can revel in the knowledge that the date will soon end. But in your case, you'll constantly have two children of the same age in the house, and therefore you'll need a solution to this whole competition thing. Luckily, we have a few.

Strategies for Avoiding Competition

Label Everything

Mollie labeled everything in her home with either "K" or "T" from the time Kevin and Tommy were about eighteen months old. For more information on this strategy, see "Fighting over Toys" within the "Addressing the More Frustrating Behaviors" section for one- to two-year-olds.

Give Each Kid "His" Day

Mollie implemented "Tommy Day" and "Kevin Day" when the boys were about two and a half. Even-numbered days were Tommy's and odd-numbered days were Kevin's. On each kid's respective day, he got to do and choose everything first. He got to get out of the tub first, walk out the front door first (unless he wanted to be second), get out of his car seat first, use the "better" nebulizer (their breathing treatment machine), pick the first story at bedtime, and later on choose whether he napped in his room or in the guest room (more on this in a few pages).

Separate Them

If the kids aren't getting along, ask them to play in separate rooms. This isn't a punishment; it's an acknowledgment that they aren't getting along at the present moment and therefore need to spend some time playing separately.

IMPULSIVE BEHAVIOR

What is the percentage of twin toddlers who make it to their third birthday uninjured?

—Heidi, mother of twin boys

Toddlers are insanely curious. They are curious about

what everything is, what everything does, and what they can do with everything once they think they know what it is and what it does. There were times when we all thought, "Holy cow, this kid really is going to climb on top of the table!" In many cases, you'll notice what appears to be curiosity run amok in your house (or in public).

My friend Heidi was changing her son's diaper one day when she noticed his twin climbing up onto a chair and then onto the kitchen table. She was frozen in a moment of uncertainty. She was unsure as to which was more dangerous: changing her son's diaper quickly and praying that in the meantime her other son didn't fall off the table, or rushing to get her son off the table and leaving his brother flipping around in an unsecured, massive Code Brown diaper.

There will be days when laundry baskets are emptied of a week's worth of freshly folded clothing. There will be days when entire contents of unlocked drawers are deposited all over the house. If you can imagine it (and even if you can't), it will probably happen. So if you can't stand folded laundry being unfolded, put it out of reach or keep it behind a closed door. If you can't handle finding your Tupperware in a drawer in the dining room buffet table, lock that particular cabinet door.

Kids this age have little to no fear. They'll walk right into the street. They'll climb into a fireplace (that's lit). They'll jump from the top step, sure that they can fly. Mollie is convinced that the anxiety she experienced during the No Fear phase has taken at least eight years off of her life. Just getting the kids in the car some days without one darting into traffic was a miracle. Many moms wonder how on earth to go anywhere fun such as a park or children's museum without ending up in the ER.

When Olivia and Kambria were young and newly mobile together, it was wintertime. They were about eighteen months old before the weather permitted them to go to the park on a regular basis. Thankfully, by that point they were no longer freshly walking and superbly curious. It wasn't as hard to keep them corralled in public as it might have been earlier on.

Barb did have her fair share of curiosity-run-amok moments, however. One day, she found the girls covered in permanent black marker. Strangely, they didn't get any of it on the walls, the carpet, or the furniture, but they themselves were covered from head to toe. After scrubbing and scrubbing, Barb accepted that she had no choice but to wait for it to wear off. One day when the girls were closer to three years old, Barb walked into the bathroom and found that Kambria had cut not only the ponytail of her Cabbage Patch doll, but her own ponytail as well. At this point, the child-friendly scissors were taken out of the craft drawer and put up so high that even Barb needed to stand on a chair to reach them.

Strategies for Managing Curiosity

Choose Wide-Open Spaces

When choosing a park to attend with new walkers and/or ultra curious kids, try to find one with wide-open spaces where the kids can run without crashing into a million other kids or one becoming interested in the slide while the other is eyeing the rock-climbing wall. If you do choose a park where the kids are likely to become interested in the play structures, take someone with you so you can each be responsible for a child. If you want to take your children to a park where playsets are involved and you do not have an adult companion, give it a whirl (no pun intended) and pray for the best. Remember, if all else fails, you can go home!

Lower Your Expectations

Regarding in-house curiosity, if it isn't dangerous and you can stand the results, just go with it. There were days when I'd *hand* the freshly folded basket of laundry to the boys to give them something to do besides yell.

Turn It in a Positive Direction

It is through curiosity that everyone learns. If you weren't curious about something, you would not explore it or ask questions about it. Kids are no different; they just don't always know what's appropriate to play with and how. If you can provide a few structured activities that encourage them to explore sensations in ways that aren't familiar to them, it'll likely keep them entertained and happy for quite a while. For suggestions, peruse *The Toddler's Busy Book* by Trish Kuffner or *Wonderplay: Interactive & Developmental Games, Crafts & Creative Activities for Infants, Toddlers & Preschoolers* by Fretta Reitzes and Beth Teitelman.

THE FOURTH YEAR
(THREE- TO FOUR-YEAR-OLDS)

Aye Carumba!
—Me, several times a day

Barb called me one Monday morning to report on her family's weekend adventure. She and Tim had taken the girls to a lakeside cabin in Wisconsin. As she described their experience, I felt like I was watching a Calgon commercial. They built a campfire, roasted marshmallows, and told ghost stories. The girls swam in the lake all day long while Barb and Tim read on the beach. They kayaked as a family all around the lake. "And you'll never believe this, we even saw a swan!"

My response: "You mean they didn't throw wet sand at each other? Or fight over who sat where in the kayak? Or argue over who got which life vest even though they were exactly the same? Or push each other *out* of the kayak?" Clearly, while I love her to death, Barb's family and mine cannot go on vacation together anytime in the near future because Barb and I would hate each other by the end for completely opposing reasons.

After Barb finished describing the Dream Weekend, I regaled her with the details of *my* end-of-the-week adventure. On Friday I had taken all four kids to Costco, and after pulling into my spot I opened my purse to retrieve my membership card (you don't want to be fumbling for this magic key at the entrance with three out of four kids on the loose). Suddenly, in my peripheral vision, I noticed that the green minivan next to me was backing up. "What's the big deal?" you ask. Well, *there was no one in the driver's seat of the minivan!* If you haven't already figured it out, the reality was that the minivan wasn't backing up; I was moving forward. I was so frazzled trying to grab the membership card with all four kids yelling in the back seat that I'd forgotten to put my own car in park. I realized this just as I smacked the poor little Saturn in front of me head-on (thankfully, no damage was done).

Whenever I think about the fourth year with our twins, the thought that will probably always come to mind is *Groundhog Day*. Do you remember that movie starring Bill Murray and Andie MacDowell? Murray's character wakes up every single morning to the exact same series of events he experienced the day before. In a big way, that's the perfect analogy for my life during this year.

I knew with absolute certainty that each morning at 7:06 I'd hear Jack yelling at Henry about getting clothing out of the wrong closet. At 7:11 Henry would begin yelling because he could not get his pajama top off. At 7:13 he'd thank Jack for helping him take it off. At 7:14 he'd yell at Jack, who was trying to help him put on his shirt. At 7:22 they'd barrel down the steps side-by-side shouting, in unison, "Me first. *I'm first!*" At 7:24 they'd be arguing over who got which cereal bowl.

At 8:04 they'd begin debating who got to open the car door. At 8:12 after battling it out to get into the car, they'd argue over who got to close the car door. At 11:58 Henry would tattle on Jack. At 11:59 Jack would tattle on Henry for tattling. And so it would go until 7:34 p.m. when they were finishing up their bedtime routines and Jack was whining about wanting one more story and Henry was crying because stuffed animal number twenty-three was missing from the foot of his bed. At least I knew what to expect. At least it was consistent. At the same time, knowing what to expect made it quite difficult many mornings to crawl out of my warm bed after being awakened by the Henry-those-are-*my*-pants-take-them-off-*now* alarm.

There were many days when I ran my home like a well-oiled machine. I'd stand in the middle of the house, feet firmly planted, arms gesturing with the precision of a national champion cheerleader as I barked orders such as, "Jack, your cup is on the carpet. Grace, your shoes belong in the laundry room. George, don't eat that. Henry, please stop spinning. Jack, I mean Henry, I mean Grace . . ."

There were moments—many of them—when I appeared not to be able to match my kids with their given names. One day, amidst the chaos of trying to feed lunch to my kids plus Olivia and Kambria, I referred to Barb as "George." Even worse: she answered, "What?" immediately!

The frazzled monotony of daily life is the struggle that seems to permeate the lives of most moms of twins I know. The good news: there are ways to deal with this challenge. I wish I'd known what they were when I was going through it, but since we each figured out a good number of solutions an hour or a day or a week too late, with any luck you'll benefit from all of our "If only I'd known that" or "Hmmm, if only I'd *tried* that" moments.

The way I summarized my relatively static state of mind one evening to David was by explaining that I felt like my silo of energy (my Sanity Silo, if you will) was being depleted by this Groundhog Day existence, and I was having trouble finding ways to refill those reserves. I had to find ways to refill them or I'd have nothing to work with.

Be sure to identify what fills your reserves. Realize that it's different for everyone. If the activity that works for your best friend doesn't work for you, don't do it. If the activity your husband suggests doesn't seem viable (as in, "What about a once-a-week dinner at Hooters, honey?"), don't do it. If a trip to the salon for a facial leaves you questioning the efficiency of the aesthetician as it did Mollie, *please* don't do it, I beg of you.

You must find something that works for you. I have friends who joined book clubs. I have friends who joined knitting groups. I have friends who joined gyms (gyms without the benefit of free childcare, which I truly don't understand but support nonetheless because they are my friends). I have friends who found part-time jobs in the evenings or on weekends or during the week when they could get a sitter. I have friends who took basket weaving or floral arranging or cake decorating classes at the park district. I have friends who went back to school on a part-time basis to pursue the career they finally realized they were meant to have (how many people truly know what they want to do for the rest of their lives when they are eighteen anyway?) The next time you are really low on sanity, ask yourself what would make you feel better. Then find a way to do it at least once a week so that you stay ahead of the Sanity Silo Sucker instead of run ragged behind it. Replenish your reserves before they become dangerously low.

If the Sanity Silo analogy doesn't work for you, try thinking of it this way: if you wait until you are driving on fumes before you try to find a gas station, the anxiety created by worrying that you might have to get out and push your vehicle through a major intersection will suddenly not be worth the extra errands you ran before stopping for gas. Frankly, you'll pray at every intersection that a gas station will present itself, and it'll be many miles before one actually does. Analogies aside, I never let my gas tank drop below a quarter of a tank. Okay, never say never. It happens. But very, very rarely. Usually only when the kids are so crazy in the back seat that I'm too busy praying to notice the status of the gas gauge. Don't ever let your sanity reserves drop below a quarter of a tank.

Strategies for Conserving Sanity

Our ability to delude ourselves may be an important survival tool.
—Jane Wagner

Keep It Together
Don't add another meltdown to the mix any more often than necessary. When you feel like you're going to blow because of the whining, the bickering, or the lack of outdoor activity in the middle of February, let the kids know that you'll be back in a moment, and escape inside the pantry for a handful of something in which sugar is the first ingredient.

Be the Bigger Person (figuratively as well as literally)
Do whatever you must do to stay above the chaos. Take deep breaths, sit down with a good magazine, and try to ignore as much as possible the pandemonium that doesn't seem to be manageable at that given moment with any strategy ever conceived.

Speak Quietly
I often have to laugh when the kids are yelling, I'm yelling at them to quiet down, and I suddenly realize the irony in my yelling at them to stop yelling. Keep your voice low as often as possible. It's inevitable that when the kids yell, you will yell so they can hear you above their yelling. But then they'll keep yelling for the same reason. It will soon be clear that you're all yelling, but no one's listening to anyone else. Think Mr. Rogers and keep your voice as calm as possible. Worst case,

the kids will keep yelling, but you'll feel better about your approach. Best case, your voice and demeanor will bring them down a notch as well.

Speak Slowly

Speak slowly and deliberately. You're hoping for the same effect here as in the above example. If you're speaking slowly, the kids have to pay attention to find out what's coming next. The more slowly you talk, the longer they have to stay quiet to hear your entire message. I make no promises here. They may not care one bit about your message. But again, you'll feel better about the way you handled the situation, and your blood pressure will thank you for it. Make no mistake about it: I am human and there have been plenty of days when I have spent twenty minutes speaking slowly and deliberately and have then succumbed to simply yelling, "Henry, *zip it!*"

Keep Track of Your Sanity Silo

Heed the previous advice regarding the importance of identifying what you need to fill your Sanity Silo. Put it on the schedule—and stick to it. After any and all particularly challenging days, refuse to go to bed before scheduling some sort of outing for yourself in the next forty-eight to seventy-two hours.

Establish Your Own Official Time-Out Spot

Mollie is a fan of moms establishing their own time-out spot for those occasions when a three-second trip to the cookie area of the pantry just isn't going to cut it. Hers is the laundry room. When she believes she's about to lose it, she lets the boys know that she's feeling frustrated and needs to go into her time-out spot for a few minutes. (She feels that if she follows the advice of the experts, she should be in time-out for somewhere in the vicinity of thirty minutes.) She closes the door and helps herself to a few handfuls of one of the thirty-eight stealthily stashed bags of Halloween candy she purchased at a heavy discount on November 1.

It is during this year that the light at the end of the tunnel will be blazing and beckoning. Yes, there will be a lot of negotiating. There will be a good bit of bribery. There will be outright begging on occasion. In the interest of maintaining a positive perspective, let's tout the reasons this year is so great.

One of the most beautiful aspects of this time period is that as much as they'd love you to think otherwise during those moments when it can work to their advantage, three-year-olds are *very* capable creatures. At some point during this year they will become potty trained. They will learn to dress themselves. They will learn how to open and close the car door. They will learn to fasten their own seat belts. (Since Jack and Henry sit in the third row of our car, this particular moment was, in my household, more momentous than the one when they learned to hold their own bottles.)

Also extremely noteworthy, in my opinion, is the fact that three-year-olds don't truly understand the difference between work and play. What does this mean to you? That a morning cleaning bathrooms and putting away laundry is something you will no longer do alone! Take advantage of it because the minute children turn five, these activities are immediately recognized to be the unpleasant but necessary tasks they really are.

Three- to four-year-olds instinctively know what it takes to make someone smile. I can't tell you how many times Jack went outside to play in the backyard and shortly thereafter brought me a hand-picked bouquet. Some days, this bouquet was made up of weeds, and other days it consisted of hybrid roses that only develop six blooms per bush per year. Thankfully, my reaction—whether I had just been handed a bunch of weeds or a bunch of precious roses—was the same: my eyes came out of my head. Jack correctly identified this response as surprise, and whether it was sweet surprise or what-was-I-thinking-when-I-planted-*this*-bush surprise, I did my best to focus on the underlying gift. I plopped those roses (or weeds) in a glass of water and placed them on the island so everyone could admire them.

The need for a double stroller while shopping has disappeared since the kids are now able to walk the aisles with you (and with any luck, won't run in different directions when the opportunity presents itself). Their language skills are improving to the point where you can actually discuss why darting into a parking lot or writing on your mother's two-day-old flat-screen computer monitor in permanent marker is unacceptable. (If you don't believe a child would do this, talk to Barb. Obviously, the poor woman has experienced more than one unfortunate incident involving a permanent marker.) They may not heed the initial warnings, but you can feel quite confident that they are making a conscious choice not to do so as opposed to not following the rules because they don't understand them.

One mildly unfortunate tidbit regarding the three- to four-year timeframe is that within it, you'll lose a bit of the credibility you might have had during the two- to three-year timeframe when making reasonable excuses for your twins' behavior. After all, when they were two (even if it was the day before they turned three) and they poured milk on their sibling's head, you could dismiss the atrocity if you really needed to by reminding yourself (and others), "Well, she *is* only two." When they are newly three, you can pardon the behavior by rationalizing, "Well, he *just* turned three."

When they get closer to three and a half, it becomes trickier to defend their actions in those terms. And, as I found out, when they get precariously close to turning four, folks are really going to start to question to what degree you are in denial as you self-consciously ask, "They will be four next week. Do you really think it's a problem that they are still using their books as missiles directed at their walls until ten at night?" David was more likely to play the they're-not-even-four-yet card, whereas my stance was, "These kids are almost *four years old!*" (When the kids were not within earshot, that comment was typically preceded, followed, or mixed with an expletive of some sort.)

I would challenge any parent of twins—any parent period—to present me with a behavioral challenge I have neither seen nor topped, a fact that I often took solace in. I reminded myself that if all this weren't going on, I would potentially not be the proper candidate for penning a book on managing (or surviving, as the case truly was on occasion) twin toddlers.

I rarely could understand certain of the boys' behaviors. Grace never presented the same kinds of behavioral challenges at this age. Don't get me wrong, she was quite challenging from two and a half to three and a half, but even still, she never would have thought to engage in some of the activities that the boys did. Books were books, not hammers. Bookcases were bookcases, not imaginary rock walls to scale. Beds were beds, not trampolines.

However, she's a singleton—and she's a girl. I don't like to reinforce stereotypes, but based on more discussions than I can even remember with parents of both boys and girls, the ones regarding girls being able to sit quietly by themselves playing with dolls and pretending to iron while their male counterparts dart from room to room growling like lions and leaving paths of destruction in their wake seem to hold more than a sippy cup's worth of water.

Twin boys are physical, and are often reported to be more "sneaky" than twin girls or boy/girl twins. Still, Barb's girls, who can sit and play with a puzzle for far longer than Jack and Henry would need to stuff all one hundred pieces down the nearest vent, still engage in behavior and banter that you simply don't hear about nearly as frequently between singleton siblings. When I am talking to Barb and ask, "You are seriously able to give your girls forty-five-piece puzzles? And know that all the pieces but four won't be lost within sixteen minutes?" She'd say, "Yes, but remember, in nine years you'll be living the good life while I'm dealing with two prepubescent girls and all that comes with *that.*" Excellent point.

Once twins reach an age at which we believe they should be able to play relatively nicely together all day long, it can be confusing when they don't. Worse, it can be frustrating when they spend a large majority of their days bickering, battling, or otherwise tormenting each other.

Most of the free world appears to be under the impression that twins are living the high life because they always have a "buddy." I've often thought this as well. It's true that they'll likely develop different friends and interests over time, but at the end of the day, they'll always have someone the same age around to play with, wrestle with, or destroy property with. Right?

The reality is that twins themselves don't grasp the fascination with the concept of being born with a buddy. They don't know any other way of life than to be a twin. Early in their lives, they likely assume that everyone is born minutes before or after a sibling. As they grow up, they learn that's not true, but their reality is defined by the fact that they were. Their reality of always having a companion who is the same age, of always having a partner in crime, is as normal to them as it is normal to a singleton to be the sole celebrity at her birthday party. So, while my daughter is absolutely disturbed beyond belief that she wasn't the one born with a twin—a twin sister, that is—the boys seem to spend a decent amount of time wishing the other would go away for an hour or so (even though they are barely functional after twelve minutes apart).

PRESCHOOL-AGE COMMUNICATION

There is nothing worse than falling prey to someone else's confusion.
—Valerie Natress

Again, before we address specific strategies for guiding twins at this stage, it's important to understand how far their communication skills have likely come.

By three to four years of age, children should understand common verbs and adjectives, and should comprehend When/Where and Yes/No questions. Their average sentence length should be four to five words (even though it will often feel as though the entire day is comprised of just one, very long run-on sentence!).

If parents didn't believe it were possible for a child to have more to say than when she was two years old, the preschool years will prove that it indeed is. Given all the new experiences in their lives, it's easy to understand why. They want to talk to you about all that they are learning, and they want to be sure you are paying the utmost attention to every minute detail. Twins will want to express themselves simultaneously, and won't be willing to accept that you have only two ears that don't work independently of one another. I'm sure evolution will solve this problem someday (probably shortly after mothers develop a third arm), but for now, you'll have to find alternate methods for convincing them to take turns.

In the mornings, when my patience was most abundant, I worked hard to let Jack finish his thought and then said, "Okay, it's Henry's turn." After going back and forth for what felt like hours, it became clear that neither kid really had anything to say. He just wanted more airtime than his brother. One of Henry's favorite sayings during this year was, "Jack, stop erupting me!"

During this time, Tracy (my favorite speech therapist) reminds parents, "The best thing [you] can do is provide a good speech model. Speak slowly and clearly, and try to remove time pressures for speaking. Let your child know that you are interested in what he has to say and you are more than happy to stop and listen."

Katherine Cook (my other favorite speech therapist) recommends, "If hard-to-comprehend speech or other communication issues continue, become more severe, or your child seems constantly frustrated by speech and language challenges, contact a speech-language pathologist for an evaluation."

THE BEDROOM PARTY

When angry, count to four; when very angry, swear.
—Mark Twain

Should you decide, either by choice or because there are no other options, to keep your children in the same bedroom, you may quickly learn that once they are out of cribs, it's New Year's Eve every night (and most afternoons) in their bedroom. The occasional mid-afternoon or late-night pow-wow probably isn't that big of a deal, but you'll perhaps want to address loud renditions of the Bob the Builder chorus that not only take center stage around 11:00 p.m., but seem to increase in frequency. There are a slew of strategies we've found effective.

Strategies for Party Annihilation

Mornings
Many children do not have exactly the same sleep schedule or exactly the same sleep needs. If this is the case with your children, one child might wake up quite early and purposefully or inadvertently wake the other (who is not yet

ready to get up). At this point, you've got one child who is crabby because he needed to sleep longer, and you've got two kids who are convinced nevertheless that they are ready to start the day. When it's only 5:30 a.m., and you simply do not do 5:30 a.m. wakeups, determine a hard and fast time before which you will not start the day. Mollie's is 6:30 a.m. Her boys have a clock in their room, which Jack and Henry cannot have because they'd pull the cord out of the wall and swing it around over their heads like a lasso. Tommy and Kevin are starting to recognize what six-thirty looks like on the clock, but they also know that it's six-thirty because that's the time Gary gets into the shower. They are not allowed out of their rooms until they hear the shower turn on. When the boys do come out of their room before six-thirty, Mollie threatens to close the door and that is usually all that's needed to force them to climb back into bed.

Naptime

These days, Jack naps in his and Henry's room (which sadly, Henry now refers to as Jack's Room since he's banned from it every afternoon), while Henry naps in Grace's room. This wasn't possible a year or so ago because Henry would have been like a kid in a candy store in there. In fact, even at three years of age, we had to remove the lamp on Grace's bedside table at one point because in the middle of naptime, I went upstairs and heard Henry talking to himself. He was saying, "The dinosaur is wary wary hot!" I quickly thrust my head into the room to find his plastic dinosaur melting atop the light bulb.

After much frustration surrounding similar issues in her home, Mollie adopted the same approach: now one kid naps in the boys' room while the other naps in the guest room.

The kids weren't always thrilled with these arrangements. Henry would claim he was terrified of Grace's room, and Mollie's boys actually fought over who got the "good" room (that being the guest room). I agreed to leave Grace's door open, provided Henry did not come out, and Mollie lets the boys alternate nap rooms based on whose day it is. At four years of age, Jack and Henry still nap for two hours each afternoon and Tommy and Kevin for one to two hours. I can guarantee you that none of the four of them would be doing so if they were sharing a room during rest time.

Even when in different bedrooms, Mollie's boys sometimes sleep for only thirty minutes. If one wakes after a short slumber and refuses to stay upstairs, he is allowed to come downstairs so he doesn't wake his brother, but he has to sit quietly by himself and read or otherwise entertain himself. They usually follow these rules because they know that if they don't, Mollie will force them to go back upstairs. Once the other kid wakes up, both boys are allowed to resume playing downstairs. When more than two days of thirty-minute naps go by, I know it because Mollie answers the phone sounding like someone who hasn't slept in weeks.

Nighttime

If possible, separate the kids at bedtime. Let one go to sleep in their room and the other in a guest room. After she has fallen asleep, move the child who went to sleep in the alternate room back to her own bed. We did run into a bit of trouble with this particular issue. Initially, when the boys had been partying too long in their room, we'd let them know that if we heard anyone again, the person making noise would have to sleep in the guest room in the basement. It's a finished basement and, frankly, nicer than either of the other two floors, so while it might sound like punishment, it was actually more of a luxury. After a while, Jack and Henry would actually fight over who got to sleep in the basement! On one occasion in the grocery store, I asked them to please stop jumping around, and Henry said (in his typically loud voice), "Yeah, if we don't behave, we have to sleep in the basement." I got a lot of looks at that moment, believe me.

PRESCHOOL

Faith and doubt are both needed, not as antagonists, but working side by side to take us around the unknown curve.

—Lillian Smith

Typically, children start preschool—whether in a formal school environment or in a homeschool environment—when they are three years old, depending on the cut-off date of the school district in which they reside. If you choose to enroll your children in a formal preschool outside of the home, this two and a half hours or so two to four days a week will change your world in a whole slew of ways.

Logistically, one of the first questions parents have when enrolling their twins in preschool is whether or not to keep them in the same classroom or request that they be separated. For as many parents as there are who ponder this, there are as many opinions out there on which approach is best.

When Jack and Henry were born, I positively could not imagine separating them—ever. I thought, "I'll fight any academic administrator who believes that they should be separated. I'll homeschool them if necessary." But Jack and Henry could not be more different from each other. In fact, I have yet to meet a set of twins who are terribly alike in any department besides looks. I concluded that in the longer term, while they'd have fun being together, they could be together after school and on weekends. They needed to be allowed to explore their own interests and develop their own friendships without either one completely relying on the other or feeling that he needed to be there to help the other all of the time.

For my own sanity I chose to keep Jack and Henry together during preschool. I could not fathom the idea of them being in separate classes—and in all likelihood being on different floors and opposite ends of the school. That would mean I'd have to be first in line to pick up one child in order to get to the second child before he began to wonder if I'd forgotten about him. Yes, I realize I could have simply requested that they be put in classrooms that were close and on the same level, but I wasn't terribly concerned that being in the same preschool class would be detrimental. In addition, I was concerned that, emotionally, Henry would have a difficult time without Jack. I acknowledge that as he grows up, he needs to learn to rely on and trust himself more than he did when he started preschool. However, I wasn't sure that it was worth the anxiety that he would likely experience if we forced him to separate from Jack at only three years of age. And to be honest, Jack was just as anxious about the ways in which Henry needed him as Henry was. I was concerned that if they were separated, Jack would spend the entire morning wondering if Henry was okay, and Henry would spend the entire morning screaming for Jack. It seemed to present a roadblock that would prevent them from enjoying the preschool experience to its fullest.

In addition, with George being so young, it wasn't feasible to take him along when the school had an event to which parents were invited (and during which our participation was requested in addition to our presence). Therefore, either David or I stayed home with George while the other attended the event. If Jack and Henry were in different classes, whoever went would have been either running back and forth between classrooms or leaving one child without an attendant parent. The latter option was completely unacceptable.

Even before day one of their first year of preschool, I decided that for their second year, I would most likely request that they be separated. I felt relatively certain that once they reached kindergarten, they would need to be separated in order to develop their own lives independent of one another, and I figured it was better to make the change before the boys were also making a change in schools.

Many school districts (beyond preschool) have guidelines for multiples. Many stipulate that unless you press the issue, the kids will be separated. Many stipulate that *even* if you press the issue, the kids will be separated. The topic of multiples' classroom placement has recently made its way to the forefront of the more serious discussions on raising multiples. Many schools impose an across-the-board policy that requires that multiples be separated. This poses an even greater challenge when a specific grade level has only one class. Parents of multiples have become so frustrated by school policies regarding multiples that in many states, new legislation is being proposed—legislation that would give families a say in their children's school placement as well as encourage schools to look at each set of multiples on a case-by-case basis when determining whether or not it is in their best interest to keep them together or separate them.

In an article she wrote for iParenting.com, Alexandria Powell (who is a mom of twin girls) provided excellent information and perspectives on this issue.

First, she addressed some of the more common myths surrounding the separation of multiples. Many school administrators believe that separating multiples solves many problems, including competition between the children and the tendency for teachers and students alike to see them as one unit instead of as individuals with their own likes, dislikes, strengths, and areas that need improvement. According to John Mascazine, an associate professor of education at Ohio Dominican University in Columbus, Ohio, beliefs about separation of multiples are often based more on old wives' tales than on scientific fact. There's simply no research that proves that separation would be best for all multiples.

A common misunderstanding is that multiples will always struggle with comparison and competitive issues, which often isn't the case. According to Mascazine, "The challenge is to help non-twins avoid projecting their expectations to compete upon same-age siblings." And while there is no research to suggest that keeping twins together is detrimental, there is reason to believe that, in some circumstances, separating them could be. Especially when they are young, many multiples often find great comfort in knowing where their sibling is. After all, they've been together since the moment they were conceived and, many times, the anxiety they may experience when separated is taken for granted.

On the other hand, notes Mascazine, in cases where same-age siblings have different levels of ability, when one's behavior is disruptive to the other, when their competition with one another is so strong that it is unhealthy, or when the siblings have extremely different social development, separation should be considered. Notes Nancy Segal, professor of developmental psychology at California State University, Fullerton, and the author of *Entwined Lives: Twins and What They Tell Us About Human Behavior*, "Some multiples will do better being separated, of course—the point is that there should not be a single policy for multiples, just as we do not treat all non-multiples the same."

To conclude the article, Alexandria provided suggestions for parents who encounter resistance from their school's administration even after communicating that they believe it's best for their twins to be assigned to the same classroom. Most of the suggestions came from Kathy Dolan, a mother of twins in Queens, New York, who founded Parenting in Education: A Child's Entitlement—the largest of many groups asking for legislation that will give families a voice in their children's placement. Dolan suggests that parents ask for a copy of the school's written policy on multiple birth children. Most of the time, she contends, the school won't have one. It's far easier to challenge a "policy" that doesn't exist in writing. Another suggestion: speak with your children's pediatrician and/or your children's preschool teachers. In many cases, if a pediatrician can document the benefit of two children remaining together—due to an emotional attachment that, if removed, would prevent them from concentrating and performing to their full potential—it may coerce the school into bending their "rules." Testimony from a preschool teacher who has taught a specific set of multiples and can confirm that there weren't any issues may also be beneficial. A final suggestion of Dolan's is to go to www.twinslegislation.com. This site provides the latest research on multiples in the classroom, and can put you in touch with other parents in your area who are working to establish legislation that would put such an important decision back, at least partially, into the hands of parents.

Another bit of information to be aware of: The National Association of Elementary School Principals' website has an area for research. If you enter "twins" into the search box, the returned content is an article entitled "The Trouble with Twins." Written in January 2004, the article comments that with the rate of twinning continuing to rise, as of 2005, one out of every thirty-five kindergarteners will be a twin. Therefore, the association chose to address the approach that schools should take when a parent shows up to register "identical or near-identical" children for kindergarten. The article addresses the research done to date (which is ambivalent at best), special needs children, and guidelines for educating twins. To read the article in its entirety, go to http://www.naesp.org/ContentLoad.do?contentId=1144.

Assuming that parents *are* allowed to voice their opinion on whether or not their twins remain together or are separated, you can read almost as much about each option both online and in print as you can about whether or not to dress twins alike or name them in complementary ways. In my case, I went to the closest experts.

Barb and Mollie are both teachers; Barb has taught kindergarten, second, and fifth grades, and Mollie taught eighth grade. So I asked their opinions.

Mollie chose to request different preschool classes for her boys because they are so competitive at home. In many ways, Mollie believes the decision to put them in different classrooms was more for her and Gary than for Tommy and

Kevin. They wanted to do whatever they could to avoid any potential pitfalls of sharing a classroom, teachers, and friends.

Mollie believes that the two hours apart were extremely beneficial for the boys. For one, they didn't have the option of tattling on each other. Plus, the boys are each other's clones (even though they are technically fraternal), and Mollie didn't want the teachers to be confused or to—even subconsciously—compare them in any way. This way, the boys got to have their own adventure every day. Even though there were days when one or both of the boys wished he could be in the "other room" based on what his brother had gotten to do the previous day, Mollie and Gary believe that they began to learn to appreciate the benefits of having different experiences at school.

On the whole, Mollie believes that whether multiples are kept together or separated at school is a decision parents should make for themselves. She thinks that a blanket approach by a school district is fine as long as the administrators are accepting of parents' requests for a different arrangement.

Barb also split Olivia and Kambria for preschool for many of the same reasons. She wanted to foster their ability to separate from each other as well as their sense of independence and their self-confidence. Just like Tommy and Kevin, the girls asked to go into each other's room on occasion, but being separated hasn't caused any lasting issues whatsoever, and the benefits have far outweighed their occasional wishes to stay together for the morning.

The biggest issue in Barb's mind was her desire for each of her daughters to develop her own identity. She wanted to ensure that teachers weren't able to compare the girls, and also that the girls weren't able to compare themselves to one another. Barb knows full well that the girls will likely develop stronger skills in different areas, and she feared that if one saw that the other was easily doing something she found difficult, it could cause unnecessary challenges. With the girls in different classrooms, their skill differences weren't as "in-your-face" as they might have been otherwise.

When Nancy Bowers' twins started preschool, she had to keep them together because there was only one preschool class that year. The next year, there were two classes and she put one into each. Because their classes went to recess at the same time and occasionally joined together for group activities, the kids were able to see each other during the day. When it was time to register them for kindergarten, there were ten classes. Nancy ensured that they were on the same "team." In some school districts, especially where there are a large number of classrooms for each grade, teachers were grouped into teams (and, according to Nancy, this approach is still in practice today in many districts). While her kids' classes operated independently of one another, they worked on the same projects, had the same homework assignments, used the same classroom materials, etc. This way, Nancy did not have to buy poster board for one child's weekly activity and construction paper for the other's. Additionally, it made it easier to help them with homework and other projects.

At the end of the day, do you know who the person most equipped to make the right decision is? You are! You know your kids better than anyone, and while others can provide their opinions, you'll have to weigh them along with your own and determine what is best for your children. What is best may differ from one year to the next. So, take it a year at a time. And trust yourself. You must have the confidence in yourself as a parent to know that you hold the key to the best decisions for your children.

MORNING MAYHEM

A woman is like a tea bag. You never know how strong she is until she gets into hot water.

—Eleanor Roosevelt

One of Barb's first priorities when she registered the girls for preschool was the avoidance of morning chaos. School started at 8:15 a.m. That meant she had to be in the car driving at 8:02. There are many days when Olivia doesn't wake up on her own until 8:45 (don't get me started). Barb was not at all sure how she'd get both girls up, dressed, fed, and out the door by 8:02 a.m. without major meltdowns.

I was in the same boat, as Grace had to be at school at 8:25 and the boys at 8:55. In order to be successful without having one hair on your head turn gray (from this process, at least), you will need a morning routine that is executed with military precision.

Strategies for Effective Morning Management

Breakfast Prep

Set out cereal bowls, cereal boxes, utensils, cups, napkins, and whatever else you might need for breakfast the night before (but not the milk; the kitchen won't smell good in the morning). If you are feeling particularly adventurous and plan to make pancakes, French toast, or waffles in the morning, set out the griddle and any other necessary preparatory dishes and utensils. Additionally, make sure you have all requisite ingredients on hand before you announce your plan to cook such a meal. There's not much more devastating to young children than to have the announcement of a special pancake breakfast countered forty-five seconds later with, "Oh. I didn't realize we were out of eggs. How about Rice Krispies?" I think this is why Mollie always has a box or two of frozen waffles in the freezer.

Lunch Prep

If anyone needs a home-made lunch, be sure to make it the night before. Don't forget to put it in the refrigerator if it contains any perishable items! If it does contain items that need to be kept cold, stick a Post-it note somewhere near your car keys with a reminder to place an ice pack in the lunch box before leaving the house.

Clothing Prep

I hung sweater racks in the boys' closets and on Sunday nights, I fill each slot with a days' worth of clothes: pants, shirt, underwear, and socks. We call it their Clothes Butler, which is particularly hilarious when we are entertaining out-of-town guests and the boys start the day by screaming, "Mom, there are no clothes in my Clothes Butler!" When they wake up each morning, they are to put their pajamas in their laundry basket and get dressed. They can then come downstairs. Many mornings still, *I* am the one who puts their pajamas in their laundry basket around noon after I find them strewn about the upstairs hallway, but we're working on it.

Don't Talk, Just Eat

While my kids are eating their breakfast, I set the timer on the microwave to go off exactly twenty minutes before we need to walk out the door. When the timer goes off, breakfast is over. I give updated reminders to finish before the timer goes off, and if they don't make it (they have thirty or so minutes to finish breakfast, which is more than enough time in my opinion), the kitchen closes. I'm pleased to report that it's not yet closed in the middle of anyone's breakfast.

The Grand Finale

After breakfast, the kids go upstairs and brush their teeth, or I help them do it downstairs. They then put on their shoes and coats. We are out the door at 7:55, which allows four minutes for arguing over who opens the garage door, who opens the car door, who gets in the car first, who *closes* the car door, and one minute for fixing Henry's seat belt which inevitably gets stuck four out of five days a week.

Mission Accomplished

We are driving down the road at precisely 8:00 a.m. I am usually a bit out of breath by this point, but most major altercations have been avoided and no one is late.

Another more obvious solution to avoiding morning mayhem is to sign up for afternoon preschool if it's offered. Mollie almost needed a prescription for Xanax just thinking about getting her boys up and out the door before 8:00 a.m., so she signed up for the afternoon session. Some days her boys are so wiped by five o'clock that they barely know who they are, but Mollie believes she is far more capable of dealing with it then than first thing in the morning.

GETTING YOUR LIFE BACK

Change in all things is sweet.

—Aristotle

Both Barb and Mollie put their kids in a four-day preschool program since the kids were a month or two from turning four when school began. For some reason unbeknownst to me, I put Jack and Henry in the three-day program. The day Tommy and Kevin started school, I called Mollie and asked how things went. She was ecstatic; the boys had a great time and she ran all of her errands. Barb had a similar experience.

Day 2: Tommy, Kevin, Olivia, and Kambria had a great day. Barb and Mollie cleaned.

Day 3: Kids did great; Barb and Mollie didn't know what to do with themselves. Mollie, sounding somewhat defeated, said, "Well, I guess I'll clean again. I'm going to have the cleanest house on the block!" I told her that if she got really bored, I had a few rooms she was welcome to address.

I took this little bit of downtime while Jack and Henry

were at school to the extreme and expected a bit too much of myself in those two and a half hours. I also was not completely alone since I had George with me. The number of things I concluded that I could accomplish with no problem in those seven and a half relatively free hours per week made it quite clear that I had only a marginal grip on reality.

At one point, I became concerned about my anxiety level. I was so excited for just a little bit of "me" time and therefore had so many things on my to-do list that most days, I couldn't even prioritize which were the top three things on the list. David tried to coach me into prioritizing not only numbers one, two, and three, but to sub-categorize in order to create 1a, 1b, and so on. Not a bad idea, except that as far as I was concerned, everything on my list deserved to be categorized somewhere at the top, so I had 1a all the way to 1w, and I didn't feel any better about that than I did about the original long list of bullet points.

During a visit to my doctor at that time, I mentioned my concerns (I had not yet been blessed to find the doctor who writes prescriptions for fun weekend outings in addition to drugs and tests). He listened and reassured me that this was all normal. He then did the requisite check of my eyes, ears, heart . . . He stopped at my heart. "Are you aware that you have a minor heart murmur?" he asked.

"No."

"It's very minor, but it could indicate mitral valve prolapse."

"Oh!" I perked up, feeling knowledgeable. "My mom and my sister have that."

"Hmmm. I think you need to get an ultrasound to check for it."

An ultrasound. That means I get to lie down . . . and I'm not allowed to take children with me.

"I'll take the first available appointment."

He concluded, "I'm not terribly concerned. If anything, it's a minor issue. Of course, you do have an increased risk of sudden death, but . . . Come back in a few weeks and we'll go over the results."

I'm sure they were wondering exactly when I was going to leave the exam room. It was the what-do-you-mean-I'm-pregnant appointment all over again. Well, not exactly, but close. I went to see my doctor to discuss my level of anxiety and he concluded the appointment by informing me that I had a higher than normal risk of sudden death. As my sister once said, "My life is like a cartoon."

GETTING YOUR BODY BACK

I'm afraid to start plastic surgery. And my breasts are so versatile now, I can wear them down, up, or side to side.

—Cybill Shepherd

In the interest of personal longevity (after all, I want to be around when these children are calling with frequency wondering how to get their *own* kids out of the grocery mid-tantrum), I decided to incorporate a new eating regimen into my life just after the boys turned two. This regimen supposedly increases your energy as well as your life expectancy. However, it prohibits the ingestion of anything even remotely sweet, including fresh fruit. Whoever heard of fresh fruit being on the no-no list? Because I've made my feelings about chocolate quite clear, I'm sure the world will understand why I couldn't completely commit to this plan. I read the magazines (in fact, a night in bed with *People* was often as satisfying as a trip to Hawaii), and I saw how great Gwyneth looked while on the macrobiotic diet. But, as much as I dislike the nastier, more negative gossip out of Hollywood, I was pleased as punch to see the spread in *In Touch* that profiled the non-airbrushed celebrities and their cellulite. Truthfully, I would love to be a goddess—wouldn't we all—but I would be a horrible person to be around if I were because it clearly would require that I be without my chocolate. I don't want to live to be 120 if I have to give up chocolate in order to do so. Therefore, I incorporated *parts* of the diet plan in an effort to make myself feel like I was doing *something*.

Sadly, even after all of the aerobic activity involved in the prior three years—constantly chasing kids around, cleaning, and running through Target lobbing items into the cart and whipping from aisle to aisle—I still didn't seem to be in as good of shape as I'd hoped.

Several months before Jack and Henry turned four, my friend Stacey—part of that little Triathlete Trio that included Barb and Sonya—suggested that Sonya, Barb, Mollie, and I join her in a mini-triathlon. The best reason she could come up with? "Because it's a cheap race—only $24, and you just can't *find* a triathlon you can enter that cheap anymore" (as if I would know).

I don't think I was on the initial invitation—for good reason. Joan Rivers once said, "The first time I see a jogger smiling, I'll consider it."

My thoughts exactly.

Barb of course agreed right away because not only had she been on that damn elliptical every morning since her girls were four months old (she'd call me and I'd hear this whirring noise in the background and ask her what she was doing, after which she'd enthusiastically reply—not even remotely out of breath—"I'm on the elliptical!"), but somewhere between their second and third birthdays, she had also begun swimming three days a week at 4:00 a.m. (no, a.m. is not a typo). I swear, that woman puts on a tank top and I just want to deck her.

Sonya tried to dodge the whole thing by hiding behind the mountain of paperwork growing on her office desk (however, she could have successfully completed the race with no problem had she so desired). Mollie claimed that was the day she was scheduled to wash her hair.

So somehow, the force of Stacey wanting another participant landed in my e-mail in-box. I tried more than once to politely say "No." Stacey is nothing if not persistent, and she tirelessly maintained the conviction that even a word as blatant and direct as "no" could be worked with as long as it wasn't coming from a two-year-old.

"Stacey," I pleaded, "you realize that I'd be doing the swim in a skirted Lands' End I've-had-four-babies-in-five-years swimsuit; I have a very cool mountain bike I *could* ride (if mountain bikes are even permitted), but it has a child's seat attached to the back; and, frankly, I have complete and utter confidence that I would never even make it to the running portion of the race so there's no point in addressing what the issues might be related to that leg, no pun intended."

Was Stacey satisfied? No.

"Okay, let's start small then," she retorted.

"Define small."

"How about a 5K?"

"I'm willing to humor you," I conceded, "because I'm a masochist and I love a good challenge. But you're going to have to train me."

"Super. Start slow—two miles three times per week."

(Pause)

"Are you seriously insinuating that two miles is an easy run?"

"Well, one mile then," she effortlessly countered.

"Again, same question, but replace the word 'two' with the word 'one.'"

"Start with whatever you can do. Walk part of it. Build on the distance every night. You have four weeks. You can do this. And this one's even cheaper than the triathlon—only $10, and that includes a t-shirt!" Super. So I'll at least have a new t-shirt to cover my unclad, sagging breasts the next time the fire department shows up at 9:00 a.m.

I think I was just tired of negotiating. After all, I spend all day every day negotiating. She wore me down even more than my kids could because her persistence, while not necessarily logical in my mind, was laid out so nicely. It was persistence with a purpose, and it was most refreshing.

I agreed to start training. Now, that $10 race didn't happen for me, but I'm pleased to report that six months later, I'd progressed from being able to run for three minutes to being able to run for four and a half minutes, and I consider that real progress.

There is an unfortunate pressure on moms to drop their pregnancy weight as quickly as possible. This pressure is created by myriad sources: images of svelte, toned celebrities three months after giving birth (to twins), interpretations of what defines a "hot mama", and insane curiosity regarding the strategies employed by the next-door neighbor who is back in her size two Lucky Brand jeans eight weeks post-partum.

The strongest pressure undeniably stems from one source: ourselves. Perhaps we dream of *wearing* our neighbor's size two jeans (even though we haven't fit into a size two since we were seven). Some of us may want to be slim and trim new moms like Denise Richards and Liv Tyler (even though they themselves revealed that they were put through grueling training sessions in order to achieve their look). Many of us have happily traded much of our pre-baby lives for diapers, bottles, and lots (and lots) of laundry, and we simply want to look in the mirror now and then and find someone other than a mom staring back at us.

Far more important than stressing over when you'll get your pre-baby body back is being happy with the person you are today—sagging breasts, tummy rolls, and all. The big question is: what kind of physique do *you* want? And, more important, to what lengths are you willing to go to get it? The idea of a "hot mama" is all the rage these days, but it's important to define for yourself what that means. Don't get caught up in the figure society says you should have and, by all means, erase the image the celebrity magazines suggest that you *could* have (if you had a personal trainer, a chef, and a decent amount of free time on your hands).

If you are like Barb, and the endorphins begin to flow at the mere thought of forty minutes on the elliptical machine, you are naturally going to carve out time to exercise because you enjoy it—not merely to get on the scale after each session and pray that you are at least four ounces lighter than before. Women who love to exercise don't need to be told that. In all likelihood they aren't reading this section—they're exercising.

If you are like me and don't particularly love to exercise, take comfort in the fact that you'll undoubtedly lose most, if not all, of the weight you gained while pregnant. You may simply notice a little more sagging here and drooping there than you did previously.

While raising young children, what's most important is maintaining your sanity. Regardless of what magazines, talk shows, or neighbors suggest that you should be doing in your free time, be sure that your extracurricular activities are ones that nurture *you*. They may nurture your cardiovascular system or your biceps; they may nurture your spirit; they may nurture your intellect.

I have identified a compromise in my own life. I go to the gym once a week and walk on a treadmill for thirty minutes. Sometimes I walk fast enough to break a sweat; sometimes I don't. The one constant is: no matter how fast I'm walking, I'm always worried about tripping over my feet and flying off the back end of the machine.

In addition to changing my environment for an hour (to one where no one under the age of twelve is permitted) I feel good about the fact that, at least once a week, I walk approximately 2.2 consecutive miles. I also use this once-a-week visit to justify my portion of our membership cost! Alternately I read, do a crossword puzzle while soaking in a bubble bath, watch the previous week's episodes of *Days of Our Lives* on TiVo, write, or simply sit quietly and stare at the wall. My entire self is much better rested after engaging in activities that relax my mind than it is after lifting free weights for an hour.

Now, when it gets precariously close to spring and the short shorts and itsy, bitsy, teeny, weenie bikinis are on prominent display in any and all stores, I become temporarily more motivated than usual. The first seasonal sighting of Barb in a tank top elicits the same reaction. In these moments, I make a pact with myself to get in shape. I venture to the gym *twice* a week for approximately three weeks. I then find a reason—any reason—to make a pan of brownies and revert to my old schedule.

DROPPING THE AFTERNOON NAP

Life is something that happens when you can't go to sleep.
—Fran Lebowitz

Many children lose their need for an afternoon nap at some point during this year. Many will still require one (even if they don't realize it), and many will need one now and then depending on the day's or week's activities. It will undeniably be clear to you on which days this is the case. If not, remember this: if either of your children has thrown himself into a heap on the floor and is crying because a bird flew away from the backyard tree before he had a chance to go out and try to pet it, he needs a nap.

Whether or not your children actually fall asleep in the afternoon, we in the sorority are huge proponents of "rest time." This is an opportunity for children to read, play quietly, or even watch a cartoon should you deem that appropriate, but the key is that it's *quiet time.* The knowledge that rest time is on the schedule has saved my sanity many, many times. There have been plenty of days when, if I'd had to manage the household (and everyone in it) from 7:00 a.m. until 8:00 p.m. with no break whatsoever, I would have lost my mind.

Jack and Henry still nap every single day. Barb really resents this, as Olivia and Kambria rarely, if ever, sleep while the sun's up. I quickly remind her of the days of fecal fascination, at which point she acknowledges that her girls' refusal to sleep is a small price to pay—especially because they are more than willing to sit quietly in front of a movie for ninety minutes or so each afternoon while Barb cleans, reads, or works on the 150 handmade, frighteningly ornate holiday cards she creates each year. And when I say ornate, I mean ornate. The proof: she got all worried last year when her forearm started badly hurting in mid-December. She said she could barely raise her arm, and stormed her internist's door convinced that something was horribly wrong with her. Turns out she had tendonitis from overusing the paper cutter. I'm still laughing.

Mollie's boys nap most days, but only for an hour or so. Mollie claims she needs only an hour, so this works fine. In my case, it takes me an hour just to get my blood pressure back down to a normal range, so I need more time than that. Thankfully, Jack and Henry are often unconscious for two to three hours each afternoon.

The most important part of rest time, unless the boys are watching a movie in the family room, is that they are in separate bedrooms. Otherwise, the quiet rest time will turn into a time for loud debate over who gets which book and to whom the Goofy stuffed animal really belongs. Once that occurs, the point of rest time is lost (for strategies on separating kids who share the same bedroom at naptime, see the "Naptime" portion of the "Bedroom Party" section). Frankly, even occasionally allowing Jack and Henry to watch a movie during rest time necessitates that they occupy separate rooms. The debates over who gets to sit on which couch cushion, who gets which of the seven available blankets, or who has control of the remote put me over the edge.

At six years of age, Grace still has a rest time in the afternoon on days when she does not have school. She uses this time to work on her scrapbook, read, or just relax on the couch. As far as she's concerned, she's *far* too old to actually be in a bedroom while her brothers are napping! The point is that she does something independently and quietly. I'm quite sure this little two-hour block of quiet time will be part of the routine in our house until all four kids are in school full-time. At that point, I personally plan to sleep all day long.

GUIDING YOUR
THREE- TO FOUR-YEAR-OLD TWINS

Always end the name of your child with a vowel, so that when you yell, the name will carry.

—Bill Cosby

While guiding your three- to four-year-old twins' behavior patterns, you may often feel as though you're swimming down a murky stream. Focus on the fact that while the water may be cloudy, slimy, and a bit chilly, you are swimming downstream, not upstream. Sometimes I pretend that this whole guidance thing is nothing more than a game of Candy Land. I hope with each newfound approach that it'll be the one that lands me on Gumdrop Pass or, on a really good day, Rainbow Trail—allowing me to skip ahead quite a few steps. On the more difficult days, I think about Gloppy, who, if he could talk, surely would tell me that I had to go steal a handful of chocolate chips out of the pantry, or Princess Frostine, who I just know would sweetly tell me to go bake a whole cake, grab a fork, and retreat to bed. I get sent back a few steps with frequency, but I try to remind myself that my goal is to get to the finish line, and in my version of the game—when I'm playing in my own mind (as opposed to playing with the kids for real, when I of course always ensure that they win)—that goal involves getting to the finish line *before* my kids do so that it's clear that I outplayed them and not the other way around.

There are several truths about this year in terms of behavior. I shall try to put as positive a spin on them as possible.

The Reality of the Three-Year-Old Mindset

Responsibility Skills

During this year, your children not only hear what you are saying, they truly start absorbing it (and it will come right back at you many days). I've heard Jack say, "No, I'm making the right choice and being 'propriate" when Henry's requested that he engage in questionable behavior. I think I've heard it only once, but I've heard it, and that's good, isn't it?

Comprehension of Acceptable Behavior

There were no doubt many instances when your twins were younger when you wondered if they truly understood whether what they had done was wrong and why. Trust me, they now know when they are doing something wrong. One of Jack's favorite phrases during this year: "I did not *see* myself do it!" Now, he never uttered, "I *did* see myself do it," but I realize I should expect only so much in the "taking responsibility" department in one year.

Impulsive Behavior

Kids this age are impulsive, as evidenced the day we were in the store and Henry kept saying from about twenty feet back, "Look at me! Look at me!" and I continued to respond, "Henry, stay with us. Henry, walk faster please." Finally, eager to get him to stop asking us to look at him, and painfully aware that he was now about sixty feet behind us, I turned around to find Henry just standing there with his pants around his ankles laughing hysterically. Sadly, this surprised me so little that I just rolled my eyes, told him to pull his pants up, and continued on. Jack and Henry laughed their way through that shopping trip instead of argued, so in the end, because this little flashing episode was seen by no one except us, it admittedly created a relatively peaceful shopping excursion.

Listening Skills

Kids this age hear what they want to hear. One day on the cartoon *Arthur*, Arthur was talking about New Year's, which Henry heard as "nude ears." He found this perfectly hilarious and laughed for days about the fact that Arthur was talking about nude ears. So, that's funny and kept Henry positively entertained for quite some time.

Negotiation skills

Three- to four-year-olds will hone your negotiation skills. I've felt most diplomatic as I've informed Henry that if he wanted to have dessert, he needed to stop playing with the lamps in Costco. His reply: "That's okay; I don't want dessert." On another occasion, I informed Henry that the flowers he was attempting to lick were faux, and I asked him to please choose to stop licking them or give up that evening's bedtime story. His response: "That's okay; I'll read to myself." I learned that when negotiating with a three-year-old, parents oftentimes must be more clever than their child. It's not always as easy as you might imagine.

Entertaining Shopping Excursions

Shopping excursions can be filled with entertaining dialogue with perfect strangers. In Costco one day, I was getting lids and straws for the lemonades I'd purchased for three obviously impatient kids. George was signing "milk," but everyone around us thought he was waving hello. They all began waving back, at which point he began screaming at the top of his lungs because it was all-too-apparent that no one understood him. Amidst this chaos with which I'd become all-too-familiar, an employee on a snack break looked up and said, "Are they all yours?" I said, "Yes." He asked, somewhat sympathetically, "Are you having a long day?" I said, "Sir, my *life* is really just one very long day!"

Proactive Identity Development

When they get to be between three and four years of age, twins begin to do things in order to prove they are different. One example is a child who demands the exact opposite of his brother's order in the drive-thru at Burger King only to have a fit at the pick-up window because he's suddenly decided that his brother indeed ordered the perfect meal.

Quick Thinking

The minds of children this age work far more quickly than adults sometimes give them credit for. One day in the grocery store, Henry said his stomach hurt. He was a little hunched over, so I let him ride in the big part of the cart. I cut about twenty items off of my list and headed straight for the checkout lane praying he didn't throw up (he did not). For several months thereafter, the boys believed that they could cut short any shopping trip or otherwise unpleasant outing by claiming illness. Jack and Henry got more stomachaches in the next several months than they'd ever had—stomachaches that mysteriously disappeared the second I headed for the exit. I got wise to their little plan somewhere along the line, and now refuse to leave no matter how badly they claim their stomachs are hurting. I'm sure that at some point, Henry will actually puke somewhere, but . . .

During this year, it is important to be fair regarding just how much of your children's behavior truly is age-appropriate—albeit frustrating and a bit annoying at times.

And as usual, know that it could always be worse. I spent a good bit of my boys' fourth year asserting to anyone and everyone that I could not even take them to the grocery store to pick up a pack of gum because they would fight the entire way in, whine about not being able to push the kid carts, push their way in front of each other to get directly behind me, and then blame each other when one of them (whoever was walking less than three inches behind me) stepped on my shoe, sending me full-force into the candy display.

I was reminded that the reality is that they are generally pretty good kids (fake stomachache incidents aside) the day we were in the furniture section of a very nice department store. As I tried out a fluffy, velour chair for comfort, I suddenly felt as though I was mistaking the bedroom section for a zoo. Two children suddenly appeared on a double bed right next to us (a Martha Stewart bed no less). They had removed their shoes and were jumping on the bed as though it were the latest and greatest trampoline. I looked around, wondering if perhaps their mother had left them there for the afternoon, mistaking the bedroom department for a glorified drop-off center. Sadly, she was nowhere to be found.

My next concern: the employees were going to think these kids were mine! We slowly moved toward the escalator, and I spotted the kids' mom admiring a dining room table. She briefly turned, saw what her kids were doing, and much to my horror, said simply, "Guys, be careful," at which point they continued to test just how resilient the springs in that bed were. I do not think that Martha would have considered this a Good Thing at all. While I would not put a lot of things past Jack and Henry, I know they would not do *this* in public. In their own room? Absolutely. But not on the Irvington nickel-plated bed from Martha's Turkey Hill collection. Thank goodness.

A friend recently told me about an adorable, hand-painted sign in a boutique window that read:

*Unattended children will be given
an espresso and a free puppy.*

The bedding departments of all stores that sell the Martha Stewart collection would be wise to put this sign in a very obvious place.

It was during this year in my life that ABC began airing *Supernanny*. I was glued for weeks. Many of Supernanny's clients had multiples in the family, which provided another reason to watch with interest and hope. One of Jo Frost's (aka Supernanny) claims to fame is her use of a "naughty chair" or "naughty mat" or otherwise "naughty" spot. Basically, it's a time-out spot that Jo insists children are put in when they misbehave. After the requisite time in the naughty spot is up, the child must be reminded why she was put there to begin with and she must apologize for her actions. I liked the fact that Jo used the time to give the child a break from the dynamic that caused the problem to begin with, and I especially appreciated that Jo ensured that the child understood what she had done wrong. However, I didn't like the word "naughty." I figured the moment was already tainted with enough negativity. So our spot of choice became the Thinking Couch. When someone was having trouble behaving appropriately (i.e., would not stop whining, was beating on a sibling, insisted on blowing bubbles in his milk during all seven minutes that we sat together at the dinner table, etc.), he would have to go sit on the Thinking Couch for a few minutes and consider an alternate approach. We did our best to discuss their actions with them, discuss the alternate approach they came up with, perhaps propose one of our own, and then move on. We didn't always have success with the Thinking Couch, but more often than not, it worked well because it removed the child from the situation, allowed him to think about what had happened instead of just be punished for it, and identified a way—at least in theory—to handle the problem differently the next time.

Specific Approaches to Behavior Modification

Time-Outs

Provided they're used as an opportunity to take a break from the people and the dynamic that's caused a problem, time-outs generally work well during this time period. Be sure to explain to your child beforehand and afterward why he's been sent there. Afterward, identify an alternate solution. Ask your child to do the same. Then pray that he remembers to use it the next time!

Counting

If you are counting at this point, I bet you're uttering a *lot* of numbers each day. The only way counting worked at this point for us was when someone was really having a hard time following directions. If I said, "One," that was all that was necessary for the kid to begin complying. I've no idea why it suddenly clicked. But I used it very rarely, and I rarely got to "Two." If I got to "Two," I knew I could continue all the way to one thousand and the child was not going to comply. I usually used this approach when we were putting on coats, or when I otherwise needed a child to follow directions immediately so that we could go somewhere. Sometimes, the child was so headstrong in terms of dealing with whatever problem he had that he didn't even hear the thirty-seven requests for him to put on his coat. For some reason, the word "one" typically worked like hypnosis. This really was a mystery to me because, again, I never really counted to begin with so they had no reason to identify my getting to "three" with a consequence. Frankly, they had no idea what would happen after I said "One" if they didn't comply (honestly, neither did I!). But, when necessary, it worked and I suppose I shouldn't spend too much time trying to identify why that was the case.

Encouraging Responsibility for Actions

Continuing to enforce the power and importance of choice is especially important during this year (and probably forever more). The return on investment takes time, but this approach, in our opinion, does work. Your children will learn a lifelong lesson: they have the power to choose how they'll respond to any situation. Whether they want you to realize it or not, three- to four-year-olds absolutely understand the concept of choice. I know this because while they put on their best I-don't-get-it face when I ask them to choose between no longer licking their boxes of Animal Crackers in the store and putting them back on the shelf, later that day I'll hear Henry in the back yard informing Jack, "If you choose to kick my ball again, you're choosing for me to sit on you."

Beyond asking children to choose a different approach, choose not to yell, or choose another toy, Mollie encouraged her children to choose their own consequence. If Tommy or Kevin were fighting or behaving poorly, Mollie would ask them to pick a toy and give it to her for the day. Typically, their behavior improved after this because they just could not believe that Mollie would take away a toy! However, they also quickly realized that they just needed to pick a toy they didn't like that much or didn't feel like playing with that day, and suddenly, the consequence wasn't quite so painful. Nowadays, Mollie chooses which toy gets put away for the day.

Undoubtedly, during this year you will want your children to learn to handle on their own any issues that lead to whining and/or fighting. These two behaviors seem to go hand in hand and occur almost constantly. As Mollie acknowledges, "I completely sucked at this. It was a total 'needs improvement' area." She admittedly did not have the patience to request over and over again that her boys identify another solution, explain their problem in detail to one another, etc. Her one consistent approach was simply to tell her boys that she didn't understand them when they whined. After that, she ceased to pay attention. Tommy and Kevin knew she wouldn't back down, so they changed their tone. When one bothered the other, she still felt that it took less effort on her part to intervene and assess who did what, get them to reenact the entire dialogue that occurred just minutes ago, and then decide who needed to go where, apologize to whom, etc.

If the boys were physically fighting within her line of vision and she could determine that no one was going to get killed, she didn't interfere unless she was called for (at which point she went through the reenactment exercise described above). Some days, she didn't know whether to punish everyone or just go get ice cream. More often than not, when it was the thirtieth time she'd reenacted the same scene in a day, the boys were split into separate rooms, or if the weather was nice they headed outside or ran an errand. The trick she pulled out of her hat when she was at her most despondent was stating "I'm very disappointed in your behavior and Santa is watching." This seemed to have as hypnotic an effect in her house as the declaration of "One" did in mine.

Most days, my kids continued to whine no matter what I did. I spent a lot of time during this year reiterating the importance of not whining or yelling, and instead explaining one's feelings to the antagonist. I should have just had a central intercom system that played an incessant recording of "You need to work that out on your own. Use your words." Most of the time after receiving this direction, the kid who had come to me to report on the actions of another would run into the other room and say, "Please do not hit me!" (even though he then sometimes hit the perpetrator in order to make his point more clear). So that's something to feel sort of good about, I suppose. I knew we were making mild progress the day Henry calmly walked into the room in which Jack was destroying his carefully built tower and proclaimed (without hitting), "Jack, I'm feeling very frustrated!"

At one point, someone suggested that I purchase one of those blow-up punching bags for the kids to hit when they were feeling angry or needed to relieve themselves of some aggression. I was initially opposed to this idea because I feared that it encouraged violence. After I realized that Jack was going to continue to punch and kick the walls during his moments of extreme frustration (which occurred every eleven minutes or so), I acquiesced.

I bought a Disney punching bag (there's something fundamentally wrong with merging the Disney brand with this concept, don't you think?). I told the kids that when we get frustrated, we sometimes believe it might feel really good to hit something. Frankly, I have a few moments of my own each day when I think, "I would really love to just smack the crap out of something right now!" I explained that we do not ever hit people, walls, doors, or windows. When we are feeling frustrated, the appropriate thing to hit is the punching bag.

It worked great . . . for eight days. On the eighth day, the punching bag was dealt such a blow that it broke. Not sure what I should think about that. Should you decide to try this approach, prepare yourself for the fact that for the first week or so, it's probable that every kid in the house is going to "feel frustrated" constantly so that he or she can go at the bag. Henry would seriously wake up in the morning and say, "Good morning, Mom. I'm frustrated. Where's the bag?" But the novelty quickly wore off and then the thing was able to serve its intended purpose only when truly necessary—again, until the eighth day.

Barb's approach to whining and fighting is the easiest to implement. She picked up the phone, dialed my number, and said through clenched teeth, "I am going to Lose. My. Mind. Can you *hear* this? What the hell?"

THE CHILD WITH A SELECTIVE PALATE

Ask your child what he wants for dinner only if he's buying.
—Fran Lebowitz

Even in the later toddler years, children will probably continue to appear fickle about what foods they find appealing from one day to the next. Many times, children at this age love a particular food one night and can't stand it the next. Our kids went through a phase when they loved sausage. So each time sausage went on sale, we bought it up and froze it. We ate sausage two or three times a week because we knew that if we put it on the table, no one would complain. In fact, everyone would cheer! Then suddenly, for no apparent reason, sausage moved to the no-no list. I put it on the table one night and Jack informed me that he didn't like sausage. Henry and Grace followed suit. I told them it was just like a big hot dog, and they love hot dogs. "No, it's different," they argued. "It's spicy." I told them they could let it take a swim in a bowl of ketchup, but even that wasn't enticement enough. So we'll have about fifteen sausages in the freezer from now until kingdom come, but hey, who's counting? Perhaps in a few months, sausage will again be all the rage in our house.

One night, they loved salmon. The next week, they acted like we were trying to poison them by serving salmon. One evening, Jack sat down in his seat and noticed that his plate contained salmon. He said, "Excuse me," and went to the refrigerator. He brought the vat of ketchup over to the table, put it down right next to his plate, and proclaimed, "I'm ready to say grace now." Told ya, ketchup is a must. I just wish it still worked on sausage.

When I was younger, I'd ask my mom each afternoon what we were having for dinner. Her response was always, "You'll know when we sit down to dinner." This always drove me insane. Why couldn't she just tell me what we were having? I vowed that when I had children, I'd always tell them what we were having for dinner when they asked. I'll admit that I broke that vow. Here's why: my mother knew that nine times out of ten, I'd say, "Yuck," and she was trying to put that off as long as possible. I now understand her approach completely.

When I placed a meal on the table and the kids sat down and announced, "I don't like chicken," or "I don't like bread," or "I don't like anything green, orange, or brownish," our rule was that they needed to eat what was on their plate in order to have dessert. Jack truly doesn't eat a lot of meat, so in many cases, he simply needed to eat everything else on his plate, which included some vegetable, and then he could substitute a banana or other item that he could access on his own. But there was no debating. If the meal was not eaten, the kitchen closed. The only dessert available was something healthy and easy such as a banana, apple, or yogurt.

We worked so hard to provide a few meals a week that we thought the kids would love. I spent a few Saturday mornings at the freezer-cooking establishments of which I spoke earlier because that way we could pull out an entrée, cook it, and ensure that we could eat as a family. But inevitably, the meal didn't appeal to anyone but David and me, and the point of freezer cooking parties is lost when you're baking one frozen entrée for yourselves and another entrée from scratch for the kids.

One evening, we had a bit of a miscommunication over who was cooking what, and David ended up putting peanut butter sandwiches on a plate, with broccoli in between the sandwich halves. He hesitantly put each kid's plate in front of him (or her), just waiting for the complaints. Henry took one look at the contents on his and proclaimed, for the first time, "Now *that's* what I'm talkin' 'bout!" Peanut butter and broccoli—who knew?

POTTY TRAINING

Fear knocked at the door. Faith answered. No one was there.

—Old saying

It occurred to me midway through writing this book that perhaps I should have given this activity its very own chapter. Potty training probably is not the most difficult or the most frustrating (though admittedly not the most joyous either) challenge you'll be faced with as a parent of twins, but it is the toddler milestone about which I receive the most questions (questions regarding the challenges involved in having another baby after twins fall only slightly behind in popularity).

In many ways, I think parents anticipate the process of potty training any child with both dread and excitement. The dread comes from the assumption of the amount of work involved, the prospect of the "Clean up in Aisle Five" announcement bellowing over the airways in any store, and the irrationally lurking fear that their child might turn ten and still not want to go to the potty where he should. Let me assure you that the latter is not going to occur.

I read an article recently in the *New York Times* about a new practice whereby parents are beginning to potty train their children from the age of ten weeks. I thought maybe it was a joke, but the *New York Times* rarely, if ever, prints material in such fashion. Apparently, there are support groups all over the place encouraging this sort of effort and singing its praises. I don't know; somehow, in the midst of everything else that is involved with tending to newborn twins, I can't figure out exactly how or when one would work in the requirement of holding a kid over the sink or potty every hour with the hope that he or she would void in it. However, should you be interested in this concept and have success with its techniques with your twins, please contact me. I'd like to profile you in some article—I can't promise it will be an article depicting sane mothers, but I'd like to profile you nonetheless.

The point at which a child is officially potty trained (whether at seven months or four years) marks a kind of crossing over into a new way of life. A way that does not require you to change diapers each morning, afternoon, and evening. A way that alleviates any anxiety over opening a box of wipes to find that there's only one left (and no refills anywhere in the house). And most importantly, a way that allows you to fund a mini vacation each month with the money saved from no longer having to buy diapers!

To be honest, I'm feeling as overwhelmed by the thought of writing about the process as you may be feeling about beginning it. So, we'll go through it together, step by step. Step One: Take a deep breath. Exhale. Repeat three times. Okay, here we go.

Getting Started
What to Call "It"

The first step in potty training is deciding how you will refer to your children's most private body parts. You're going to be referring to them all day long, and your kids need to know how to refer to them as well—or at least know what the heck you are talking about when *you* refer to them.

One thing that makes me feel quite badly for preschool teachers is that each kid in the class calls his head his head and his nose his nose, but each calls his penis or her vagina something completely different. I swear, I've heard it all: pee-pee, wee-wee, thingy, Peter (which makes me terribly sad for any kid whose name actually is Peter), willie, ah-ah, and unit (clearly a father taught his son this one), for starters.

"Penis" and "vagina" are not words that typically roll off of our tongues unless we are medical practitioners. However, if you choose the time during which you're potty training to make them part of your everyday vocabulary, they soon *will* roll off your tongue as easily as "vaginal discharge" did when you were pregnant and explaining your symptoms day-in and day-out to your obstetrician.

David and I always used the textbook names for body parts. We rationalized that, after all, we call our ear our ear and our toe our toe; why should we not call a vagina a vagina? If it looks like a vagina and it works like a vagina, why call it a "thingy"? But there's a reason why many kids refer to their private parts in different ways. It's a "private" part, and therefore, as adults, we've become quite sensitive to being private about it. And we should be. But in this case, we're just talking about it, not showing it to the world.

Grace referred to her vagina as a "majahnia" for years. I had a friend whose daughter was riding on his shoulders at a neighborhood picnic and suddenly shouted out for the whole world to hear, "Daddy, this is hurting my 'gina!" Seriously people, that's funny. And in my opinion—and I do have a few that I'll share without remorse you know—it sounds a lot more acceptable than, "Daddy, this is hurting my wee-wee!" But again, you're going to be using the word a lot, so you've got to be comfortable with it. I'd say the best way to decide what you want to call their more private parts is to decide what word you are most comfortable with *them* using if and when they need to tell a teacher or doctor or whomever that it hurts (and remember, the teacher, doctor, etc., has to be able to understand what the kid is talking about in order to appropriately help him!).

Mollie is also a big proponent of calling body parts by their real names and not showing any embarrassment. However, I like to portray another perspective as often as possible, and for another perspective on this topic, I only needed to go as far as fabulous Barb.

Because Olivia and Kambria have a female cousin who is only slightly older than they are, they heard with regularity the way in which she and her parents referred to her more private parts. The word they used was "peeps," as in, "Don't forget to wipe your peeps." Olivia and Kambria picked it up and ran with it. It was simply too easy, and Barb saw no need to add one more thing to the process. In her mind, they were thrilled about doing what their cousin did, and if they could share with her the excitement of this whole peeps-wiping thing and be excited about it, rock on.

Just before they turned four, Olivia and Kambria started asking Barb what the exact term for the peeps region is. Apparently, it was hard to believe that any part of the body was actually called "peeps"! Of course, Barb told them, and now they know. So weigh the options, decide how you feel about each, and go from there. For the record, even though they might use the term when discussing it with their sons, I don't know of any grown man who would go to the doctor and mention that he was having an issue with his unit. So, if you feel strongly about using a euphemism, know that in the end, your child will more than likely know what it's really called and use that term when appropriate.

When to Start

Next, you must decide when to start training your children. With one child, many parents make this decision based upon gender. It has been said (another stereotype, I know) that girls are ready earlier than boys. I've known several girls who were potty trained long before they turned three, and I've known some boys who weren't trained until they were four or older. However, I've also known some girls who took a little longer and some boys who were all too pleased to use that potty well before anyone imagined they would be.

The onset of a preschool program for which the kids must be potty trained is often one of the greatest factors for parents in determining when they will get ultraserious about beginning this process. This can be especially challenging for parents whose children turn three a month or two before school starts. In this case, if parents are truly nervous about whether or not they'll be able to get their kids trained by day one (and are having to make that decision when registration commences, often eight months before starting school), an option is to seek out a preschool for which they do not have to be potty trained. They do exist, but they are not nearly as common as their must-be-potty-trained counterparts. Also, remember that you just need to get to a point where the kids do not have consistent accidents for the few hours when they are in school. In many cases, if you've been working with them for a while, and you make sure they use the bathroom just before leaving for school, they'll be fine, especially since they will get a potty break during the morning.

Many preschool teachers are sensitive to the fact that children are still mastering this concept. Many kids who are doing wonderfully at home refuse to use the potties at school. The preschool teachers I've known were quite understanding and patient early on in the school year regarding these sorts of issues, especially for newly turned three-year-olds.

We started working with Jack and Henry at about the same time George was born, so they were two months or so from turning three.

Training Children Simultaneously Versus Separately

With multiples, many parents wonder, "If one child appears ready to begin potty training and the other does not, do we start one before the other?" As always, I advise gathering as much information and advice as you can, and then making an informed decision.

An advantage of starting to work with the kids at different times is that you'll be able to concentrate on working with one child, and perhaps the second child will gain interest in the process. A disadvantage is that the process may—and I emphasize *may*—take longer in total because you'll be working with one child for a few months, and then just when he or she is trained during the day, the other will be ready and you'll begin Act Two.

While we started Jack and Henry simultaneously, Jack

thought the whole process was superbly fun and Henry wanted nothing to do with it. After a while, we backed off with Henry. Then one day Henry just decided he was ready. He wanted to do it on his terms, apparently, which should not have surprised us at all because this is who Henry is on all fronts. He was completely trained during the day within five days. Jack, who had been working quite hard for six months, took another month or so. In addition, Henry was trained through the night about a year before Jack was. So the fact that one child starts the process later than the other does not mean that he will complete it later.

Mollie also started training her boys at the same time. At times one would progress further than the other, and then they'd switch (they did this switcheroo in every other area; why should the potty be any different?). One approach she vowed never to take was comparing one child to the other. It's just not effective to say, "Your brother can do this, and you can do it, too," or "Your sister can do it; why can't you?" It might occur to you that a competition to "get there first" might motivate your children. You do not want to make potty training about competition. Train them both simultaneously if you choose, but treat them as individuals as you move through the process.

Potty Chair or Toilet?

Again, a personal decision entirely. We tried the potty chairs initially and found them to be sort of a mess. Cleaning them is not at all fun. However, the kids can sit on them on their own (you don't have to lift them onto the big potty or help them turn around after they utilize some sort of stool to climb up to the big potty), which takes away some of the work on your end.

With four sisters, Mollie had positively no experience with potty training little boys (or doing much else with them, frankly). She felt as though she was grasping at straws many days trying to figure out exactly what was the best way to teach them. Remember, Mollie is the one who advises anyone with a question about anything at all to call the 800 number provided by the company. Therefore, I'm sure it will come as no surprise that she did not feel that any of the books—even those with illustrations—sufficed in their explanation of how to tackle this challenge. She wanted a DVD. She wanted visuals. She claims that if she had had boy/girl twins, she would have needed an on-site therapist to assist her with understanding their different body parts and exactly how they work and feel when each has to go to the bathroom.

Mollie's use of the potty chair ended abruptly when Tommy decided one day that it would make a cool helmet (and yes, Mollie did find him wearing it on his head). From then on, they used the little cushion seats that you place on top of the big toilet seat.

The boys saw Mollie sit on the potty, but she urged them to stand. However, when they had to poop, it was awkward to say, "Okay, stand to pee; then quickly turn around, put the seat down, and sit." It was like a bad game of "Pat your head and rub your tummy." Apparently, a book by T. Berry Brazelton urges parents to have their sons sit before they stand, but Mollie read that too late. A bonus to the ignorance to this advice: at three and a half years of age, they could go either way! After ridding her home of the potty chairs, Mollie put a stool in front of the big potty for times when the boys needed to sit on it, and they had no problem getting up on it when necessary.

The only major problem we had with the boys sitting on the potty was that they often did not "aim" properly. One day, I found Henry screaming in the bathroom, hysterical over the fact that he had, in effect, parted his hair with a stream of urine. He hadn't yet mastered the skill of peeing while standing, so he was sitting, and he was so busy watching the process unfold that he didn't realize that he wasn't aiming down, but instead sort of up/out. I thought it was hysterical; he did not.

To be clear, the aiming issue is not just a sitting-down-on-the-potty problem with boys. Kevin called Mollie into the bathroom once and said, with great pride, "Look, Mom, I made a circle!" Sure enough, he had drawn a perfect urine circle—on the wall. Kevin truly enjoys pulling his pants down to his hips and just letting the thing (I know, I said "thing," but in this case, I think it works) go like a fire hose, flapping it all around.

Once our boys started standing up (which they learned at their Parents' Day Out program, ironically enough), they too quickly learned that their penises could be used as fire hoses. I drew the line there. I got lucky (the universe owed me after all the poop-in-the-carpet incidents), and one very stern warning was all that was needed.

They do sell flushable pellets, called Piddlers Toilet Targets, that you can put in the potty and at which boys are supposed to aim. We fervently believe that boys have no problem with aim. It's just that aiming is no fun unless you're playing basketball. We didn't try the aiming gizmos, but perhaps in the beginning they would be effective to help boys get the general idea. If you think they might work, give them a shot (no pun intended). Who knows?

Barb also opted against potty chairs. In her mind, they added yet one more transition. First you go from diapers to the potty chair and then from the potty chair to the big potty. She was interested in as seamless a process as possible.

How Many Potty Chairs Do You Need?

If you choose to use potty chairs, you are obviously going to have to have at least one, possibly two, in each bathroom. If this sounds cluttered to you, think about this: I distinctly remember the magazine that profiled Bobby McCaughey on the cover alongside a headline about potty training the septuplets. The magazine carried an article written by Bobby regarding the manner in which she approached this task, and it did involve, I believe, storing five potty chairs in the middle of her living room.

You can buy two potty chairs (or four, or whatever so you have two for each bathroom) if you'd like. Or, you can start with one, see how that goes, and determine if you need another. Initially, the whole potty activity is fascinating to the kids—more than anything because there are potentially treats involved with success (or at least trying). If your kids are at all like mine, they will therefore want to be on the potty practically all day long because they are trying—and therefore deserve another M&M. So, if you have only one potty chair and one kid's on it, there will be a squabble. If there is one place you do *not* want a squabble, it's on a potty chair while one kid is actually producing something!

Initially, Mollie was adamant about having two potty chairs in each bathroom. They have three bathrooms and, yes, they had six little potties in total. She realized that it was almost certain that, at least initially, both kids would have to go (or would want to try) simultaneously, so she figured that if she didn't have two seats, she'd have to take one to one bathroom and one to another. Now, if you have bathrooms the size of Gibraltar, this decision might not be as difficult. Perhaps you might like to have a little potty chair in there for yourself as well, especially since most of them now sing to you and possibly by this point even flush themselves for real!

Training Pants, Underwear, or Diapers?

Diapers versus training pants versus underwear versus the birthday suit; it always makes for a fun debate. But beyond providing a topic to discuss for hours on end, it really doesn't matter terribly much which way you choose. There's no "right" way other than what makes sense to you.

Barb put her girls in underwear right away so they would know what was happening when it happened. She let them pick out their own panties at the store and made a huge deal out of how pretty they were. Again, her goal was to avoid an additional transition (I do hope I've mentioned that Barb is very brave; remember, she's the one who never put away her crystal and it's all still in one piece).

I refused to put our boys directly into underwear because I knew that they would just pee all over themselves and the entire house and think it was completely hilarious (and then probably demand a treat—because after all, they went potty).

Many believe that training pants are so absorbent that kids can't even tell when they've urinated in them. They now have newer ones that supposedly help a child feel when she's gone, but I've not heard of anyone who thinks they are remarkably better. Another product I've heard of is called PODS (see http://www.pottytrainingsolutions.com), which you put inside a child's underwear or training pants. It helps kids feel when they've gone because it actually becomes cool to the touch.

In our house, once the boys were out of diapers, they were out of diapers. Once training pants were in season, that was all we used because going back and forth from diapers to training pants was, in my opinion, too much of a pain. We had to at least take a step toward underwear, even if it was as minor as going from true diapers to more glorified ones.

In Mollie's case, the training pants weren't very effective because when one of the boys had an accident, everything spilled out of them. They used Huggies Convertibles and loved them, and used them at night until the boys stayed dry through to the morning.

Worrying That You Started Too Soon

If you determine, using whatever logic, that you were a little overzealous in your desire to begin this process, you can certainly stop without causing irrevocable damage. We had to do this about six times with our daughter. With Jack and Henry, we didn't start until they were almost three years old, but when we had a setback or two, we backed off.

Be sure you're clear on whether you think you started your children too soon or whether you may have started yourself too soon. Having potty trained three children, I am quite clear on the fact that many times the process of potty training isn't nearly the issue for kids that it is for the parent doing it. Why? Because the parent's schedule is at the mercy of the child's while this is all going on. When the child announces in Target that he has to go potty (or worse, when one child announces this need and then the other agrees merely because the Target bathroom is so fun and there might be an M&M at the other end of the activity), many parents want to just say, "You're wearing your training pants; go ahead and go in them—just this once." But that's not a particularly realistic approach because you're only half-training the child. It's not fair to expect a child to know when it's okay to "just go" and when she needs to let you know that you need to find a potty.

After a few days of potty training, Barb realized that she had perhaps started the process with Kambria and Olivia before Olivia was truly ready. Initially, she didn't believe she had any choice but to keep going because she saw no feasible way to train one and not the other. The girls just were not happy doing different things, but Kambria was completely ready to use the potty and doing it very well. Barb will tell you with complete conviction that potty training was a long and sometimes difficult journey.

Shortly after the potty was introduced, Olivia experienced episodes of extreme constipation—to the point that she needed a daily dose of an over-the-counter laxative to keep her system flowing. It was just awful, and I understood it firsthand because we went through the same thing with Grace. I believe that in both cases, at least initially, while appearing as though they were struggling terribly to poop, both Grace and Olivia were actually struggling to ensure that they did *not* poop, either because they were frightened of doing so in the potty, or because they'd had a less-than-joyous experience during a recent episode and were, therefore, afraid to do it again. It didn't take long for this activity to set off a chain reaction; their systems backed up, they became truly constipated, and then they would not poop because they were terrified of the discomfort caused when they did. After a few months on the laxative, both girls let go of their fear of going and became more regular. It became clear to me, as it did a couple of years later to Barb, that while Grace was peeing in the potty all day on her own, I would have to let her determine her poop-in-the-potty timetable all by herself. And she did, much more quickly than I would have imagined.

The bottom line for Barb was that Olivia was not going to be ready until *she* was ready. There are two things, in my mind, that kids ultimately have control over: when/where they go to the bathroom and when they fall asleep. As parents, we can encourage certain behaviors or use reward/behavior modification strategies to motivate our children to follow certain rules, but in the areas of sleeping and voiding, we have little to no control. It's not a war worth waging, trust me.

As I've mentioned, Henry is also a child who does things only when *he* wants to. We tried so hard in the beginning to encourage him to try to use the potty now and then. But we could have offered him a train set the size of Jupiter and it would not have been enough to make him sit on that potty (or actually produce on it)—until he made the decision that it was his time. So sometimes, it's important to just back off. You don't necessarily have to revert to diapers if you don't want to. Just let your child do his or her own thing. You may be surprised by what happens next.

In the end, Barb decided to back off completely with Olivia. Barb didn't use training pants with either of the girls, and it wasn't going to work for Olivia to pee and poop all day in her underwear, so back to diapers she went. (Barb did put the girls in training pants at night, however, a fact that allows me to believe that while brave, she's not completely insane.) True to the pattern that's surely existed through the ages as parents weathered the challenge created by a child with a mind of her own, shortly after Barb decided to give Olivia her space, she made the transition all by herself.

Mollie held to a zero-pressure theory in her house. She didn't care if the in-laws were over kvetching that her boys were too old to be in diapers. She stood strong in the knowledge that she was the mom, and if the potty was a stressful issue, what on earth would she do when the boys were fighting over curfews and car keys? (The woman's perspective really is top notch.) Because her boys both have extreme asthma, Mollie's area of control had to be their breathing treatments; there is no negotiation over the necessary administration of twice-daily medication in her house. So, using the potty? No big whoop. She figured it would happen when they were ready. If they wanted to continue wearing diapers in the beginning, fine. If they didn't want to sit on the potty some days, she didn't raise an eyebrow. In their case, once one boy sat down and produced on the potty, that was all that the other one needed in terms of motivation. But it was the boys who set the standard of "competition," not Mollie or Gary.

It should be noted that once Tommy and Kevin were relatively well trained, they refused to wear underwear because they said the tags bothered them. She cut out the tags; no go. She bought them boxers; no dice. She called Hanes and requested tagless underwear; they told her where she could purchase them. She bought the store out, and the boys said, "No way." One day, I knew it was time to return the "Liz, if you go get those babies every time they cry they are going to play you like a fool for the rest of your life" lecture that she so brilliantly delivered to me when our babies were around five months old. I tactfully informed her that she was being played. She knew it was true, so she told the boys, "These are your underwear, and you are going to wear them!" She must have had the this-is-the-way-it-is-and-don't-even-try-to-mess-with-me look on her face because that was it; they were in underwear—with tags—from that point forward.

There are one thousand approaches to potty training, and probably one thousand minor variations of each approach. The point on which to focus is that we each had different approaches and different perspectives, even if only slightly so. And we are pleased to report that all of our kids are indeed potty trained.

Do what works for you. Be flexible when an approach ceases to work—or fails to work at all. I wonder how many more times I will deliver that piece of advice before I'm one hundred.

Basic Training
Nitty Gritty Details of the First Few Days

Wait. Back up a second. Before I dive into what to do *in* the potty, I need to mention something very important about what to do even before you *get* to the potty. Rid your child's wardrobe (at least temporarily) of all overalls! Pants with an elastic waist are best initially. Even zippers and snaps (not to mention buttons) can cause real and unnecessary frustration at this point in the process. I hope to spare a few of you the trauma experienced in many a home when a kid really has to go badly and no one, not even the mother, can get those darn overall clips undone.

Whether you use a potty chair or not, it's probably a good idea to talk the whole plan up for a few days before starting so that the kids know what to expect. Let them know that they're going to try sitting on the potty several times a day and let them know what they are supposed to do on it.

Mollie had the boys sit on the potties a lot in the first few days. They played or read a lot in the bathroom. She offered them the chance to try every thirty minutes or so, but acted as though it was really no big deal if they didn't want to or had an accident.

Barb's strategy was to pump her girls full of water and juice all day long so that they would learn to get the feeling of having to go to the bathroom. They basically incarcerated themselves in their home for the first few days to a week, attempting only extremely short errands.

Nancy Bowers, author of *The Multiple Pregnancy Sourcebook*, offered each of her twins a cup filled with half water and half juice. She set a timer to go off twenty or thirty minutes later. The buzzer signaled that it was time to go to the potty. This approach worked nicely because the kids didn't perceive their mom as the one asking them to stop whatever they were doing *again* to go to the bathroom. The message was being delivered by the buzzer!

Establishing a Daily Schedule

The best bet early on is to establish a bathroom schedule. Some recommend putting the child on the potty every fifteen minutes until she produces to teach her to recognize the sensation she'll have before she has to go. I swear, I could have put my boys on that darn potty every two minutes and in the ten seconds they were off, they'd go. It was exhausting. So, I recommend a more liberal schedule, like every hour or two. In the very beginning, you're really just trying to get them to understand cause and effect, not stay dry all day. Once they get the basics down, it'll be far easier to graduate to a schedule that makes more sense, such as using the potty upon waking up, at mid-morning, after lunch, after their nap, right before dinner, and right before bed.

Barb gave her girls reminders every twenty to thirty minutes. She'd gently ask, "Does anyone need to go potty?" Or she'd ask one of the girls specifically if she needed to go. Sometimes, kids do need to go, but they are so involved with whatever activity they are engaged in that they don't realize it—until it's too late. A gentle reminder is sometimes all it takes to trigger a child's awareness that she does indeed need to go (and the light bulb that goes on in her head reminding her of the treat to follow her success doesn't hurt either).

Providing Rewards for Success

Offering an incentive is one tactic that rarely fails to work with children. Many times, if they don't have an incentive, things ain't gonna work right, and when they do, the sky's the limit as far as the miracles they might perform. Face it, everyone needs an incentive to get out of bed in the morning. Mine is the Starbucks Frappaccino drink chilling in the refrigerator and the Pepperidge Farm cinnamon bread sitting on the counter calling my name. What works for each person, however, is different.

Some parents give children an M&M each time they try to go to the potty, and then each time they are successful they might get two M&Ms. Some parents offer mini marshmallows. It does have to be something your child really wants and rarely gets; offering a carrot for attempts and an apple for success aren't likely to get you anywhere. (How is it that kids instinctually love chocolate and don't love vegetables? That whole dynamic makes no sense to me. If McDonald's were good for us, we'd all be healthy as horses.) Be sure to be fair about rewards, especially in the beginning. If kids are trying their hardest, but just not going in the potty for whatever reason, you do not want them to perceive that they are being punished. This will end the enjoyable potty training process in a hurry.

We rewarded the boys' efforts with M&Ms initially, but Jack was going in and sitting on the potty every six seconds just to get an M&M. We went through a pound in two days. So, that strategy had to go. Same with juice snacks.

Barb had to offer the most creative rewards (in large quantities) to get Olivia to poop on the potty. At one point, they needed rewards to get Olivia to poop anywhere! When things were at their worst with Olivia, rewards were of zero value. She just wasn't going to go. This was when Barb had to back off completely and let the issues run their course.

Mollie offered matchbox cars. The boys were allowed to pick one from a big bucket if they peed and a prize from the dollar store (stashed in the laundry room) if they pooped. After they mastered the former (which took about two weeks), Mollie only rewarded pooping on the potty. That reward went away after they mastered that process as well, which also took about two weeks. (Mollie must have had a serious system going on over there because it took two weeks in our house just to convince Henry that the potty would not swallow him.) The tantrums that ensued over the receiving of—and ultimately the removal of—treats were, in Mollie's house, minimal because once again she was utterly and completely consistent about only giving a prize for producing. Once the boys had begun to demonstrate potty proficiency and Mollie didn't feel that they needed prizes anymore, she was stoic about the fact that prizes—for strides in that department, at least—were being retired. The new reward was that they could again leave the house!

In our house, once the boys had mastered peeing in the potty, but were still working on pooping (which frankly, is the one you really want them to master), the process became more difficult on every level. They just did not want to poop in that potty. So we did what Mollie did and went to Target and got a bunch of matchbox cars when they were on sale. Each time they pooped in the potty, they got to choose a matchbox car or another small, inexpensive item from a treat box. This worked quite well. However, when Henry turned four and had been completely potty trained day and night for about seven months, yet still wanted a treat each time he pooped in the potty, we thought we might lose our minds. Perhaps the problem was that I was not as consistent (or better yet, convincing) as Mollie was.

Some parents choose not to offer rewards as incentive for using the potty. Bowers fell into this category. In her family, attempting to use the potty was simply something that needed to be done, much the same way children are expected to hold an adult's hand in a parking lot. Not offering rewards clearly didn't hold her children back; her son was out of diapers and completely trained in one day (I think she needs to go into business as a potty-training coach).

Preparing for Trips in the Car

I always kept a potty chair in the trunk of my car. When a child learning to use the potty declares that he has to go, asking him if he can wait five minutes until you get home (or to a Burger King) is usually not going to get you the answer you want. When they gotta go, they gotta go. With a potty chair in my trunk, I could pull over in a parking lot if I needed to, whip it out, and let the kid go. It was quite convenient. It was highly convenient when we were returning from a weekend out of town and were stuck in Saturday-afternoon traffic entering Chicago. We were at a dead stop on the Eisenhower when both boys (and then Grace) announced they had to go potty. I whipped that chair out, popped them onto it, prayed that it didn't overflow, poured its contents into a bag, and the minute traffic began moving again (which was about forty-five minutes later) I pulled off to find an infrequently if ever walked on grassy area.

Mollie was resolute; there was no way in heck ("heck" was not the exact word she used when we discussed this) she was going to venture out *anywhere* during the first week of potty training. Forget it. She had a colossal fear of public restrooms, and vowed to hold off on using them for as long as possible. She put the potty chair in the car once, but made the mistake of telling the boys that she had it. She ended up pulling over every mile for the kid who was screaming, "Mom, I have to go potty *now!*" only to giggle while sitting on it in the back of the Jeep. Of course, neither boy ever produced on the potty in the car; it was nothing more than a huge game for them. It didn't take long for Mollie to permanently remove the potty from the car.

Preparing for Trips to Stores

I have no idea why, but kids are fascinated with public

restrooms. Barb made it a rule to hit the bathroom whenever she and her girls entered a store or just before they left so there were no accidents in Aisle Five and no exploding bladders at a red light.

Whether they truly have to go to the bathroom or not, be prepared for your children to announce in Home Depot, the grocery store, and every fast food joint that they need to, if for no other reason than to check out the restroom. I suppose this fascination is akin to the one that piques my curiosity regarding the differences in the penthouse suites in every four-star hotel in the world. Many times, you may not believe that the kids truly have to go, but in my experience, it's not wise to argue.

For visits to public restrooms, you might want to check out disposable potty seat covers such as Potty Toppers manufactured by Neat Solutions. (These are much like another of their products called Table Toppers, which are great to put down on the table in a restaurant so that your child isn't eating his food directly off of the table.) You can carry these Potty Toppers in your purse for visits to public restrooms. After the kids are finished, you just throw them away. Charmin also recently began selling a product called Charmin To Go Toilet Seat Covers. They offer a travel size of five disposable toilet seat covers stored in a tiny purse pack that would fit in a large wallet. I can think of no purse this package could not fit into. The covers retail for around $1 per package and can often be found in the sample section of a store. (For a whole slew of products in travel sizes small enough to fit into a purse—for use everyday or when traveling—check out http://www.minimus.biz.)

A non-disposable toilet seat cover also exists that can be folded up to fit inside your purse, but my theory is that when you're stuffing something that's been sitting on a toilet seat into your purse (even into a plastic bag in your purse), you aren't really avoiding the bacteria you were trying to avoid in the first place.

Personally, when dealing with any public restroom, I am like the woman in the commercial for Dial Complete who opens the department store door with her foot in order to enter without having to touch the door handle. My rule is: touch nothing. I keep antibacterial hand sanitizer everywhere: my purse, my glove compartment, my pockets. I'm like a walking hand sanitizer bottle. Barb and I believe we should have bought stock in Bath & Body Works years ago because between the two of us, we've probably upped the value of their stock price significantly just from our many purchases of their bottles of Just for Kids Anti-Bacterial Instant Hand Foam (which kids love because they smell great and are "fun to pump"). When we return home from an errand during which someone had to use the public restroom, the kids wash their hands once again. These days, Grace comes out of a public restroom stall and says, "Okay Mom, stealth mission time. I shall now turn on the faucet like a surgeon . . . " I wonder if I've gone too far?

Mollie actually lied and told her boys that only certain places had restrooms—and those places were limited to their house and their friends' houses (did I mention that she is seriously terrified of public restrooms?). Once the boys had mastered the potty, she did succumb to visiting public restrooms on occasion. By the time the boys were almost four, she admitted that they'd visited one in all major, frequented stores. However, her cardinal rule still stands—everyone must go to the bathroom before leaving the house. Period.

What If One Child Regresses?

When Barb was working with her girls on using the potty and Olivia was showing signs of regression, Barb was terrified that if she did indeed regress completely, Kambria would as well. As we all found out, this did not necessarily happen. In fact, it didn't happen in most cases. The fear of it happening is certainly not a reason to forcefully halt the kid who is doing well. Be patient with both kids; remember to view them as individuals learning at the same time, not a unit learning together. A subtle difference, yes, but an important one.

STILL MOVING . . .

When you get to the end of your rope, tie a knot and hang on.
—Franklin D. Roosevelt

As I complete this manuscript, we're smack dab in the middle of the Christmas season. It's a time when I can reflect from morning until night on what a true blessing—albeit a chaotic one at times—my children are.

I had a lovely experience in the post office the other day. I had all three boys with me. I was carrying George, who was none too pleased and therefore screaming, grabbing at anything, and otherwise trying to escape. That was okay though; after all, he's only one and that kind of behavior at his age is to be expected.

His brothers, on the other hand, are *four,* and have assumed aliases as of late: Baby Dog and Papa Dog. Seriously, some days if you do not address them as such, they will not respond. Anyway, after 6.3 minutes waiting in line with every single second of that time spent negotiating, bribing, or flat out begging the boys to stop spinning, whining, removing insurance forms from their slots, and being otherwise disruptive, I opted to zone out and pray that their less-than-stellar behavior would cease on its own.

It did not.

I intervened once when Henry started swinging monkey-style on the ropes that kept the line from becoming an uncontrolled herd.

"Seriously Henry," I admonished in an extraordinarily annoyed voice, "are you kidding me?"

The man behind me, who was clearly uncomfortable, asked me how old the older boys were. I wanted to say "two," but they are quite tall even for four and the answer would not have passed.

As all this was going on, Jack started whining, "Mahhhmmm, I have to go pahhhhtty."

"Hold it!" I responded through clenched teeth.

When I finally made it to the counter, I realized I appeared to be missing a kid. I turned around to see Henry lying splayed out on the floor, seemingly quite content, but splayed out nonetheless as though he'd just run 183 miles. I think he was actually using his left arm as a pillow. Jack was next to me jumping up and down as though he'd sucked a five-pound bag of sugar through a straw just prior to leaving the house. As predicted, he ultimately jumped right up into the counter. He then began wailing. Of course, there were no fewer than thirty-seven people in line behind us, all holding holiday packages that they, too, had waited until the last minute to mail. They were all looking at me as though they either felt horribly sorry for me or thought I was the worst, most incompetent mother on earth.

It was a sitcom. Except that no one was laughing, and I wasn't being paid a cent (though most of the people in there likely would have paid me a small fortune to mail my package the next day and pay extra for rush shipping).

In that moment, I thought, "What the heck am I doing

writing a book on how to manage this stuff? I live in an area with an extraordinarily high rate of twins, and if anyone in here recognizes me, I'm finished." But seconds later, it dawned on me that I've never claimed to have *all* of the answers, and certainly not to be the perfect parent. I would hope no one would attempt to assert that they could solve every problem of every child in every situation all of the time. If we all put our thoughts and our experiences together, however, surely we can solve the world's most devastating crises. After all, we're moms, and that's what we do. Most days, I'm just another mom. Just another mom who's learned one heck of a lot in the last four years about parenting twins (parenting period, frankly), and marriage, and cleaning products, and baby equipment, and negotiation tactics, and when to attempt Bob Evans for dinner solo with four kids versus when to call and beg Mollie to meet me there.

Once in a while, Barb receives a poem, story, or joke through e-mail that she can't help but pass along. A few days ago, she passed along the following letter to Santa from some mom somewhere. Once again, the author is unknown (I really wish people would start putting their names on these things; at a minimum, they'd become instantly famous given how prolifically these e-mails circulate!). Apart from the story included earlier in this book about the husband who came home to find the house in disarray, I don't believe I've ever come across any group of words that so perfectly summed up my mindset, not just this time of year but all year round. I bet it does the same for millions of other moms out there.

Dear Santa,

I've been a good mom all year. I've fed, cleaned, and cuddled my children on demand and visited the doctor's office more than my doctor.

I was hoping you could spread my list out over several

Christmases, since I had to write this letter with my son's red crayon on the back of a receipt in the laundry room between cycles, and who knows when I'll find anymore free time in the next 18 years.

Here are my Christmas wishes:

I'd like a pair of legs that don't ache (in any color except purple, which I already have), and arms that don't hurt or flap in the breeze, but are strong enough to pull my screaming child out of the candy aisle in the grocery store. I'd also like a waist, since I lost mine somewhere in the seventh month of my last pregnancy.

If you're hauling big-ticket items this year, I'd like fingerprint-resistant windows and a radio that only plays adult music; a television that doesn't broadcast any programs containing talking animals; and a refrigerator with a secret compartment behind the crisper where I can hide to talk on the phone.

On the practical side, I could use a talking doll that says, "Yes, Mommy" to boost my parental confidence, along with two kids who don't fight and three pairs of jeans that will zip all the way up without the use of power tools.

I could also use a recording of Tibetan monks chanting "Don't eat in the living room" and "Take your hands off your brother" because my voice seems to be just out of my children's hearing range and can only be heard by the dog.

If it's too late to find any of these products, I'd settle for enough time to brush my teeth and comb my hair in the same morning, or the luxury of eating food warmer than room temperature without it being served in a Styrofoam container.

If you don't mind, I could also use a few Christmas miracles to brighten the holiday season. Would it be too much trouble to declare ketchup a vegetable? It would clear my conscience immensely.

It would be helpful if you could coerce my children to help around the house without demanding payment as if they were the bosses of an organized crime family.

Well, Santa, the buzzer on the dryer is ringing and my son saw my feet under the laundry room door. I think he wants his crayon back. Have a safe trip, and remember to leave your wet boots by the door and come in and dry off so you don't catch cold.

Help yourself to cookies on the table, but don't eat too many or leave crumbs on the carpet.

Yours always,
Mom

P.S. One more thing . . . you can cancel all my requests if you can keep my children young enough to believe in Santa.

Man, I love this! I love it because I know how many women read it and could cry at the validation it provides of the job they are doing. And then it makes them cry harder because after acknowledging that as moms, we all muddle through some relatively difficult days—moment by moment by moment—it clarifies that those challenges aren't what make us whole. They are merely peripheral details that come with the job. What makes us whole is the immeasurable love that we maintain for our children no matter what, and the fact that in the end we'd sacrifice every inch of our own sanity for their happiness and health and never-ending belief in the magic of Santa Claus, the Easter Bunny, and the Tooth Fairy.

Whether our hearts are overflowing from the corners of

our eyes, or we're praying for the sudden appearance of that magic compartment behind the crisper to which we can steal away to make a phone call or—on the more challenging days—into which we can escape at full speed hoping to find our own Narnia for six hours (which in real-world time is only six seconds), in the end, the essence of Santa perfectly represents the true reality of motherhood: it is better to give than to receive. For what we give always comes back to us. What we give, we receive ten times over.

Therefore, I suppose that at the end of our days, it's nothing short of a miracle that by design, the first and foremost responsibility in a mom's job description is to give. Our day-to-day, minute-by-minute challenges may differ, but as moms, we are all cemented to one another by that one common truth.

It's Christmas Day. Don't gasp and think poorly of me; I'm not really working. I'm not running for a thesaurus or researching the many ways other moms have successfully encouraged their children to taste the brussels sprouts floating in their ketchup soup. I'm merely taking a quick break from the festivities (the truth: three kids are arguing over three Lite Brites that are the exact same color so I ran for any excuse that would force responsibility on David for a few moments).

Grace is six. Jack and Henry are four. George is one. Holy cow, why don't I weigh less? At this precise moment, the yelling seems to have ceased, and the boys are working nicely together to build a fort with their new brick blocks. They chose aprons (excuse me, construction uniforms) without fighting, and they're using my best Calphalon spatulas to lay bricks, not beat each other over the head. And, to prove that other relationships have, after much work, come full circle (I don't want anyone worrying about me any more than they already might), I must reveal that last night, I happily kept David's favorite beer coming as he played Xbox to his heart's content. And as of 9:13 this morning, I am wearing Jeanine Payer. Well, not Jeanine exactly, but one of her creations. Truthfully, it's not one of the seventeen I suggested.

It's better.

I also finally summoned the courage to take the dreaded What's Your Real Age? test. The results: my calendar age is 33.4 years. My real age (drum roll please): 33.1 years. So my body is functioning as though it's .3 years younger than my birth certificate says it is. Of course, I secretly hoped to learn that my mind and body were operating as though I were a twenty-two-year-old. Twenty-five would have been an equally nice surprise. Heck, anything under thirty would have been cause for celebration. But I'll look on the bright side: I knew there was a chance, however slim, that the result could be seventy-five, so with that in mind, 33.1 isn't too bad!

Even though I grudgingly accept that the public "incidents" during which I pull the bill of my baseball hat as low as it will go will occur here and there until the end of time, I do think we've finally gotten there. "There" being that place where I get to relax a bit. Where I don't have to follow everyone around and worry all the time about what might be destroyed, about who's about to hit whom, or who's whining about what.

I can hear Grace reading to George. George is laughing. Grace has stopped to sound out a word. It's taking a while. The silence has me a bit concerned. George is still laughing. That has me even more concerned. Uh oh, the yelling has begun. Four kids, lots of yelling. Can't really decipher much of it. What I can tell is that there is a bunch of tattling going on even though I'm not in the room with them. I should let them try to sort it out on their own.

"Sounds like you guys have a problem! Would you please choose a different way to handle it?" (two of my most often used phrases; thank you so much, Mr. Moorman). I don't think they heard me. Or perhaps they just don't care.

Still screaming. Okay, I've understood a few words. Something about a cat in the dishwasher.

We don't have a cat.

Where the hell is David? Maybe he figured out how to get behind the crisper.

I hear someone running toward the office. I think it's Grace.

She's breathless.

"Mom. We have. A problem."

"Grace, I know you can work this out. Where is your father?"

"I don't know. Probably in the bathroom, which usually takes, like, twenty-two hours. Seriously, Mom, I think you'd better get out here."

"Is anyone bleeding?"

"Well, no, but . . . " she adds while stealing a quick, frantic glance toward the kitchen.

"Is anything on fire?"

"*No!*" she responds as though I've asked her if she'd like to have cauliflower and beets for dinner.

"Okay, well then I'll be there in just a minute."

"But Mom," she concludes with a sense of urgency that has me wondering what on *earth* could be going on in there, "the boys . . . put . . . your coat . . . in . . . the dishwasher!"

Okay, I'll get it in a second.

"But they turned . . . the dishwasher . . . *on!*"

Sorry sisters. Gotta go!